Philip Warner, well known as a military historian and lecturer, joined the Army after graduating from Cambridge in 1939, and served throughout the war, mainly in the Far East. Among his works are *Panzer*, *Alamein*, *The D-Day Landings*, *Auchinleck*, *The SAS* and *The SBS*. These last three titles are available from Sphere Books.

Until recently Philip Warner was a Senior Lecturer at the Royal Military Academy, Sandhurst.

Also by Philip Warner in Sphere Books:

AUCHINLECK: THE LONELY SOLDIER
THE SAS

Horrocks
The General Who Led
from the Front

PHILIP WARNER

SPHERE BOOKS LIMITED

SPHERE BOOKS LTD

Published by the Penguin Group
27 Wrights Lane, London W8 5TZ, England
Viking Penguin Inc., 40 West 23rd Street, New York, New York 10010, USA
Penguin Books Australia Ltd, Ringwood, Victoria, Australia
Penguin Books Canada Ltd, 2801 John Street, Markham, Ontario, Canada L3R 1B4
Penguin Books (NZ) Ltd, 182–190 Wairau Road, Auckland 10, New Zealand

Penguin Books Ltd, Registered Offices: Harmondsworth, Middlesex, England

First published in Great Britain by Hamish Hamilton Ltd 1984
Published by Sphere Books Ltd 1985
Reprinted 1987, 1988

Copyright © 1984 by Philip Warner
All rights reserved

Printed and bound in Great Britain by
Cox & Wyman Ltd, Reading

To Sir Brian and Lady Horrocks whose
friendship and co-operation made writing
this book a great pleasure

Contents

Foreword

When I began this biography I had certain questions to which I hoped I would find the answers. Was Sir Brian Horrocks, for example, an underrated general? I had always understood that his genius had flourished under Montgomery's protective shadow; but was Horrocks' debt to Montgomery greater than Montgomery's to Horrocks?

Secondly, was Horrocks an English Rommel? Could he, if given a completely free hand, have emulated the deeds of the 'Desert Fox'? There were many similarities between the two, but similarities can be dangerously misleading when making assessments. Both were front-line soldiers, both were brave, often taking unnecessary risks, both were known and admired by their men. Rommel's command was approximately the same size as Horrocks', but his task was different and he had a known flair for fast, mobile, mechanized warfare. Unfortunately Horrocks was never in a position from which a fair comparison can be made. His most Rommel-like acts were at Mareth in 1943 and in the drive across Europe in 1944. Both men suffered from recurrent, nagging illnesses; both fought with chivalry. Rommel, of course, had more worries than Horrocks. When not bluffing his own high command about his urgent need for more supplies, he was trying to deceive the Eighth Army that he was better equipped than they were.

Thirdly, I wondered whether Horrocks' astounding drive had been equalled anywhere else. Patton, certainly, was not one to hang back, and O'Connor displayed a genius for moving his troops forward in unpromising situations, but neither appeared to have been able to sustain the momentum in the way that Horrocks had.

Finally, did the subsequent career – Black Rod, TV programme presenter, journalist, writer, director of a large industrial company – show that there was more in Horrocks than the Army had managed to bring out? If he had not been wounded, or later invalided out, what rank could he have attained? He was always very firm about his limitations – that he could never have become CIGS or a Field Marshal. 'I am a subaltern-general,' he would say, 'and that is my right place.'

When I began research for this book I was perturbed by two discoveries. Horrocks' memory at the age of eighty-six was fragmentary. But when he did remember something it was crystal clear. I felt that somehow the loss of memory was almost deliberate. He remembered the excitement of trying to escape from German prisoner-of-war camps but could hardly recall anything about Arnhem. He said that he had been asked so much and so often about Arnhem that he had now completely lost interest and forgotten it.

On the other hand he had written extensively about himself and his wartime career. His autobiography *A Full Life* contains a mass of tightly packed information and many enjoyable stories. In old age he remembered all that was in that book but very little outside it. When questioned about certain periods he would repeat almost word for word what he had said either in that, or his later book *Corps Commander*. After a time, and particularly when I had talked about his TV programmes with his former producer, Sir Huw Wheldon, I realised why that was. In his own mind he reduced everything to the minimum and discarded the rest. On the same principle he had got rid of all his papers and letters, casualties too of the many moves of house he had made. He had never kept a diary. He reduced information to essentials, built it into his memory, and threw away the scaffolding. This was ideal for wartime but made the task of the historian and biographer rather difficult.

But he was always helpful, always happy to talk about what he could remember. And, of course, there were still, when I could find them, many friends who had known him well. These too were invariably helpful. Perhaps the most outstandingly generous contribution was made by Leo Cooper, who lent me the entire correspondence between himself and Horrocks from 1966 to 1973. This covered the whole of the 'Famous Regiments' and also Horrocks' own autobiography. The autobiography had first been published by Collins but then passed to Leo Cooper. A revised and lengthened edition had therefore been produced in 1974. When in 1981 I mentioned to Leo Cooper that I was contemplating a biography of Horrocks he was considering re-issuing the autobiography. On hearing of my intention he promptly discarded the idea and instead gave me every assistance in writing a book which could not be anything but detrimental to his own interests.

Many other people have given me great help and encouragement. If I gave them all the thanks they deserve I should make this foreword unduly long. I have therefore simply recorded their names. If there are any omissions or mistakes I alone am responsible and offer my sincere apologies: the late Lt-General Sir Terence Airey, KCMG, CB, CBE; Lt-Colonel A. D. Andrews, MC; Dr S. C. Aston;

Mr Christopher Bailey, Headmaster, Bow School, Durham; Mr J. N. Baines; Mr Correlli Barnett; Mr Eversley Belfield; Maj-General H. A. Borradaile, CB, DSO; Lt-Colonel M. H. Broadway; Brigadier F.M. de Butts, CMG, OBE, DL; Mr A. J. Coventry; Major P. Critchley; Major N. Denny, MC; Mr A. C. Edwards; Mr Edward Fox; General J. M. Gavin; Mr R. B. Goodall; Brigadier P. W. P. Green, CBE, DSO; General Sir John Hackett, GCB, CBE, DSO, MC; Sir Denis Hamilton, DSO, TD; Mr John Herbert; Squadron Leader H. E. Hervey; Major D. N. Hopkins, MBE; Sir David Hunt, KCMG, OBE; Mr J. W. Hunt and the Library Staff at the RMA, Sandhurst; Mr B. E. Hutton-Williams, MBE; Lt-Colonel R. Leyland, OBE; Captain D. Lynch, MBE, DCM; Lt-Colonel G. Macdonald; Professor Sir Robert Macintosh, MA, DM, FRCSE, DA, FFARCS; Mr B. Matthews (Archivist, Uppingham School); Mr J. A. Nasmyth; Colonel G. Powell, MC; Mr J. McN. Shelford; Lt-Colonel G. A. Shepperd, OBE; General Sir Frank Simpson, GBE, KCB, DSO; Dr J. S. Sweetman; Colonel A. V. Tennuci; Mr M. Varvill, CMG; Mr N. Vincent; Sir Huw Wheldon, MC; Dr M. H. Wright; Mr Harold Young; Brigadier P. Young, DSO, MC; and Maj-General A. E. Younger, DSO, OBE.

The Record of Service of Sir William Horrocks was taken from the roll of Medical Officers of the Army, 1660-1960, Vol. 1, provided by the RAMC Historical Museum, to which I would like to express my gratitude.

Philip Warner

Chapter 1

Early Days

'Two fresh Corps Commanders arrived out, Leese and Horrocks. They were Montgomery's choice, and I'm sure he never regretted it. They were both great commanders, possessing drive and enthusiasm – in fact all the right qualities. Leese was more methodical and thorough, whilst Horrocks was more spectacular and colourful. I always used to think of him as Marshal Ney.'

Thus said Major-General Sir Francis de Guingand, Chief of Staff, Eighth Army and 21st Army Group. The comparison with Marshal Ney is a curious one and suggests that de Guingand knew less about the French general than he did about Horrocks. For although Ney was described as 'the bravest of the brave' and had a number of brilliant victories to his credit, he was prone to be over-venturesome on one occasion and too hesitant on another. But perhaps de Guingand was merely thinking of the Frenchman's style rather than his whole career. Both were men who led from the front, but Ney was originally a cavalry officer. Horrocks came from the infantry. Ney was executed on a trumped-up charge at the age of forty-six: he had been a marshal for eleven years. At the same age Horrocks had just become a corps commander.

Which of the two was the better commander would make an interesting debate. Ney, of course, had the greater opportunities, although they all turned to defeat and ashes at the end. Horrocks was more fortunate when his military career ended, for he was able to display outstanding abilities in other fields. A fortnight after he had retired he was offered the post of Black Rod in the House of Lords, an appointment he held for fourteen years. It appears to be a job of simple ceremonial, requiring nothing except the ability to walk about in an elegant uniform. In fact, like many ceremonial posts, it requires considerable tact, diplomacy and stamina. At times of potential disaster it can be very tense and exacting. Horrocks was fifty-four, and had been invalided out of the army following various wounds. When he eventually found the long hours too exhausting and resigned at the age of sixty-eight, however, it was not to slip away into peaceful retirement but to begin another career, or series of careers, in industry and television for the next fourteen years. That

1

took him to the age of 82. And before finally retiring he had written two books – and edited a series of books on famous regiments.

One of the keys to his ability to lead such an energetic life was the ability to relax. The other keys will become apparent later in the story. But about relaxation his own words are particularly relevant: 'Today any man who leads a well-filled life should have a private lane down which he can escape to his other world – preferably far removed in feeling and tempo from his everyday existence.

'For some, the lane leads to a garden, or shelves of books, or a workshop in which hours can be spent with wood, tools, glue, nails and screws. The essential thing, I think, is that the lane should lead away from ever-ringing telephones, radio, TV, pavements filled with hurrying elbowing crowds, and roads congested with impatient, hastening drivers. For many years, my lane led down to a quiet water's edge, where a small boat lay at her moorings. At the age of sixty-one, I attended with my wife a course in small boat sailing, first of all at Bosham and then at Emsworth Sailing School. Thus we found something which occupied all our spare time more happily. I only wished I had taken it up many years before.'

Sailing came late in the day. Before that there had been many other ways to relaxation, mostly through sport of one kind or another. But the ability to relax is more widely conferred than the ability to create a life from which relaxation is a paramount necessity. For the impression conveyed by Horrocks was always of super-abundant, dynamic, thrusting energy. Even in an ordinary conversation with a stranger he could convey this impression of intense interest, a man like a coiled spring. Where did that come from?

He himself does not really know. It seems to be a combination of hereditary factors and a happy upbringing. As he put it, 'Unlike, as it would seem, many children of today, I had an extremely happy childhood.'

He was born on 7 September 1895 at Ranniket, then an Indian hill station much favoured by the British Army. His father was William Heaton Horrocks, formerly of Little Bolton in Lancashire, who, after graduating at London University in medicine, had joined the RAMC as a surgeon in 1887. William Horrocks subsequently had a distinguished career which was recognised by a knighthood in 1918 and the honorary rank of major-general, although his real military rank was colonel.

One of his greatest achievements was in his work with the Royal Society Commission on Malta fever. Malta fever, otherwise known as brucellosis or undulant fever, is carried by raw milk or imperfectly cooked pork. Nowadays, because milk is pasteurised it is less frequently encountered, but it was a scourge in the nineteenth century.

Rarely fatal, it is a weakening and depressing disease. Horrocks assisted in the discovery that the main carrier was infected goats' milk.

Another notable contribution to health in the Army was the 'Horrocks box'. By the outbreak of the First World War in 1914 Horrocks had already acquired a high reputation for his publications on the contamination of water. One of these explained how bacteria from sewage could find their way into ventilation pipes. Very early on in the campaign it became clear that unless all drinking water was sterilized disease would become widespread. Horrocks therefore devised and perfected sand filtration and chlorine sterilization plants which could be assembled on lorries and barges. These were found to be practical and indispensable; it is said that the remarkable freedom from water-borne disease of the Allied forces was principally due to the Horrocks box.

From water purification against natural contaminants it was a short step to research against poisons introduced by the enemy. Water supplies were not often poisoned but Horrocks and a colleague named Professor Baker found a foolproof way of removing poisons in case they should be. He also helped design the first gas mask.

Many soldiers owed a debt to William Horrocks, of whose existence they were doubtless unaware. As Director of Army Hygiene in the First World War, he laid down principles which saved many lives in the Second. The Horrocks approach was simple, clear and direct.

In 1894 William Horrocks married Minna Moore, daughter of the Reverend J.C. Moore of Connor, County Antrim. Their marriage was a happy one, although the early irresponsibility of Brian must have worried them at times. Brian had a sister, Jean, who never married and who died a few years ago. Like her brother, she was a keen games player and a skilful golfer.

For young Brian Horrocks the nomadic life of a service family was all tremendous fun. He was very happy and secure at home. He loved both his parents deeply and later marvelled at their tolerance of some of his escapades, escapades mainly of idleness and extravagance. By the time he was reaching school age his father had been posted to Gibraltar. From Gibraltar Brian was sent to a preparatory school, the Bow School at Durham, which still flourishes.* He does not know why they chose Durham, nor even why later he went on to Uppingham. All he remembers is that he enjoyed his time at both enormously. Life in Gibraltar as a young schoolboy is something he

---

* A picture of Horrocks' medals hangs in the school hall.

remembers vividly nearly eighty years later. He describes it as 'a small boy's paradise'. He travelled back and forth by P & O, his only worry being whether his money would last out. His mother would meet him and he would tell her of his adventures or, as he puts it, 'as much as I thought was good for her to know'.

By the time he was due to move on from Bow School his father had been posted to the War Office in London, so the journeys between home and school were less interesting.

Uppingham, which until 1974 was in Rutland and proud of it, is now in Leicestershire (the county of Rutland having ceased to exist). The school had been founded in the sixteenth century by an Arch-deacon of Leicester, Robert Johnson, who had also established a similar school at nearby Oakham. There were hundreds of such small grammar schools scattered all over the country. Oakham* was the better known and respected of the two schools until 1853 when Edward Thring, a Somerset clergyman, became headmaster at Uppingham. When he arrived it had twenty-five pupils and was virtually unknown; when he died in 1887 it was one of the major schools in the country with 300 boys on the roll. Thring was appointed headmaster at the age of thirty-two after a distinguished university career in which he had been elected a Fellow of King's College, Cambridge. However, his memories of his own turbulent schooldays at Eton caused him to establish a different system at Uppingham. Although a keen disciplinarian and upholder of academic tradition, Thring was a reformer. He gave each boy a study, partitioned off the beds in the dormitories, built a gymnasium, introduced handicrafts and the arts, established the first Public School Mission for poor boys in London, and founded the Head-masters' Conference in 1869. Although a fervent upholder of the Classics, Thring also believed in the importance of accurate know-ledge of English grammar and expression. He wrote several books on this and other educational matters. In consequence, when boys like young Horrocks went to the school in the early years of the present century, they were given ample opportunity to enjoy school life instead of hating every minute of it, as boys did in many other schools.

Horrocks had ten terms at the school; he arrived in September 1909 and left in December 1912. Although Thring's headmastership had ended twenty-five years before he arrived at the school, the head-master's standards and ideas were still a powerful force.† Thring had

* Oakham continued to flourish and in the 1970s was one of the first public schools to become fully co-educational.
† This was not an unusual phenomenon. Arnold's ideas long outlasted his time at Rugby, as did Sanderson's at Oundle, as did Grundy's at Malvern and Almond's at Loretto. But bad examples could be as durable as good examples.

always emphasised certain principles which, consciously or uncon-sciously, Horrocks practised later when he became not merely a first-class army instructor but also a nationally known TV per-sonality. Thring used to say: 'The teacher considers the worse the material, the greater the skill in working it. Pouring out knowledge is not teaching. Hearing lessons is not teaching. Hammering a task is not teaching. Lecturing clearly is not teaching. No mere applying a knowledge is teaching.

'Teaching is getting at the heart and mind, so that the learner begins to value learning, and to believe learning possible in his own case.'

Although Thring did not invariably practise what he preached – he would become indignant if some of his sixth-formers did not always show the same enthusiasm or perhaps merely could not keep up – he left his pupils with a series of valuable precepts. He believed in a vigorous style of teaching, using vivid examples and practical comparisons. He believed firmly in success. In school games, when he played with the boys as he did frequently, he played to win.

He also understood how authority should be used. 'Unpunctuality makes authority grate' was one of his dicta and, later, Horrocks was always so determined never to be a second late that he would set out for an assignment early, and then wait around the corner until he was due. 'Little changes make authority con-temptible and little interferences make it hateful.' In military life Horrocks liked to give clear instructions and then stand back. (He did not, however, make the mistake of assuming that everything would always go well; he had ways of finding out unobtrusively.) But he learnt much from the traditions of Thring who, before his success, had suffered appalling setbacks. Just when he had built Uppingham into a much-admired school, for example, he saw it nearly ruined by epidemics, first of scarlet fever, then of typhoid. The town blamed the school for the epidemics; the school had much to say about the local drainage system. Eventually, at the point when boys and masters were looking for places in other, less afflicted schools, Thring moved the school to Borth, in North Wales. The expense and worry were horrific but the school survived.

Horrocks looks back on his days at Uppingham as being thoroughly enjoyable. In distant retrospect he feels he could have applied himself more rigorously to academic studies; instead he drifted into the Army class and coasted along with the minimum effort. Games were a different story: he took part in those to his heart's content. In consequence, when the time came for Sandhurst entrance, he scraped in bottom but one. Perhaps the authorities took into account the fact that he had been a drummer in the Officers'

Training Corps Band at Uppingham. He was also a left-arm bowler in the 1st XI and fly-half in the 1st XV.

Few people would have predicted a distinguished military career from Horrocks' beginnings at Sandhurst. In each company intake a few cadets were promoted to various posts of minor responsibility, senior under-officer, junior under-officer, cadet sergeant, etc. None of these came Horrocks' way; he stayed firmly on the bottom rung, distinguished only by being a good all-round games player and something of a rebel. 'Let me be quite honest about it; I was late, careless in my turnout – in any parlance scruffy – and, due to the fact that I am inclined to roll when I walk, very unsmart on parade. Throughout my military career I have always been allotted a position on ceremonial parades where I was least likely to be seen.'

He entered the Royal Military College, Sandhurst on 12 February 1913 and left on 15 July 1914. In that time he studied administration, military law, riding, musketry, sanitation, French, map reading, history, physical training, tactics, engineering and signalling. It was a very practical course. 'Sanitation' dealt with field hygiene. The British Army had learnt some bitter lessons in the three-hundred-year history of fighting everywhere from the bitterly cold forests of Canada to damp and oppressive areas in the tropics. The causes of many diseases were imperfectly understood but the Army, largely from the efforts of Horrocks senior, had learnt the best ways to prevent them. Campaigns such as the Crimean had emphasised the importance of dry clothing, cleanliness, properly sited cookhouses and latrines, a balanced diet, and adequate drainage, both human and material. Engineering dealt with such matters as fortification and bridge-building. Musketry was probably the most important subject of all. The strength of the British Army lay in its marksmanship. When the 'Old Contemptibles' confronted the advancing Germans in 1914 the latter thought they must be encountering machine-guns, so accurate and rapid was the fire of the British riflemen. Fifteen rounds a minute does not sound very much nowadays, but great skill was required to fire two five-round clips of .303 ammunition in a minute, let alone three. Cadets would not normally attain a very high standard of proficiency, but would certainly learn how to supervise the training of marksmen. Horrocks was, as it happened, a good shot, an ability which would be useful later when he engaged in the pentathlon. In athletics he specialised in the mile and two-mile events. His company was Champion Company in 1913.

In his last three months at Sandhurst he managed to get himself 'restrictions' for the entire period. Restrictions is a punishment which usually means that the officer is confined to barracks, makes periodic appearances at the guard room in full kit, and gets additional fatigues and parades. A fatigue in the army can mean any of many irksome tasks. It can involve checking kit, collecting marker flags after parades or exercises, carrying ammunition or water. Some NCOs have a positive genius for thinking up tedious and often unnecessary tasks. Every cadet has some experience of punishments and fatigues, and it is right that he should have, for the men he will later command will have their share of them too, usually more fairly earned than those which fall to a cadet. A cadet may turn up on parade immaculately tidy (as he thinks) with rifle and boots as near to perfection as can be. But under the eye of the inspecting officer or NCO he may be found to have 'dirty flesh', an 'idle' rifle, or unclean boots. 'Take his name.' There is no appeal against the inevitable sentence, nor is any cadet so foolish as to try to make one. Standards were made almost impossibly high at Sandhurst and the Royal Military Academy at Woolwich; when the two colleges were merged in 1947 to become the Royal Military Academy, Sandhurst there were many changes, but standards remained as high as ever. The factor which made this necessary tyranny bearable, and accepted by cadets (who came from many countries other than Britain) was that it often seemed humorous, even to the victim.

Horrocks' crime was, of course, more serious than having a speck of dust on his rifle or a button which did not shine like a mirror. He had tried to evade payment of his railway fare. He was not the first nor the last officer cadet to prefer such a risk to a forty-mile walk, but he was caught. As a senior who should have had more sense than to get himself into such a mess, he received a severe punishment. Unfortunately for Horrocks a friend had told him of a horse which was certain to win the three o'clock race. It was such a cert that neither he nor his friends bought return tickets: instead they took singles and put every penny they could muster on the unbeatable horse. Disaster inevitably followed. But even the loss of all his money and the three months' restrictions were not the end of his troubles: his marks on the course had not been high and when the final exams came he was far from certain that he had done well enough to obtain a commission. Final results would not be published till mid-August.

In the end the results did not matter at all. On 4 August 1914 Britain found herself at war with Germany and, instead of the usual careful and lengthy process of commissioning and posting, those who had completed the Sandhurst course were promptly made second lieutenants and despatched to the regiment of their choice. Horrocks was relieved that Sandhurst was safely behind him, but had another pressing problem. He had borrowed his father's revolver – and pawned it. Worse still, he had lost the pawn ticket. Was his father very angry? 'No, he took it terribly well. He wasn't too pleased though.'*

His regiment was the Middlesex. The Middlesex, although one of the younger regiments of the British army, has a magnificent fighting record. It had been founded as the 59th (later to become the 57th) regiment in 1756, for use against the French invaders of Canada. During its lifetime it had fought with distinction on many fronts, in India, in Spain, in the Crimea, during the First World War when it had raised twenty-three battalions and won five Victoria Crosses, through the Second World War, in Korea and in Cyprus. But in the 1960s and 1970s, when the numbers of the army were being drastically reduced and there was a widely held, though equally widely questioned, belief in the virtue of large regiments made up of amalgamations, the Middlesex came to the end of its distinguished career. Faced with the problem of deciding which regiments must go, for some *had* to go, the War Office chose to decide it by seniority. It was at first a question of merge or disappear; later the mergers became so complicated that many of the original regiments disappeared altogether. It ceased to exist in 1973 when it was fully absorbed into the Queen's.

When Horrocks joined the Middlesex, the idea of such a regiment ever coming to an end would have seemed ludicrous. He was, and still is, enormously proud of his membership of it. The regimental nickname was 'The Die-hards', earned in the battle of Albuera in 1811. The 57th as it then was, for the county names did not come into use till later in the century, had fought several gruelling battles already in the Peninsular campaign. On 16 May 1811 they were the centre of a division facing a determined French attack. The commanding officer was Colonel William Inglis, who had been with the regiment since 1781. He was a keen disciplinarian – as he needed to be to prevent looting, rape and desertion in such a campaign – and he led by example. Early in this battle his horse was shot and fell; Inglis managed to land on his feet and carried on deploying his men as if nothing had happened. The French had the advantage of fresher troops and much superior numbers, but these were not the worst of the British troubles. In the early stages of the battle mist had obscured the relative positions. When it lifted the 57th, on a forward slope, were being slaughtered by concentrated cannon fire well out of range of their own muskets. All they could do was to edge forward and hope that enough would survive to hold the position and eventually make an attack. Inglis was wounded in the chest by

* As a member of the RAMC and thus a non-combatant, his father would not normally bear arms. However, RAMC personnel serving in areas where the Red Cross was not recognised were permitted the means of self-defence.

grapeshot. As he lay on the ground he called out steadily, 'Die hard, 57th.' Although there was a constant noise of cannon, shouting, cries of pain, Inglis chose his moment well. He continued to give the rallying cry and propped himself up on his elbows in front of the regiment, refusing all medical attendance. The hours passed; rain fell. On the right flank the Royal Fusiliers were now beginning to edge their way forward. As the French began to waver, what was left of the 57th gradually began to move forward too. There were shouts of 'Stop them − they'll all be killed,' from General Beresford's position, but they were not heard. The 57th had held, and now they too advanced.

The cost was appalling. Out of 600, ninety-one were dead, 333 wounded, and a mere 176 still on their feet. Inglis, though badly wounded, survived; he was the only officer to do so, and he lived to become Lt-General Sir William Inglis. Inevitably, the regiment became known as 'The Die-hards'. It was a title they would merit again in the future, more than once. It was certainly an inspiration to Horrocks. Even when his memory had faded, that incident at Albuera remained clear and vivid in his mind. In his own military life there were numerous occasions when the recollection of it sustained him.

In general, the effect on serving soldiers of valiant events of the regimental past is probably not very great. In many instances it probably has no effect at all. In every regiment, soon after a recruit joins, there is a detailed lecture or series of lectures about the history of the regiment. Many recruits, weary from endless marching and physical training, nod off as soon as they are comfortably seated in a warm lecture hall. Even those who are apparently awake may merely have acquired that useful army habit of looking alert and interested while in reality their thoughts are far away − if existing at all. But, as service with the regiment lengthens, the message seeps in, however remote in time and concept the original events may have been.

Officers, particularly young ones, are much more receptive to the lessons of military history than NCOs or soldiers, even if only to avoid showing ignorance when questioned. Some will be inspired: undoubtedly Horrocks was one. Inglis belonged to a period in military history when commanding officers varied from the excellent to the deplorable. One cannot but contrast the Charge of the Light Brigade in 1854 with the Middlesex at Albuera in 1811. Cardigan showed examplary courage when leading his men, but that was the limit of his contribution. After the charge, all he could do was grumble, then retire to his yacht, drink a bottle of champagne and go to bed. There was little difference in the casualties, for the Light

Brigade was only the equivalent of a regiment in numbers: 673 took part in the charge, 113 were killed, 134 were wounded: it all took twenty minutes. Proportionally the Middlesex would seem to have suffered more, for they sustained their losses through a day's dour fighting under more continuous strain.

In his own campaigns Horrocks never forgot the value of personal example, the willingness to take risks. He knew that soldiers would be frightened, more particularly if they had never been in action at all. In the desert (the story comes from his ADC Captain H. Young) he would say, 'These chaps moving up will be pretty scared, particularly if it's their first time. Now *we*'ll go right up and then drive slowly back, taking our time. When they see the general coming back from where they're going, without a scratch on him, they'll feel better about it.'

Horrocks always knew that – to use the cricket expression – 'if you can stay at the wicket the runs come'. There were times in his career when wounds, ill-health, financial strains, and bereavement, might have crushed him. But, like Uppingham and Inglis, he survived.

As a teacher he had absorbed much of his school's practical philosophy. In 1956, Major P. Critchley recalls being present at a lecture Horrocks gave at Devizes. Horrocks arrived on the platform, surveyed his audience which had had all too much experience of visiting lecturers, and began: 'Now, gentlemen, it's after lunch, and it's a warm afternoon. And I'm not much of a lecturer. So if you feel you can't avoid it, don't worry about dropping off for an occasional nap. I've often done it myself and I shan't feel at all hurt.'

Then he began. For a few minutes some of his audience took him at his word and settled themselves comfortably. Ten minutes later all were sitting on the front of their chairs, determined not to miss a syllable.

On 8 August 1914, 2nd Lt Brian Horrocks reported for duty with a militia battalion at Fort Darland, Chatham. The Middlesex mustered ten battalions. At that time battalions normally numbered 1000, including officers and men. (Modern regiments who often have to make do with little more than half that number in a battalion envy their forebears.) Four of the ten battalions were regulars, 1st, 2nd, 3rd and 4th; two were reserve, 5th and 6th, and four were territorial, 7th, 8th, 9th and 10th. The 1st, which Horrocks would join, was at Woolwich, but the 2nd was at Malta, the 3rd was in India, and the 4th at Devonport. The Depot was at Mill Hill. In view of the fact that war had been declared on the fourth, it was no mean achievement to have something like 10,000 men equipped and ready for war four days later. The reserve battalions, the 5th and 6th, had mobilized at Mill Hill, been equipped, and sent to Chatham: they would be used as reinforcements and for replacing casualties. Meanwhile the 1st battalion had been sent to the Mons district, which they had reached after a series of gruelling marches. After a brisk opening battle they were ordered to take part in the general retreat and soon found themselves back in Le Cateau. There, after days of marching on the paved roads under a hot sun, they were required to dig in and hold the Germans. In order to make marching easier they had been told to throw away all surplus equipment, including entrenching tools. They were now required to dig in on hard chalk with no more suitable implements than mess tins. The thoughtful originator of these orders had justified them by saying 'they were too tired to march further but not too tired to lie down and fire their rifles'. And fire their rifles they did, at fifteen rounds to the minute. Then orders to retreat once more, another 150 miles. By 28 August, when Horrocks was setting off from Chatham, the 1st Middlesex were at Pontoise which they had reached after a period of three weeks' continuous marching and fighting; their casualties had mounted accordingly. And the great German attack which was to encircle and engulf Paris had still not been stopped.

Horrocks, aged eighteen, now had ninety-five men under his command. They were all reservists, all old soldiers who, though somewhat softened by life away from the colours, knew all the tricks of the trade. There is a saying in the army: 'Any bloody fool can be uncomfortable.' In contrast the experienced soldier can extract some trifling degree of comfort out of almost any conditions. There is no military virtue in enduring hardship if you can be warm, dry, properly fed and not be exposed to unnecessary danger. Horrocks learnt more from these men than he could ever have guessed at. To his surprise, when he reached Southampton and counted them, the ninety-five had become ninety-eight. Everyone was so firmly convinced that the war would be over by Christmas, with the Germans well beaten of course, that men could hardly wait to get to the front and three unofficial extras had joined the ranks. Nobody had the slightest idea of what conditions were like in France, but even if they had it would have made no difference to the enthusiasm, except perhaps to increase it. Horrocks retained his unorthodox command all the way through France until they arrived with the battalion just in time for the battle of the Aisne. An early memory was of the ability of soldiers to 'live off the land'. Since leaving England they had travelled in the French railway trucks designed to carry eight horses or forty men in equivalent standards of comfort. Whenever the train

11

halted the officers looked around keenly to make sure no pillaging of local crops – mainly carrots – took place. No soldier, he says, was ever seen to approach a carrot, yet in the stew that same evening tasty carrots seemed to be the principal ingredient.

He retained his command of the ninety-eight reservists for a few days after arrival on the Aisne, but then they were taken from him and allocated to companies as replacements. Horrocks was given command of a platoon (No. 16), less than one third the strength of his original detachment, and now, with a good company commander and an experienced platoon sergeant, he began to learn the essentials of military life. At first it was the tactics of how to fight on the retreat, then how to keep going when he was so exhausted that he was almost incapable of thought. 'I had never realised before that it was possible to go to sleep while the legs continued automatically to function.'

Confused though these days were, clear memories from them never left him. Not least was the Cockney sense of humour with which his regiment was well endowed. This ready wit that thrives on adversity is not of course restricted to Cockneys, but the shout from a raucous voice during incessant bombardment asking the Germans to 'Give over a bit, Jerry. Our gun's broke,' is a valuable antidote to the strain of front-line fighting.

The official history summarised the events of these days: 'They were hastened forward by forced marches to the battle, confronted with greatly superior numbers of the most renowned army in Europe, and condemned at the very outset to undergo the severest ordeal which can be imposed on an army. They were always short of food and sleep, for thirteen days, as has been told; at the end they were still an army, and a formidable army. They were never demoralised, for they rightly judged they had never been beaten.'

This was Horrocks' introduction to war. But worse was to come.

Chapter 2

Into Limbo

The retreat from Mons did not end until 5 September 1914. The 1st Middlesex had then reached Grisy, a village to the north of Melun. The right wing of the German master plan (*Schlieffen*) had been deflected from its route to encircle Paris from the west and had instead come on to the eastern side. The 1st Middlesex had fallen back from Mons through Le Cateau, St Quentin, Noyon, Compiègne, Senlis and Lagny. Now they would be required to push up in a counter-attack and reach the Aisne, near Soissons. This they did, and then settled down to trench warfare. But before the long grinding war of attrition in the trenches could begin there was some further desperate fighting in the north. Here, it seemed, was an opportunity to push the Germans back by a drive towards Menin. Hopes were not to be realised. When Haig sent the British Corps forward, it ran into unexpectedly heavy German concentrations. These, with equal desperation, were trying to break through to the Channel ports. The key point of the British forces was at Ypres. Strategically it was of no great importance, and if it had been evacuated little would have been lost and many lives saved. But Ypres, dangerous because it was a salient, became a symbol of territory which must not be yielded, if only for the sake of morale. The battle of Ypres was a heavy price to pay for that morale.

The official history of the Middlesex Regiment described the events of those days as follows. The 1st Middlesex marched out of St Omer at 7 a.m. on 11 October. On 12 October 'touch had been established with the enemy about Strazeele. On the 19th [after marching and fighting] they set out with orders to reach Laventie. This entailed a long march of some 27 miles at the end of which tired troops trudged into Estaires at about 2 a.m. on the 20th finding only *very bad billets*. At 12 noon the whole brigade received orders to move on to Fromelles. Half an hour later the Middlesex marched out of Estaires, taking up position on the left of the Royal Welch Fusiliers, then posted along the road to Pont Pierre in support of the French cavalry. All night long the Middlesex men were engaged in digging trenches and in putting the position into a state of defence. The two battalions (Royal Welch Fusiliers and

Middlesex) bivouacked about a mile north-west of Fromelles for the night.'

Orders were then given for Fromelles and Le Maisnil to be occupied. The Cameronians now joined the 1st Middlesex and both moved into Le Maisnil. The 2nd Argylls were already in the town, and their sector soon came under prolonged and accurate shell fire. 'B' and 'D' companies of the Middlesex moved up to support the Argylls. 'They themselves were shelled heavily and had a number of casualties.' The Germans now launched a very strong infantry attack on the town. Orders were issued for the brigade to retire, but the shelling continued as the regiments moved back. The Middlesex suffered particularly badly. When the regiment took up its new position in Bas Maisnil its casualties amounted to over one hundred officers and men. Among them were two officers reported wounded and missing. One of them was Horrocks. His platoon had been surrounded by large forces confronting them and after a brisk fight in which most of them, including Horrocks, had been wounded, they were taken prisoner.

(The 2nd Argylls, whom the Middlesex were supporting, were also badly cut up. But they were to triumph over worse disasters than this. In the Second World War they fought with relentless determination in Malaya until what was left of them was finally taken prisoner on the surrender of Singapore in 1942. A new 2nd battalion was promptly reconstituted and fought vigorously and tenaciously under Horrocks' command in 30 Corps in North-west Europe in 1944.)

But for both regiments, in spite of heavy casualties, this particular battle in October 1914, which came to be known as the Battle of Armentières, was ultimately a triumph. In the final stages, now supported by the 2nd Argylls, and having pressed everyone into service, cooks, pioneers, batmen, runners, they killed 200 Germans and drove many more back. It was in the best tradition of the regiment.

'Die hard, boys, die hard' would be heard many more times before the First World War was over, but never more poignantly than when spoken in the dying moments of Lt-Colonel E.V.R. Stephenson who commanded the 3rd battalion when the Germans used gas at Ypres. Following the gas attack the battalion was almost wiped out by machine-gun fire but the survivors joined up with the Canadians and held the line.

•

But for Horrocks active service had ended on 21st October. He had been shot through the lower stomach (there are not many parts of his anatomy which Horrocks has not been shot through at one time or another). He was taken to a military hospital near Lille and put in a bed next to an Argyll private who had lost a leg. Unfortunately for the two, the Germans were particularly hostile. The hospital existed in name only for them, for during the whole month in which they were there neither their sheets nor their blankets were changed. Their clothes were still soaked in blood and as the wounds began to suppurate they began to smell very unpleasant. Periodically the Germans accused them of using dum-dum bullets (which Horrocks had never heard of at the time). A dum-dum is a bullet which has been cut or blunted at the end so that it spreads on entering a wound. Accusations were bellowed at the two as they lay helpless. Horrocks says he has associated Germans with shouting ever since.

The misery of this life was a sharp contrast to his life of three months before. Fortunately for him, that three months had been full of lessons. As a green-as-grass second lieutenant he had seen the way old soldiers can make something endurable out of the most impossible conditions, and when in action had had the advantage of a company commander who knew all there was to know about 'man management' long before the term was invented. Officers would share the hardships of their men and would not eat until all their men had eaten. He learnt to admire his men's virtues and understand their weaknesses. He was eighteen. When the war finished he was only twenty-three in chronological age but a veteran in experience.

Later he decided that his prisoner-of-war days, which were just beginning, were some of his most valuable experiences. 'Being a prisoner of war was probably the best apprenticeship for command in war. The lessons were there for learning and unquestionably the most important was self-reliance.'

He certainly needed it in his so-called 'hospital'. When the First World War began there had immediately been stories about German atrocities in Belgium. Later these were mostly dismissed as war hysteria. In fact, although the German Army behaved reasonably well in most of the First World War, behaviour in Belgium, and particularly in Louvain in the early stages, was as bad as any of the horrors perpetrated by the SS in the Second World War. Horrocks' hospital seemed to be staffed with people who would have made ideal recruits for the SS. All through his life Horrocks has recalled the fact that neither man was allowed to use a bed pan or bottle and therefore had to crawl along the floor – for neither could walk – and along a stone passage to the lavatory at the end. As their only garments were their shirts, their semi-naked state was a source of much unpleasant mirth from the other (German) patients.

After a month, although he could now walk only with the utmost difficulty, he was judged fit enough to be sent to a prisoner-of-war camp in Germany. To his joy his escort was a front-line soldier, a *Feldwebel* (sergeant) of the Imperial Guard. Horrocks always drew a clear distinction between what he described as 'the most exclusive club in the world' – the soldiers who fight in the front line – and those who follow them when the hard fighting is over. It is a delicate distinction. Certainly line-of-communication troops tended to be of inferior quality and often were only too ready to work off their spleen on helpless prisoners or wounded. But equally not all front-line troops behaved with impeccable chivalry. The SS provided guards for concentration camps but also sent units to fight in the front line, and little compassion was to be expected from those troops. Japanese front-line troops behaved abominably in Burma and Malaya too, Russian soldiers were usually as bad as the Nazis they replaced and even Allied troops could be vindictively brutal, although not as a matter of policy.

But Horrocks was lucky with his escort. When they came to one station, a German Red Cross girl was walking along the platform carrying a large bowl of soup. She was going to offer some to Horrocks when she realised he was an Englishman. She drew back, spat in the soup and threw it down on the platform. This infuriated the *Feldwebel*. However, he used cunning to defeat the system. He told Horrocks to sit down out of sight and then collected food from everyone who passed the carriage. Every single item was given to Horrocks. At another station when they went to the stationmaster's office to enquire about trains, there was no one in it. The *Feldwebel* gave Horrocks a chair. Then in came the stationmaster, fat and pompous. He bellowed with rage at seeing Horrocks sitting in his office and shouted for him to get up. But before Horrocks could move the *Feldwebel* advanced menacingly and said, 'This is a British officer who was wounded fighting – which you will never be. He will remain seated.' And Horrocks did.

On one occasion, which he recalls joyfully, a German troop train arrived on one side of a platform while a trainload of British prisoners of war arrived at the other. They included wounded and were dirty and hungry. But they were cheerful. When a German general in full regalia walked around to have a look at them, a Cockney voice called out, 'All tickets, please.'

The *Feldwebel* and Horrocks became good friends and, when they parted, exchanged addresses. Some years later Horrocks received a letter from the man's father to say that the *Feldwebel* had been killed in 1915.

The camp he eventually reached contained British, French, Russian and Belgian officers, all from their various fronts. He spent the first few months in hospital, cared for by a highly skilled Canadian doctor. After a long time his wounds healed and the swellings subsided. The camp was the severest test of morale so far. The routine never varied, and the scenery never changed. The sight of the barbed wire and German sentries marching up and down outside it was so depressing that he felt he must escape at all costs. This ambition did not make him over-popular. The inmates of the camp fell into distinct groups. There were the older ones who pined for their families but who were reluctant to do anything which might jeopardise their safe return to them; the career-conscious who now realised that their hopes of promotion had gone for ever; the ones who were only too glad to be out of the war with a whole skin; and those like Horrocks, mainly but not invariably young, who spent every waking moment plotting and pondering how to get out and what to do when they did so. This group made itself very unpopular, for every time they attempted an escape, whether successful or unsuccessful, there would be reprisals on everyone by the camp commandant. Usually the recreation area would be closed off and exercise restricted. The German government decided to play on the desire to escape boredom at any price by offering transfers to camps in neutral Holland where prisoners could move around freely, but only after having given their parole not to escape. It was a temptation, but to succumb to it meant that they would have to give up all ambition of returning to their regiments and once more taking part in the fighting.

Horrocks' early attempts at escape merely resulted in his being sent to Fort Zorndorf, Custrin. This camp was for prisoners who had made themselves a nuisance to the German authorities, and were likely to continue to do so. Nevertheless it was a hive of escape activity. All the prisoners' spare time was occupied in making devices which might be useful to an escaper. They included home-made compasses and home-drawn maps, clothing altered to look like German civilian dress and even dies to counterfeit German official stamps. There was a brisk market in all these commodities.

Fortunately – or perhaps unfortunately for the success of their ventures – the German commandant had a lively mind and a sense of humour. When a search party discovered that the bars on a window had been sawn through but skilfully disguised, he merely hung a notice on it saying (in German), 'useless'. On another occasion he discovered a specially drawn map. He was much intrigued by it because he could not identify the area. Finally he summoned the British officers in whose room it had been found and asked for an explanation. They gently indicated that it was of Berlin and led to the central lunatic asylum.

But his patience and humour was not unlimited. As Horrocks had been captured as early as October 1914, he was selected for repatriation, provided he signed the parole form. This Horrocks flatly refused to do. 'You will be sent to Holland, whether you like it or not,' the commandant stormed. 'Then if I am,' said Horrocks. 'I shall escape.' 'We shall see about that,' said the German grimly, and promptly allotted an escort of an NCO and two soldiers who never let Horrocks out of sight, even when he went to the lavatory. He arrived at their destination safely.

The new camp in the frontier town of Aachen looked formidable but had its weaknesses; Horrocks lost no time in finding them. That night he climbed over the wire, turned his British warm* inside out, and set off with the navigational aid of a small compass which he had managed to conceal through numerous searches. He knew the Dutch border was not far away but the first part of the journey seemed to consist of endless, dreary streets. It looked encouragingly devoid of guards, but when he tried to get under a railway line by taking a way through a small tunnel he ran into two who grabbed him so promptly they might have been waiting for his arrival. Subsequently he discovered that the area was always well guarded, partly to stop smugglers but more particularly to apprehend would-be deserters from the German Army. He was taken back into Aachen and interned in a civilian gaol.

Although he was in solitary confinement he soon found himself in contact with many of the other inmates. To his surprise they approved of him. They were either deserters or petty criminals, and supplied him with maps, useful information, and even files. By the time he left to go back to Fort Zorndorf he was an authority on the best escape routes and German military methods. But the information proved even more useful to others than himself. Although he tried to get away on many more occasions he was never successful.

He quotes various examples of the ingenuity shown by escapers. One concerned a Russian general who had died inside the camp. It was suggested that his body should be returned to Russia for burial and the German commandant agreed. The body was put in a coffin ready to be returned to Russia via Sweden. During the night the Russian officers cut a hole through the floorboards of their room, crawled along underneath the floor level until they were below the room where the dead general was lying, and then emerged into the room. The old general was hauled out of his coffin and a Russian captain took his place. Two days later the Germans received a message from Sweden saying, 'In place of one dead general, one live

* Military overcoat.

18

captain has arrived.' The dead general was then dug up from under the floor and buried by the Germans.

This type of escapemanship depended on the Germans playing the game by the best British sporting standards. The history of the treatment of prisoners of war makes an interesting study. In earlier times the richer ones had often been taken into families and treated like sons until their ransoms arrived. The lower ranks were usually given the option of joining the conqueror's army or being shot. Usually they chose the first and deserted at the earliest opportunity. In the Second World War the Japanese beheaded any would-be escapers. There were no jolly games such as tended to occur between British prisoners and German guards during the two world wars.

Horrocks used his enforced spare time to learn languages. He became quite fluent in French and German but his most interesting language proved to be Russian. When he was sharing a room with Russian officers they had a habit of spitting on the floor. Resolved to shame them out of it, he used to leap up every time they did so and draw a chalk circle round the offending deposit. Then he would say, 'Thank you,' in Russian. At first there would be a further shower of spitting, but gradually the habit diminished though it never ceased entirely. Years later when he was Black Rod at the House of Lords, Kruschev and Bulganin visited Britain and were shown the seat of parliamentary democracy. Before Kruschev could speak, Horrocks greeted him in Russian. 'Good heavens,' said Kruschev, 'where and why did you learn Russian?'

'I learnt it in a prisoner-of-war camp in Germany,' said Horrocks, 'in order to stop your officers spitting on the floor!' He doubted whether Kruschev believed him.

However, in case they should become too friendly with the guards, or too advanced with undetected plans, the prisoners were moved periodically to other camps. One of these was Holzminden, where the commandant was one Niemeyer. Niemeyer knew some English, but not as much as he thought he did. On Horrocks' arrival he addressed the assembled guards and prisoners. 'Any German speaking to these criminals,' he threatened, 'will be sent straight to the front.' Then he lost his temper and shook his fist. He shouted, 'You are very clever? Yes. Well, I make a special study of this escaping. You will not escape from here. You think I, the commandant, know nothing. You are wrong. I know damn all.'

The yell of laughter which greeted this made him angrier than ever, but conscious that he might have made a mistake in the English speech he was so proud of, he stalked off, red-faced and still muttering threats.

He was even more furious when, three weeks later, he found that eighteen officers had escaped. He doubled and trebled the sentries but still two or three prisoners got out each day. Niemeyer had appalling visions of being sent to the front himself. But the method of escape was perfectly simple. The escapers were simply walking out of the main gate at dusk when the guard was being changed. They had disguised themselves in a garb which looked approximately like a German soldier's fatigue dress. In the dim light they were taken for stragglers from a working party. Once past the main gate they knew they had the rest of the night to travel in. Their absence would not be noted till roll-call the next morning. Horrocks was one of the first to go. But the attempt was doomed to end in failure. After eight days tramping in continuous rain, they were discovered sheltering in a barn forty miles from the Dutch frontier.

He was now a marked man. Periodically, to teach him a lesson, he was sent back to Fort Zorndorf, from where no escape was possible. He was there in March 1918 when, for some reason which Horrocks never discovered, the Germans decided to send the British officers to other camps. He had now made friends with three officers from the Royal Flying Corps, and the four were sent to Clausthal, a camp in the Harz mountains. They were a remarkable quartet. One was Robert Macintosh, later to be Professor of Anaesthetics at Oxford. During the Second World War Macintosh rejoined the RAF and became a consultant in anaesthetics, and when Horrocks was operated on in 1944, after being wounded in Bizerta, one of Macintosh's staff was present at the operation. When they were being transferred to Clausthal, Macintosh had managed to jump off the train and escape just outside Berlin. He was carrying plenty of money (for there was no shortage of money in the camps) and having been advised by the Russians, headed for the red light district. There he knocked on a door and when it was opened pushed his way in and said to the woman inside that he was an escaped British prisoner of war and that he would pay £30 if he could merely shelter there for the night. She agreed and the next morning even went out and bought him a suit of German clothes. Dressed in this, he boarded the train again and set off for Freiburg. However, before he reached his destination, his leather boots attracted the attention of another occupant of the carriage: all genuine Germans were wearing a form of composition boot at the time.* The suspicious passenger contacted a station guard and Macintosh was arrested.

Another member of the quartet was William Leefe Robinson, VC, the first airman to shoot down a Zeppelin. Robinson survived the war and in 1919 encountered Macintosh in Jermyn Street. They

* He was also wearing a belt, which was not a normal article of German dress at that period.

arranged to meet for lunch a fortnight later, but before the date arrived Macintosh opened a newspaper one day and learnt that Robinson had died of influenza.

The last member was Squadron Leader Tim Hervey. In 1983, when I saw him aged 87, Hervey had just had his ballooning licence renewed. He was also making and painting miniatures, using only ordinary reading glasses to do so. The workmanship was so delicate he had built up an export market to America and Australia, in addition to buyers in this country.

On arrival at Clausthal Horrocks had an unpleasant surprise. The commandant was another Niemeyer, brother of the one at Holzminden. It was a large and comfortable camp but escaping was not only difficult materially: there were other obstacles. Not for the first time, Horrocks was told by a senior officer that there was no point in trying to escape. Attempts were certain to end in failure and the only result would be that the Germans would make life more disagreeable for everyone in the camp. He went even further and said that if Horrocks disregarded this warning he would recommend the War Office to court-martial him after the war. Escape was impossible; the frontier was 200 miles away.

Horrocks was relieved to discover that there were several other officers, of equal rank to the one who had warned him, who told him to take no notice. However, the disapproval of a senior officer was not the only problem Horrocks had to bear with. He and his friends from the Royal Flying Corps were experienced 'professional' escapers, even if they had not yet quite reached their intended destination. Most of the inmates of the camp had a plan for escaping but few had genuine experience. The danger was that amateurish attempts might give away, or at least hinder, more professional plans. Eventually these difficulties were sorted out and one central planning organisation was created, with Horrocks and his friends directing it. Through this they managed to assemble a miscellany of useful tools. Food parcels were coming in regularly and compasses, maps, and even wire cutters were concealed in hams, the backs of brushes or soap. Hervey still possesses an ingenious pair of wire-cutters which were irregularly shaped to seem like the bone in a piece of ham. Fortunately for the prisoners there were then none of the modern electronic detector devices which would have made short work of finding such subterfuges. However the Germans had their suspicions and insisted that every tin must be opened in the presence of the German staff. The contents of tins would then be probed or cut into pieces. To make sure nothing went astray all food parcels were put into a 'tin room', and drawn out when the owner requested them. They were then opened and examined.

This was an excellent precaution but somewhat invalidated by the fact that the prisoners had made a duplicate set of keys for the 'tin room'. Anything known to have unusual contents was therefore abstracted during the night.

But the Germans soon began to notice that less tins came out of the tin room than they had checked into it. To counter this the prisoners constantly complained that their tins were being stolen by the staff. The result was that the Germans kept changing the tin-room guards in spite of their protestations of innocence. (Some parcels were of course stolen by the guards, too.)

As time passed Horrocks and his friends became more desperate and venturesome. At one point Hervey and Horrocks hid in large sacks which their friends helped to conceal in the camp rubbish cart when it left for the outside area. But this failed. An attempt to cut a hole in the wire was detected before it had made much progress. The use of ladders by which to leapfrog over the perimeter fence was also found to be too optimistic. They were making good headway with a tunnel when an escape from another camp caused their own guards to search Clausthal meticulously. The tunnel had been a laborious effort. A major difficulty had been concealing the earth tunnelled out. This had had to be hidden under the floors of other rooms, and was discovered.

In the event of a break-out being successful an ingenious collection of passes had been forged. These were of the type issued to Belgian immigrant workers, and each bore a photograph. Cameras were, of course, forbidden to prisoners, but a combination of bartered food from the Red Cross parcels and bribing with cash (of which there seemed to be plenty in the camp) had suborned a German guard. To allay his suspicions of its use they took a few photographs of each other in uniform but its main purpose was to take photographs of each other dressed in clothing made to resemble that of immigrant workers. With these photographs, the forged passes looked entirely genuine.

Finally, an idea of Hervey's which involved brazenness rather than duplicity proved successful. Their camp was inside a perimeter fence and adjoined a camp for British NCOs and soldiers. From the latter each day came a party of batmen and orderlies who performed domestic duties in the officers' camp. At the end of each day they returned to their own camp. Hervey noticed that when this movement took place a sentry from the outer (perimeter) gate came into the soldiers' camp, leaving both the outer gate and the gate into the soldiers' camp unlocked and unguarded. He unlocked the gate between the officers' and soldiers' camps and locked it again when the orderlies had passed through. He then retired to the outer gate, locking the gates behind him.

Horrocks and Hervey mingled with the orderlies returning and when they were inside the soldiers' camp made a dash for the outer gate. The sentry spotted them and gave chase. Hervey tripped over a bucket of tar (it was dusk) and fell headlong. The sentry ran up, aimed a shot at him as he lay on the ground but missed. Horrocks dashed for the main gate but, before doing so, knocked the sentry to the ground. He ran on, assuming that Hervey was now following. As he plunged into the darkness beyond the arc lights, he heard more shots. At the appointed rendezvous he waited for Hervey, but no Hervey came. Apprehensive that his friend had been killed or wounded, he crept back towards the camp. A tremendous noise which included cheering, suggested that an unruly roll-call was taking place. Then, as he put it, 'I heard a more sinister noise, the baying of police dogs.' With a 200-mile journey ahead of him, he dared wait no longer. These particular dogs were alsatians and provided they kept close to their keepers, as they were trained to do, he could probably outstrip them. But he also took the precaution of walking along the bed of a stream for a hundred yards to put them off the scent. (In later years, although Horrocks was a great dog-lover and had several boxers, the dog he could never tolerate was a Doberman pinscher. On too many occasions his escape attempts had been frustrated by these agile, intelligent and persistent dogs.)

He walked by night and slept all day. At first he used to walk round the outskirts of every village he came to, but this took so long that he felt his food would be finished before he reached his destination. Although he was increasing the risk, he now began to walk through the middles of villages. However, every German house seemed to have a dog and as Horrocks crept by every single dog began barking. 'Dogs,' he said, 'became the bane of my life.' Once one discovered his daytime hideout and he had to run to escape; in the process his clothes were badly torn. And it rained. He was never dry. Eventually he had a bad cold and when he took his boots off his feet were so swollen he could not get one boot back on. By the time these disasters overtook him he was only four miles from the frontier. He hobbled as close to it as he could, but by then another dawn was beginning to break. Fortunately there was a convenient barn, even if the farmhouse was fairly close by. In the barn was hay – dry warm hay. It made him cough but although bouts of coughing nearly tore him apart nobody appeared to hear it.

His downfall came from a different reason. Inside the barn he had found a nest of hen eggs. He had taken several and eaten them raw, leaving the shells nearby. While he was lying in the hay, waiting to cross the frontier in the dark of the following night, the farmer had gone into the barn, seen the rifled nest, guessed the reason, and decided to call the guards and their Dobermans. When the German bayonets began to prod the hay methodically, Horrocks decided he had better emerge if he wanted to keep a whole skin. As he came out into the daylight he could see the Dutch frontier 500 yards away. The Germans paid him the compliment of detailing four soldiers to escort him back to the camp although by this time his feet were in such a bad state he could scarcely walk.

Back in the camp he was overjoyed to see Hervey alive and unhurt. The sentry whom Horrocks had knocked over had fired off all his rounds at Horrocks' back and missed, then he aimed at Hervey again. All he heard was a click, for he had forgotten to reload. Others had now joined him so he could scarcely reload and shoot Hervey in cold blood, and Hervey was escorted inside again to solitary confinement.

Solitary confinement was Horrocks' lot too when he returned, fourteen days of it in a dark cell, for having struck a German sentry. Solitary meant a wooden shelf for a bed, and bread and water for a diet. But he had hardly arrived in the cell when a note was pushed under the door. It came from British soldiers whose camp adjoined the 'solitary' cells. They suggested he should go to the latrine at a certain time every day. There, down by the bucket, they had concealed a parcel of chocolate, cigarettes and biscuits from their own Red Cross parcels. One was there, every day, although he had never met his benefactors.

Even when he emerged from the punishment cell he was still kept in 'solitary'. He was there on 11 November when the armistice was signed.

Had he succeeded in escaping, he would doubtless have rejoined his regiment and probably been killed in one of the murderous slaughterhouses of the war – the Somme, Passchendaele, Ypres, Chemin des Dames – in all of which the Middlesex took fearful casualties. Instead he had frustrating, though useful, experience. As he put it, 'I had learnt in a hard school to stand on my own feet and make my own decisions, often in a split second. I had also acquired the useful habit of thinking things out from the enemy point of view so that I might always be one jump ahead.'

He did not therefore feel that those four years in captivity had been wasted. Although he did not suggest that that sort of experience was an essential for high command, it certainly had its value.

The lessons, of course, went far deeper than playing hide and seek, escape and evasion, with the enemy across hostile country. That sort of experience may be gained in many ways. The essential ability he acquired was an accurate assessment of his fellow soldiers. In a prison camp when the inmates have settled down through months of boredom and discomfort, which may have been preceded by intense experiences, including being wounded, they show themselves as they really are. Those who are genuinely stoical and good-humoured continue to be so, whereas the actors become withdrawn and morose. The more fortunate are able to live on memories and hopes. Horrocks could look back on a cheerful and successful life (on his assessment of success) and he could visualise a future which would be even better. Although his efforts at escaping sometimes made him unpopular because of the retribution it brought to others, the fact that he was constantly engaged in it kept him alert, lively and companionable. Around him he would see men revealing their weaknesses. Those unfortunate to have had an unhappy home life had no pleasant memories to sustain them; optimism would not be ingrained, and the future would not hold much promise.

The selfish would become more so, the shallow more irritating; in unguarded moments men would reveal more of themselves than they intended. In later life Horrocks would look at men, assess them in the light of their inner reserves as well as their record, and recommend them for promotion – or dismissal. Lt-General Sir Terence Airey said of him: 'The first time I saw him was on manoeuvres on Salisbury Plain in the early 30s. He was the Brigade Major to General 'Jumbo' Wilson and a model of practical efficiency. The "*on dit*" then was that Horrocks as a brigade staff officer had got more brigadiers made generals than any other staff officer in the army.' But if he was good at spotting the winner he could be quite ruthless with the weakling, however kindly the latter process might be.

The other lesson he learnt from being a prisoner of war was that, however overwhelming a misfortune there will ultimately be a recovery. Nothing is unendurable, or past endurance. You can endure anything if you have to, while you are still breathing. Horrocks could easily have given up and died in the Lille hospital. He could have died too after the series of wounds he received at Bizerta. But he endured.

In later life, Montgomery and others used to call him 'Jorrocks'. In the PoW camps his nickname was 'Dog'. In his first camp he had been so much junior in rank to his fellow officers that they had called him 'Pup'. When he was twenty-one at Clausthal it was decided by his friends that he had now come of age and could be called 'Dog'. So 'Dog' he became, and 'Dog' was now about to come home.

Chapter 3

Russian Roulette

When Horrocks returned to England at the end of the war he found his troubles were not yet over. Like all servicemen at the end of a long war, often years spent in conditions which could never adequately be described or explained, he found himself almost equally inured to pleasure and pain, and restless as well. He was doing many of the things he had dreamt about when a prisoner of war – eating elaborate meals and wearing fresh clothes – but deriving little pleasure from these long-wished-for joys. He was too fidgety to settle to anything, even games. Instead he 'lived it up' in London, spending his four years' back pay in a frenzy of pretending to himself he was having a wonderful time. His parents observed it benignly and made no criticism. Subsequently he thought they must have been somewhat distressed by his wild behaviour but they never mentioned it. Later when he had to administer justice to some young tearaway under his command, who had kicked over the traces with less justification than Horrocks, the memory of his own past behaviour made him take an understanding, even if firm view.

The fact that at one time he had been the sole Englishman sharing a room in a prison camp with fifty Russian officers now proved very useful. The War Office asked for Russian-speaking volunteers to go to Russia to help the White armies. The background to this needs some explanation. On 3 March 1918, when the Czarist government and the Mensheviks had in turn been overthrown, the Bolsheviks signed a peace treaty with Germany. The Bolsheviks were anxious to get out of the war and accepted terms which were harsh by any standards. During the following months Russia became increasingly chaotic as different areas struggled to form independent republics.

The Allies were, not unnaturally, angry with the Russians for having made a separate peace treaty, but would have preferred to leave them to sort out their own internal tangles while they themselves dealt with the heavy German offensive on the Western Front. That simple solution was not possible. Huge supplies of munitions had been shipped to various Russian ports for use against the Germans. These had been unloaded and were stored in various depots, principally Murmansk, Archangel and Vladivostok. There was now considerable apprehension that those supplies would fall into German hands, either through a successful German drive to Murmansk or a deal with the Bolshevik government. There were other fears too. One was that Germans and Turks might attempt to reach the oil town of Baku.

The Allies were quick to react to the signing of the Brest-Litovsk treaty, partly because they had realised it was in the offing and were prepared. In late March 1918 British troops were disembarked in Murmansk, to be followed in April by others, and some Japanese, at Vladivostok. In August a contingent of British soldiers arrived in Arkangelsk (Archangel). By the end of 1918 there were 15,000 Allied troops in Russia, and these were joined by a force of some 7,000 White Russians. Meanwhile two anti-Bolshevik governments had been established, one in Turkestan and another in Arkangelsk. There was also a Czech army, formed from deserters and prisoners of war from the former Austro-Hungarian army, which had been intended for reinforcing the Russians fighting against Germany, but for which there was now no use. Trotsky (the Commissar for War) had attempted to disarm the Czech army but it had turned against the Bolsheviks, seized the Trans-Siberian railway and settled in the Urals. The United States declared itself to be against intervention on principle but sent 5,000 American troops who landed in August and September 1918; their justification was that they were supporting the Czechs and also keeping an eye on the Japanese. The latter continued to put in more troops and eventually had 17,000 on the territory of their traditional enemy. A small contingent of Italians was also landed.

When the armistice was signed on November 11th 1918, the Allies no longer needed to fear an alliance between Russia and Germany which would be turned against them. Instead they had to occupy those areas of Russia which the Germans had recently acquired through the Brest-Litovsk treaty. This manoeuvre involved some delicate diplomacy between the British and French, whose dispositions were divided by the river Don. The French contingent amounted to 45,000 men.

The Allies then had to decide how far intervention in Russia should go: i.e. whether the Bolshevik government should be overthrown and the original government restored or whether the Russians should be allowed to settle their own differences as best they could.

The British view, proffered by Lloyd George, was that the war had gone on long enough, and the British Army would not take kindly to a further campaign in Russia; the French had taken a more positive view but Foch's ambition, darkly suspected as being almost

Napoleonic in concept, had been frustrated by Clemenceau. President Wilson, on the advice of his special envoy, William C. Bullitt, had decided to oppose actual intervention as it would only strengthen the hand of the Japanese, of whose intentions and ambitions the Americans were deeply suspicious.

The natural consequence was a decision that Allied troops should now all be withdrawn from Russia. The French were the first to go. A mutiny in their Black Sea fleet, where a red flag had appeared at a masthead, quickened their thinking.

In Britain, which had been more closely concerned with Russia than the French had, there was some doubt about this hasty withdrawal. Churchill was so strongly opposed to it that he despatched a further contingent of troops to Arkangelsk. These were then attached to the White Russian Army under General Miller. In other areas, such as the Caucasus, Baku and Tiflis, British troops were withdrawn.

However, the Allies were still supporting the anti-Bolshevik government headed by Kolchak which aimed to restore the monarchy but which had no policy likely to make that restoration an enduring success. Kolchak, and other anti-Bolshevik leaders, at first were victorious but a combination of poor generalship, lack of Allied support, and disagreements between the principals, soon whittled away their gains. Meanwhile the Bolsheviks were becoming more organised. Their strongest card was that they offered a new, and presumably better, future; the White Armies merely fought for the restoration of the past system. Both sides used terror to intimidate their opponents.

Whatever Horrocks had experienced in prisoner-of-war camps was as nothing to what confronted him now. Vladivostok, where he landed in April 1919, was crowded with refugees, many of whom had been swept in one move from extreme luxury to the utmost poverty and squalor. The women were standing the shock much better than the men. Horrocks found it a new experience too, for he had just travelled half-way round the world in a comfortable Blue Funnel liner calling at such outposts of unravaged civilisation as Suez, Colombo, Penang and Singapore. The harbour, he noted, was full of ships still bringing in war material for the White Armies.

His initial briefing on the situation had informed him that the Allies were supporting the White Armies against the Red Bolsheviks. He was now taken to British headquarters and given a fuller, but not particularly encouraging, account of the current situation. Kolchak's successes had apparently been achieved by the Czechs. But the Czechs had had enough and wanted to go home. It was therefore the task of the Allies to train and equip the White

Armies raised in Siberia to take the place of the Czechs. The explanation, as he would discover later, erred on the side of simplification.

The British force in the area was a small one. It consisted of a territorial battalion of the Hampshires, a battalion of the Middlesex which was on its way home from garrison duties, and two military missions. The task of one mission was to transfer military equipment to the White Armies and train them to use it. The second mission contained transport experts and had the not inconsiderable task of restoring order out of the chaos on the Russian lines of communication. Horrocks was assigned to the first. In addition there was a small French military mission but the effort was principally a British one.

Both regiments and missions consisted of experienced officers and men, all of whom had learnt their task during the war. There was an enormous quantity of war material which had been manufactured for the Western Front but which was quite useless after the armistice. With this and the expert tuition they were receiving the White Armies should have been able to make short work of the Bolsheviks. However, it was not to be. Horrocks soon realised that the Russians doggedly refused to accept advice of any sort but, when the stores were handed over, misused and wasted valuable equipment and supplies. Horrocks and his friends were warned to exercise the utmost tact, as the Russian officers bitterly resented their presence and were suspicious of their motives. The inexperienced Horrocks was puzzled by it all but subsequently recalled that an elderly British colonel had told him that intervention was a great mistake. The colonel prophesied that the Allies would regret that they had ever embarked upon it, for it was always a great mistake to intervene in the domestic affairs of any other country. The colonel felt that the Bolsheviks were certain to win and that the Allied support for the White Armies would be a cause of endless bitterness in the future. Horrocks felt that if the people they were trying to help were resentful and suspicious, a future diplomatic relationship with the Soviets, if they should win, looked distinctly unpromising.

But for him it was still a great adventure. Vladivostok was a highly dangerous city and a man was unwise to move around at any time without a stout stick and a loaded revolver. It was suicidal to go out alone after dark.

His first task was to accompany a consignment of ammunition to the town of Omsk, a mere 3,000 miles away. The party consisted of fourteen British officers and thirty NCOs and soldiers. The ammunition train was made up of twenty-seven wagons loaded with shells. It looked a simple enough task; at least it seemed simple to Horrocks.

Of course, not everyone would consider that twenty-seven wagons full of ammunition, none the better for having been shifted half-way round the world, made ideal travelling companions. The ammunition was probably stable enough to withstand any bumps on the track but if one of the trucks caught alight from sparks from the engine or was hit by a stray bullet, the situation would quickly become interesting. Thirteen companions at ten miles an hour in a box-car for 3,000 miles might not be to everyone's liking either.

Unfortunately, although the shells had no commercial value, the railway wagons could be sold for a considerable price. A similar train had recently arrived at its destination about twenty wagons short of the original complement. The process of thinning out the train was delightfully simple – mechanical trouble. This was usually an overheated axle-box, a fault not difficult to develop with a little experienced sabotage. Horrocks would tackle the stationmaster at the next station and enjoin him to have the offending box repaired. This, regretfully, the stationmaster was unable to arrange as that particular day was a holiday and no workmen were available to work on a holiday. Horrocks noted that, by some coincidence, every day on which he wished to have repairs done was a holiday. He enquired about a replacement wagon. Regrettably that too was impossible: there was no empty wagon in the area. The stationmaster himself had not seen one for months. He suggested detaching the offending wagon and continuing with a wagon short. After all, what was one wagon out of twenty-seven?

Horrocks saw his point of view but was quite firm. Their train would wait until the necessary repairs could be done, however long it took. Meanwhile the train would wait in the siding, causing the stationmaster great inconvenience. On every occasion the stationmaster would depart, then come hastening back with the information that he had just found an empty wagon which he had inadvertently overlooked.

The box-car in which the fourteen officers travelled was cold in spite of a continuously burning stove but they stopped at various stations and there, he found, as he put it, 'The station is the centre of the social life of the district.' When the train arrived the peasants came in from miles around and the platform became a small market place. Once, on a longer stop caused by engine trouble, three of them went off to explore the delights of Manchuli, on the frontier between Manchuria and Russia. To their surprise they found it contained a night club complete with a gipsy band, dancers, Russian officers, and plentiful vodka. They were promptly greeted by a Russian colonel who invited them to his table.

This seemed excellent but almost immediately they ran into

trouble. The band began to play a tune which made everyone get up. As they got up their host said, no, they must continue sitting as they were his guests. So with the two gipsy girls who were with the colonel they sat there.

Suddenly a Cossack colonel came up to their table and demanded they should get up. Their host slapped him across the face and said: 'These are my guests and will remain seated, you Cossack dog.'

The incident clearly must have a sequel, and their host turned to Horrocks and said: 'Will you honour me by acting as my second in a duel which I now propose to fight with this Cossack?'

Horrocks agreed with enthusiasm, though not having the least idea of what his duties might be. In the event, he never discovered, for a party of military police now entered and arrested their whole party, including the Cossack. Then they were taken into a private room for a court of inquiry.

Horrocks felt it was up to him to take the initiative and so, before the formal inquiry could begin, he addressed the gathering in imperfect but emotional Russian to say that he and his friends had come all the way from England to help the Russians but because of their ignorance of local customs had caused a quarrel to break out between two distinguished colonels, both renowned throughout the world for their courage and skill in war.

It was an instant success. He was embraced by both the colonels. The Cossack joined their party and the festivities went on into the small hours. They returned to their train to find that that had not been without incident either. A Chinese looter had approached the train at dusk but had been spotted by the British sentry. The sentry, normally a poor shot, had put a bullet straight between the Chinese looter's eyes at a distance of 200 yards. They looked at the dead Chinaman with dismay.

But the Manchurian stationmaster to whom they reported the incident regarded it with indifference. 'A dead Chinaman,' he said. 'There are plenty more.'

As they came closer to the front line they were joined at the stations by contingents of the White Army whose job was to guard them. Apparently there were Red guerrilla bands now operating in the area. One night it was their turn to be the object of an attack. There was plenty of confusion, noise and wild firing; happily there were no casualties.

But they were now reaching the end of their journey. On 20 May they reached Omsk, still with twenty-seven wagons. They had been travelling for just over a month. It was an excellent performance.

But it was not the end of Horrocks' particular journey. His own destination was a further 800 miles west. The town was then called

Ekaterinburg, and is now Sverdlovsk. It was still in Siberia, but quite unlike other Siberian towns in that it was attractive and had gardens and a lake. It had its sinister undertones however, for it was where the Czar and his family had been murdered. Horrocks used to pass the house where the murders had happened every day as he went to work.

Here he was appointed second in command of an NCOs' training school attached to the Anglo-Russian brigade. The Anglo-Russian brigade had not yet been formed, but would consist of four battalions with a sprinkling of British officers and senior NCOs. Horrocks could scarcely believe his eyes when he saw the 2,500 recruits from which this brigade was to be formed. They were filthy, mainly bootless, and obviously unfit, if not physically ill. A third were promptly discharged as medically unsuitable. Training them was not helped by the fact that they were almost all illiterate; there was also a shortage of interpreters. Much had been made of the fact that there would soon be Czech interpreters with a masterly command of the language, but none of these ever appeared. The last straw was the fact that the Russian authorities were not merely inefficient but also actively obstructive.

Yet it worked. Slowly the brigade took shape. The most heartening aspect of it as far as Horrocks was concerned was that as the Russians began to realise that pay, rations, and personal welfare would all be attended to by their British officers they became unswervingly loyal and enthusiastic. Some of his concern for their welfare was, he noted, misplaced. Their feet seemed as impervious to blisters as an animal's might be.

However, the better they got on with the Russian soldiers the worse became their relationship with the Russian officers. The more the former improved, the more the latter complained about them. Part of the trouble was that the new generation of Russian officers had no experience of fighting and had no intention of getting any. It was clear that to send the Anglo-Russian brigade into action, lacking support from the Russian authorities and disrupted by internal jealousies, would be to court disaster. Then word came from Britain that the British officers must now return home. The order did not include Horrocks and his friend George Hayes, who were left behind to act as liaison officers. Theirs was not a congenial task, for the Russian population was hostile and accused the British of having deserted their allies.

Horrocks' home and headquarters was now a three-wagon train. Hayes and Horrocks lived in one, their Russian groom and their Chinese servants lived in another, and the third contained their horses. They were now 700 miles west of Omsk and had to send back reports each day to the commandant of the British mission, General Knox. They collected information for their reports by riding out on horseback. Horrocks was often away for a week at a time, spending the nights in small Russian villages. Invariably he became the guest of the village headman, which was not as luxurious a proceeding as it might seem. Every house was identical; that is, it consisted of two rooms, one full of people, the other full of animals. In the people's room was a huge stove, on top of which the oldest and the youngest slept; the remainder found a space on the floor. Food consisted of an enormous bowl of thick soup. Each person was given a wooden spoon. Horrocks found everyone else was more adept in its use than he was but he managed to survive, even if he did feel hungry. He also had the experience of drinking *koumiss*. Koumiss is a Khirgiz drink made of fermented mare's milk. Fermentation takes place in casks lined with dung. Although trying not to think of its manufacture, Horrocks found drinking it very pleasant. However it was extremely intoxicating and at times he was hard put to stay on his horse after a few cups of it.

Militarily, the outlook was depressing. The White battalions were deserting regularly to the Bolsheviks who, in consequence, found little to impede their progress. Finally even his own headquarters came under attack. Fortunately, on this occasion, the White battalion to which he was attached stayed loyal and beat off the Red assault.

But retreat was inevitable and soon they were heading back to Omsk. He had never felt so isolated. Even the Russians in the territories they were relinquishing were pro-Bolshevist, and there was no certainty that either Hayes or himself would ever see Vladivostok again. The temperature dropped rapidly; in October it was 40°F below zero. Omsk, when they reached it, was in chaos. The White front was collapsing everywhere. Hayes and Horrocks were told to make their way back to Vladivostok as best they could.

Fortunately, in Omsk, they found the remnants of the other British mission – the one which had been entrusted with the task of restoring the roads and railways. The leader of that mission had acquired two wagons and painted Union Jacks on them. This had an unexpected effect in that it promptly became the assembly point for a host of different peoples, some of whom could not even speak English but who claimed vociferously to be members of the British Empire. They included women. Dubious though their claim seemed, the mission did not feel it could leave these imperial refugees in the lurch, so they packed them into the wagons. Luckily for them all they were hitched on to a train of Polish soldiers which made good headway by the simple process of travelling on the up track instead of trying the already overcrowded down track. Needless to say there was nothing coming up to the front.

Their luck changed at Novosibirsk, some 500 miles further east. Now both lines were often blocked. Water was scarce and had to be produced by everyone collecting buckets of snow.

Another 150 miles on, Czechs, Russians and Poles were fighting for engines and using guns in the process. At this point Horrocks received a message from Vladivostok. It read: 'If the situation warrants it, do not hesitate to take complete control.' At least it raised a laugh.

On each side of the track there was now a steady procession of sleighs pulled by Siberian ponies. They were hopelessly overloaded with desperate people. Periodically one fell off and was just left to die; no one could do anything to help or prevent it.

But the Reds were catching up and their engines now finally gave up the struggle. They pushed the women and children into a wagon on a train manned by Russian soldiers and themselves took to sleighs. Horrocks realised that it was the night of 15 December. It was bitterly cold and he had had no sleep for seventy-two hours. At times he was jerked off the sleigh and had to run alongside to catch up.

But, somehow, they contrived to go on. At night they all packed into a single room in a village. The atmosphere was foul beyond belief but it was at least warm. This went on for five days and then, to their amazement, they came across the train with the wagon containing the women and children they had parted company with a hundred miles back along the line. Somehow they made room for everyone. And they went on.

But it was in vain. When they were just outside Krasnoyarsk news came that the Russians had made a flanking move, encircled them, and already captured the town. Their six-week pilgrimage had been useless.

In the general dismay which followed the realisation that they were once again prisoners, Horrocks' thoughts once more turned to escaping. He and Hayes decided that if they bought a sleigh and two horses they could probably reach the Mongolian frontier, a mere 500 miles away. Fortunately no doubt for them it was pointed out that if Horrocks departed, there would be no one in the party who could speak Russian. Horrocks decided he could not leave his companions in the lurch and decided to stay.

There was plenty to do. Although they had money, it was the wrong sort of money, for the Red Army had declared all other Russian currency illegal. The only way to obtain food was to queue for hours, half-frozen, waiting to see the commissars. The latter issued bread tickets, not enough to satisfy hunger but enough to keep the recipients alive. Not for the first time he was hungry and cold. Everybody tried his best at obtaining money or food. Horrocks managed to get himself a job teaching English to Russian school-girls. The pay was low but the job meant that he was given a midday meal of thick soup. They sold off any spare items of clothing which they did not immediately require. The buyers (or swappers) were peasants who came into the town from the surrounding countryside. These soon realised they had a seller's market for their food, and raised their prices steeply. Horrocks was mortified to see his last spare shirt go for a pair of skates and a bag of nuts, neither of which satisfied a real need.

They decided their best course was bravado. Accordingly the three senior officers, which included Horrocks and his friend Hayes, made themselves as smart as possible, walked to the head of the longest queue and, when challenged by the sentry, said curtly: 'This is an English delegation to see the Head Commissar.' Suitably impressed, the sentry allowed them into the head commissar's office.

They marched in and saluted him. To their surprise and delight, he jumped up and returned their salute. The bluff seemed to be working. Horrocks and his friends knew only too well that the Red Army was deeply suspicious of officers of all other armies and at this stage had abolished the practice of saluting their own officers. Officers were highly vulnerable: there were reported cases where, among the general cruelty, officers had had their epaulettes nailed to their shoulders. But this commissar seemed to have a different view. He asked what they wanted and Horrocks informed him that they (the British) personally held him responsible for their safety. He told them he had been unaware there were any British in Krasnoyarsk. The outcome of the interview was that they were given a generous allocation of ration cards. These, in the event, enabled them to feed a number of others as well as themselves. However, a request for early repatriation could not be granted so easily. The Red Army was now fighting the Japanese.

While they waited for further developments, Horrocks was interested to observe how the Red Army functioned. Army Headquarters was presided over by three political commissars, who shared a single room for administration. They were endeavouring to establish a tight control of the Army but were not finding it easy. The fact that the hated discipline of the Czarist army had been abolished meant that the Army itself was casual and inefficient. Horrocks subsequently compared these early idealistic days with later ones when discipline had been so firmly re-established that saluting had not merely been re-introduced between officers and other ranks but also throughout the entire army so that privates also had to salute every rank above them, and saluting was universal. Epaulettes, he noted, had come back too, and were more resplendent than ever. And as for equality of pay and conditions, by the end of World War II Russian generals were receiving not merely many times the pay of privates but several times the pay of corresponding ranks in the American Army.

It was not all plain sailing for the British. The head commissar was well aware of what they had been doing to assist the White Armies and suggested, forcibly, that they should now do the same for the Reds. He pointed out that otherwise they could very well be treated as prisoners of war and as there was an enormous p.o.w. camp nearby where the death rate was said to be 200 a day, this was a grim threat. To this often repeated suggestion they invariably replied that they were all British and were awaiting repatriation.

One day, to their astonishment they were told that they were now to be sent home. Delighted, they went to the station and got into the train which was earmarked for them. It was not a comfortable train, as became apparent when it simply stayed there, awaiting the order to move. Then, on the point of departure, disaster struck Horrocks. He fell ill, had a high temperature and was constantly sick. It was all too obvious to him what the cause was: he had typhus. It was carried by lice and there were said to be 30,000 cases of typhus in Krasnoyarsk. It was equally clear what happened to most of them, for dead, naked bodies were stacked everywhere awaiting removal and burial. The British had come to regard them with indifference in the way one does when appalling sights become familiar. Horrocks knew very well that he could easily join their numbers, but in fact he dreaded that less than the thought of being put in a Russian hospital. He had visited one and found the sick lying on the floors and the floors coated with excrement and other filth. The very smell had made him sick.

He did go into a hospital, however, the only proper one in the town. He was unconscious for six days and woke up to find himself tied to the bed with ropes. While he was unconscious he had had nightmares in which he had been tortured into betraying Britain. The first person he saw when he opened his eyes was George Hayes. Hayes had come into the hospital with him, although he knew very well the risk he was taking. It was Hayes who helped him to swallow one drop of water at a time (for the typhus had swollen up his lips and tongue). Typhus killed three million people in Russia and eastern Europe at the end of the First World War: this was bad enough, before influenza killed forty million world-wide. Against these scourges men's efforts to kill each other seemed relatively puny.

Hayes stuck by him, which Horrocks never forgot. Hayes was instrumental in getting him into the temporary hospital, which was a requisitioned school but where the patients at least had beds. It was overcrowded and many of the medical staff went down with the disease themselves. There was one Russian nurse, whom he describes as a heroine. Again by a near-miracle Hayes managed to get some milk and white bread (he could not swallow the meagre ration of black bread). Typhus, if you survive the worst phase in which the kidneys are likely to cease to function, leaves no serious after-effects. Once over the worst, Horrocks began to make progress. He was delighted to learn that nothing had been lost by his enforced absence; the train was still in the same siding at the station. He rejoined it.

Eventually, almost unbelievably, the train left on its way to Irkutsk, a mere 600 miles away. They reached it, and stopped there for two months. He now met his first woman commissar, an awesome sight, as he put it. A cigarette drooped out of the corner of her mouth, a revolver was stuck in her belt, and she looked considerably tougher than any of the male commissars.

Then they went on, accompanied by Red guards who were invariably very strict and withdrawn when they met, but who always became friendly, even weeping when they were handed over to the next batch. This time they found they were heading west. For six weeks and 3,500 miles they stayed with the railway. Optimism prevailed: this time they really felt they were going home. 'But,' he says, 'we should have known better.' Instead of proceeding further they found themselves in a prison camp. It had previously been a monastery. In it were 457 prisoners who included anyone from former generals and admirals to prostitutes and thieves. Some of the inmates, among whom were forty-five women, had gone mad. Even those who had not gone mad must have become somewhat eccentric. He remembers a distinguished Russian general who was in charge of the lavatories. He worked in them all day long, and bitterly resented intruders. The only way to approach him was to march up, stand to attention, click heels, salute, then bellow: 'Your most highest. May I have the privilege of using your lavatories to-day?' The general would also come to attention, salute, and bellow his assent. The procedure never varied.

The food, as usual, was inadequate and horrible. The small quantity of meat was usually horse-flesh. The only thing that saved the British was a French organisation run by one Madame Charpentier and her two daughters. These three, at no slight risk of incurring the wrath of the Soviet authorities, would bring in bread, potatoes, and occasionally eggs and sugar, twice a week. Horrocks never ceased to be grateful to the intrepid and kindly women who ran the risk of being imprisoned themselves. He believes that the small quantity of extra food they brought in made all the difference between starvation and survival.

Hunger and malnutrition were not their only problem; the Russian authorities were constantly demanding that they should work for the inadequate rations they received. The demand was met with a flat refusal, even though the thought of unpleasant reprisals was never absent. An intimation of what might happen was given by the occasional disappearance of selected prisoners, usually Russians; they were never seen or heard of again.

For the British, relief came when an official appeared with the news that they were to be repatriated. It was apparently due to an exchange scheme which had now been agreed. By the time it was announced they were all incarcerated in the monastery building and Horrocks recalls that his joy at his departure was ruined by the sad sight of the fellow prisoners they left behind. This, of course, was typical of Horrocks. Most people would have been so thankful for their own release that they would have had little thought for those left behind.

Another, different, regret came up in this period. Once the news emerged that the British were going to leave the country, a number of Russian women begged them to marry them. It was the only hope the Russian women had of leaving the country and they faithfully promised to leave their new husbands the moment they crossed the frontier, and never trouble them again. The British prisoners discussed the matter earnestly, but reluctantly and unanimously reached the conclusion that it was impracticable. They could not, they felt, simply abandon their new wives the moment they crossed the frontier. Perhaps they also foresaw that the wives might not so easily be deserted. The answer was 'No.'

Their problem was not a new one. Through its long existence the Army had been well aware that soldiers were often persuaded, for humanitarian or financial reasons to marry foreign nationals. British citizenship in the heyday of the British Empire conferred many privileges. Numbers of soldiers serving in the Middle and Far East cheerfully accepted the rewards, although warned of the liabilities. The most striking example of a British soldier marrying for humanitarian reasons, and never regretting it, was Sir Harry Smith who rescued and married a Spanish woman at the siege of Badajoz. (The town of Ladysmith in South Africa was named after her when Sir Harry was at a different stage in his distinguished career as Governor of the Cape Colony.)

Horrocks eventually left Russia on 29 October, and went home via

Finland and Denmark. He recalls that the Royal Navy transported them from Helsinki to Copenhagen in a cruiser, HMS *Delhi*. Their appearance as they climbed aboard after eighteen months in Russia was, to say the least, unorthodox; the Navy, used no doubt to such occasions, never batted an eyelid but did everything for their comfort. The Danes in Copenhagen overwhelmed them with hospitality. The experience seemed more like a dream than reality. A month earlier they had been starving to death with little hope of relief; now they were treated like royalty. It was an unsettling experience and it was now happening to Horrocks for the second time in his early career.

Chapter 4

A Slow Advance

His thoughts on returning to England were mixed, perhaps confused. Still a dedicated soldier with hopes of promotion and command, he faced the fact that after eight years he had gained no valuable military experience but merely an extensive knowledge of a variety of prison camps in Germany and Russia. It hardly occurred to him that as a subaltern who had joined the Army in 1914 he was remarkably lucky to be alive at all.

There were compensations. As he looked around him at his contemporaries and seniors in the 1920s British Army, he noted a rigid orthodoxy and absence of self-reliance. Such characteristics were no great disadvantage in the lower levels of the Army in the post-war period; in fact they might even be an asset. Since 1919 the Government policy on the services had been based on the 'Ten Year Rule'. The 'Ten Year Rule', said to have originated in the mind of Sir Maurice Hankey, Secretary of the Committee of Imperial Defence, assumed that as there was now no major potential enemy which Britain might have to face in the immediate future, plans could be made for a peacetime establishment for the next ten years. In 1919 this was not an unreasonable assumption, but as the rule was annually renewed it soon became a dangerous handicap to Britain when Germany and Italy were rearming. Even in its early stages the 'Ten Year Rule' was restricting Britain's ability to carry out its policing commitments in various areas of the world. The high-level debates and discussions on these matters were far removed from Horrocks and his contemporaries but they were the ones who felt the effects of the decisions.

In the early stages of the post-war period life was varied and by no means unpleasant. His rank when he arrived back with the Middlesex was captain. Some of his contemporaries in that rank had been brigadiers in wartime; many others had commanded battalions. Horrocks therefore did not feel dissatisfied. He might have been less cheerful if he had been aware that in the future promotion would be so slow that the average period of service in their ranks was nineteen years for a captain and twenty-nine for a major. There were exceptions in some regiments but no one seemed to manage less than sixteen years in either rank. The result of this was that many officers did not reach a high rank until they were debarred by age from holding it.

Horrocks' first posting was to Cologne where the 1st Middlesex was part of the British Army of the Rhine. Serving soldiers were of course in an ideal position in those days of galloping inflation. For the first time in his life he had plenty of money to spend, and did so. But Horrocks' conscience was only too well aware that his own circumstances and those of a few German war profiteers were against a background of German misery. He encountered one professional family who lived entirely off potatoes, and not many of those. The effect of runaway inflation on the German people appalled him and left him with the conviction that almost any sacrifice was justified if it avoided this economic catastrophe.

Towards the end of this period prices in the shops were being altered several times a day. As soon as a person received any wages, he or she rushed off to spend them before they lost much of their value. British soldiers were able to buy goods in the NAAFI canteen. Anything they bought could immediately be resold at a profit. During one week the NAAFI agreed to keep its prices stable and, as a result, as inflation outside roared ahead, the NAAFI shelves were cleared as fast as they were filled. Horrocks disgustedly felt that the garrison behaved like a flock of vultures. Everything was demoralising, not least the fact that when men were paid in marks the marks were delivered in sacks. Horrocks was not surprised when this chaos and desperation, of which he only saw the beginning, drove the Germans to extremes.

In 1921 the Middlesex returned to Britain. Their first duty was to be on standby to assist the police in case of rioting in the coal miners' strike which began on 31 March. 1921 was an eventful year. French troops occupied the Ruhr when Germany announced that she was unable to pay reparations. Sweden abolished capital punishment. Upper Silesia was partitioned. Although there were over twenty minor wars in various parts of the world, there were great hopes that the newly formed League of Nations would soon put an end to such events.

Hardly had the Middlesex finished with their 'aid to the civil power' duties in connection with the coal miners than they were posted to Ireland. Ireland was immersed in 'the troubles' which ended, albeit temporarily, when Britain signed a treaty giving Eire 'Dominion Status' on 6 December 1921. Horrocks, half-Irish, loathed his duties in Ireland which he described as 'a most unpleasant form of warfare'.*

* When the regiment left, the local Catholic priest came to see them off and said he hoped their successors would be as helpful and understanding as they had been.

41

Another overseas duty followed quickly. This was to supervise the Silesian plebiscite. One of the assumptions of the Versailles treaty-makers had been that wars were caused by frustrated ethnic aspirations rather than by individuals with fanatical ambitions. President Wilson had firmly advocated the principle of 'self-determination' – that people should decide by voting what their future allegiances should be. Like many other ideas prevailing at the time, this one contained much woolly idealism. In order to determine whether Silesia more properly belonged to Germany or to Poland, a plebiscite was held. Silesia had had such a long and troubled history that it was impossible to say whether the majority of the inhabitants were German or Polish. Although a properly organised and supervised plebiscite was held, it merely seemed to prove that the population of Silesia was so mixed up that a truly fair solution was impossible. In the event it was decided to award Upper Silesia to Poland and Lower Silesia to Germany. Upper Silesia contained most of the coal and iron deposits. The idea of a plebiscite appealed less to the local population than it did to the pundits of the League of Nations and for Horrocks' regiment this duty was no sinecure. To add to their problems the Polish miners went on strike against the mere presence of the Middlesex in their district. Thus Horrocks saw two miners' strikes in two successive years.

But by late 1923 these overseas duties came to an end and he was back in Aldershot in what was known as 'peace-time soldiering', an activity which contained considerable make-believe, not only in the situation of 'Redland against Blueland' but also in the equipment used. Units existed on paper, flags represented guns, and realism took second place to comfort. Under such conditions one either becomes cynical or takes an interest in something else while waiting for a change in government attitudes towards one's main occupation.

Horrocks had always been keen on games – running, boxing, cricket, Rugby football – but after his various military mishaps was less suited to boxing and Rugby football than to the others. He now found himself greatly attracted to the modern pentathlon. The old pentathlon of the Greek Olympic games had consisted of five events (a 200-yard race, long jump, discus, javelin and a wrestling match). The modern pentathlon had a more military flavour, being based on the idea of a messenger carrying despatches through enemy country. The theory is that he begins on horseback but is unhorsed; he then needs to continue by running. He may then have to swim across any rivers which lie in his path, and if attacked be able to defend himself and his burden with sword and pistol. Horrocks was already an adequate runner, horseman and shot and he set about raising his all-round standard. He proved extremely successful in winning army and national events and then was selected for the British team to compete in the 1924 Olympic Games. That year they were held in Paris but the standard was extremely high and Horrocks did not distinguish himself. It was, of course, a superb effort to be competing at that level at all after the mishaps (including being wounded) of the previous years. In old age, when moving slowly and carefully because of later wounds and old age itself, he used to look back wistfully to the days when he was fit enough to perform in the modern pentathlon.

A slightly different but equally persistent memory of these times was the aftermath. When the games were over the teams were 'shown' Paris. It must have been a remarkable occasion, for its effects lasted for a week; when he ran in the Army half-mile championships a week later he came last. His regiment was not pleased. But then Horrocks was never one to do things by halves.

By 1926 Horrocks had reached the age when the Staff College occupies – or should occupy – most of the young officer's horizon. In theory it is possible to reach high command in the Army without the letters p.s.c. (passed Staff College) after your name; in practice it is exceptional. In Horrocks' day the two Staff College courses were at Quetta and Camberley and at either the young officer (aged about thirty) listened to his seniors expounding modern military doctrine. More often than not there has been criticism that the doctrine is not modern enough; occasionally there is a plea that everything is seen against a visionary future.

Horrocks who, in his early years, had never been a studious type, did not relish the idea of long hours with books rather than long periods on playing fields, and might have let his chances slip had his father not intervened. Sir William had never been a 'heavy father', but what he said to Brian was irrefutable; it would be difficult enough to get promotion anyway but it would be virtually impossible without the Staff College. Then, for the first time, Horrocks displayed the ability to concentrate which had always been there but had never been employed in academic matters.

The entrance examination was scheduled for January 1927. At the beginning of that month news came through that his battalion had been chosen for duties in China where the Kuomintang had just established a National government. The leader of this government was the Chinese General Chiang Kai-shek and it had Britain's approval as being likely to substitute order for chaos and also to deal with a growing Communist threat. However, the Nationalists were quick to obtain from Britain a reduction in the latter's concessionary territories.

China would have been a fascinating posting for Horrocks and he was looking forward to abandoning his Staff College work and setting off, but he had reckoned without his father. Once again there was a quiet word; Horrocks took the advice. He requested being allowed to stay behind for the Staff College, and passed the entrance examination. Passing the Staff College entrance examination does not, however, necessarily mean the young aspirant eventually attends the course. A system of nomination is used and the best of the qualified candidates go forward. One way of improving one's prospects is to attend specialised courses and do well in them. Prodded by his father, Horrocks took several and worked hard at them. Eventually he received the cherished nomination and joined the course of 1931-1933. There were 120 officers on that course and they included many who would distinguish themselves in the Second World War, among them the future General Sir Miles Dempsey, the future Major-General 'Strafer' Gott (killed in an aircrash in the desert in 1942) and General Sir Frank Simpson who became Vice Chief of the General Staff and was Montgomery's principal aide.

By the time he arrived at the Staff College two other events of lasting significance had occurred to Horrocks. The first was experience with part-time soldiers, men of the type who would be in large numbers under his command later; the second was his marriage.

The part-time soldiers were a territorial battalion of the Middlesex, the 9th. As his own battalion had now gone overseas, with all his friends, he faced what he thought was a bleak future. He soon found he was mistaken. His appointment as adjutant to the 9th Middlesex began in January 1927: the regimental headquarters was in Willesden.

In those days a territorial regiment's headquarters was in offices around what was known as a drill hall. Here on Saturdays, and occasionally on other days too, would gather the local volunteers who would be instructed in rifle drill, map-reading, basic tactics and general military subjects. At intervals they would be able to fire their rifles on the nearest range, once a year they would attend a fortnight's camp, sometimes attached to a regular battalion. It was all very free and easy and sociable. Those not in the territorial army regarded the volunteers with amazement and scorn; the regulars were even more condescending.

Maintaining enthusiasm among these men who came to be dubbed 'Saturday night soldiers' was by no means easy. Volunteers had to be encouraged, and those already in retained (unless found to be more of a liability than an asset). If the equipment of the Regular Army was inadequate and dated, that of the TA was worse. The task of the adjutant and his senior warrant officer was to be imperturbable, cheerful, and full of enthusiasm. When Horrocks arrived he knew next to nothing about the territorial army and even less about the civilian world and its preoccupations. Soon he found himself totally immersed in fresh interests, not merely in his own job but also in the jobs and attitudes of those in the unit. He confessed himself amazed at the enthusiasm shown by many. Later, in the Second World War, he found this experience with the TA a valuable asset. He understood the prejudice which existed on both sides. Many territorials who were called up in 1939 were given ranks which regular soldiers had waited fifteen or more years to achieve; many of them were, initially, untrained by regular army standards. As the years passed the anomalies were ironed out, although there still remained a percentage of over-promoted TA officers to match the percentage of regulars who were too incompetent to be employed in any post requiring intelligence or foresight but who, on the 'old boy network', managed to acquire and hang on to such appointments.

Horrocks spent three years with the 9th battalion. The unorthodoxy of his career was instilling in him an understanding of the people who would later be proud to be called 'Horrocks' men'. In his German p.o.w. camps, and during the hard times in Russia he had had ample opportunity to see how different types reacted under stress; he also learnt his own strengths and weaknesses. With the 9th battalion he learnt that in certain circumstances you can do more by cheerfulness and resourcefulness than you can by authoritarianism: if he had tried the latter the battalion would probably have melted away. When a man missed an essential parade it was useless trying to discipline him; all you could do was to make him feel sorry and decide he would not miss the next one. And above all, the work of the 9th battalion must seem interesting and important. This was when he learnt to talk to the average family, an experience which stood him in good stead later when he became a TV presenter.

One of the ways in which the TA units raised money to pay for annual or weekend camps was by arranging dances or other social functions. On his way to one of these dances he decided to propose to his partner; they were passing Wormwood Scrubs Prison at the time. His partner was Nancy Kitchin, whom he married a few months later, on 11 April 1928. She was the daughter of Brook and the Hon Mrs Brook Kitchin; she had known him since his schooldays. All through his life he has admired Nancy's many qualities, though they were and are quite different types. Both have always been inclined to undervalue themselves, Horrocks because he saw himself as a not very bright philistine who had been lucky to have the success he had, Nancy because she regarded herself as a much less talented person than she was. He was an orthodox though humane Conservative; her views were well to the left of his. But they had much in common. Both had a passion for horses and dogs; even in their late 80s they took on the task of training a boxer puppy. They also learnt sailing together and enjoyed it equally.

Nancy was an artist, and at first painted conventional pictures. Later she moved on to abstracts, but in later years she decided most of her paintings were not good enough and burnt them. As Horrocks was well aware, she had a keen appreciation of beauty and good design. Horrocks had never had an eye for beauty before marrying Nancy. He did not even notice if buildings were ugly or not, although he had of course lived in some attractive architecture at Uppingham and Sandhurst.

For the first twenty years of their married life there was little opportunity for beautifying their surroundings for, 'following the drum', they lived in no less than twenty-six different houses. (This is by no means a record. A major known to the author in the 1950s had fourteen moves in two years.) Even so, until the 1939-45 war, they were separated less than modern army families. Nowadays a husband is likely to be sent on specialist courses, overseas training, Northern Ireland, or temporary attachment so often that an accompanied posting is a luxury. This, and the rootless existence, are not everyone's idea of married bliss.

A year after their marriage a daughter was born. She was their only child and when she was drowned many years later the shock and loss was almost insupportable.

The strongest influence on Horrocks at this time was the Commandant of the Staff College, the future Field Marshal Sir John Dill. Later Dill commanded 1 Corps in France, and then as Chief of the Imperial General Staff had much to do with Churchill. During the early years of the Second World War, when Churchill was full of ideas for extravagant military endeavour, Alan Brooke and Dill used to reason with him. Both understood the Prime Minister well although Dill may have been the better at handling him. In 1941 Dill went to Washington, DC as Chief British Military Representative; he died there in 1944 and was buried in the Arlington Military Cemetery, the highest honour Americans can give to a foreign national. Dill's friendship with General Marshall, the American Chief of Staff, was undoubtedly a potent influence in harmonising Anglo-American relations and co-operation. He was clearly an exceptional personality and Horrocks was lucky to have been at the Staff College when Dill was Commandant. Many sayings are attributed to Dill, though possibly apocryphally. 'He would be an excellent man in a crisis and his conduct of any operation would be likely to give him an opportunity to display this quality.' Or: 'This officer's men would follow him anywhere, even if only out of curiosity.' Dill developed the syndicate system of working which still flourishes not merely at Camberley but at other Staff Colleges too. One application of the system is to group officers in syndicates of approximately ten and leave them to grapple with problems. Very often the discussions hinge upon the subject matters of a previous group lecture. The syndicate eventually produces a collective view which is presented by one member. The presenter has to explain the reasons for the syndicate's conclusions but at the same time summarise and express any opposing points which may have emerged in the discussion and which merit attention. Syndicates are more dynamic than committees and experience of syndicate working undoubtedly makes a man listen attentively to everything which is said, and ultimately present a balanced and rational viewpoint.

Much to Horrocks' dismay he found that his first posting on completing the Staff College course was as Staff Captain in the Military Secretary's branch of the War Office. In the event he found this period of Whitehall office work both interesting and stimulating. The Military Secretary's department is in charge of all promotion, appointments, awards and ceremonial occasions. Horrocks' section of it was concerned with promotion between the ranks of second lieutenant and lieutenant-colonel. He confesses that at first he made many mistakes, one of them being to have written to an officer offering him promotion when the officer was already dead. Although a mere staff captain, he was able to read the confidential reports on every officer serving in the ranks with which he was concerned. Officers are reported on annually by three officers senior to them. Good reports are underlined in blue, bad ones in red and Horrocks noted that the same characteristics often recurred even though the reports originated from different people. The system is probably as fair a one as can be devised, but often has flaws. If an officer starts off with a good report, he tends to keep on receiving good reports; if he starts off badly he will be lucky to climb out of the rut. It is often extraordinarily difficult to think of anything positive to say about the average officer and the writers of reports are not above looking at opinions of previous report-writers and, perhaps unconsciously, taking their views into account. Nevertheless reports from originators who have not had access to previous reports, nor perhaps had very long to observe a person on a course, do average a certain unanimity. If, however, a man gets a Victoria Cross, or alternatively disappears with the regimental funds, some considerable heart-searchings are likely to take place.

Two years' experience as a staff captain brought Horrocks his next posting: brigade major to 5th Infantry Brigade in 2nd Division at Aldershot. His predecessor in this post, as in the previous one in

Whitehall, had been Miles Dempsey. The job of a brigade major is to keep the brigade commander in complete touch with the activities of the three infantry divisions in his brigade. The essential qualification for this post, which is normally much coveted, is a sound knowledge of staff procedures. Military organisation may at times seem a little pettifogging but it does provide an adequate framework in which essentials are rarely overlooked.

The divisional commander at the time Horrocks joined was the future Field Marshal Earl Wavell. Wavell was a progressive, thoughtful soldier with an acute brain. Soon after this time he gave the Lees Knowles lectures at Trinity College, Cambridge in which he said the modern soldier should in many respects be like a cat burglar. Wavell created imaginative and complicated exercises for his division; Horrocks believed Wavell had the finest brain of anyone he met in his military career. Nevertheless Wavell was not an easy man to deal with. Although educated at Winchester beneath the 'motto 'Manners makyth Man', he could be staggeringly ungracious and ungrateful. He was also socially mean. Hostesses were not a little set back when he sat through a meal saying scarcely a word and departed without a thank you. He instructed staff officers to reduce reports to the shortest possible length. After much mental wrestling he would receive one which had been pared to the bone. Wavell would then take a pencil and effortlessly reduce it by a quarter.

Horrocks deplored the fact that although Wavell impressed those who were closest to him he had no impact at all on most of the men under his command. Even in those days, long before the great public relations exponents of the Second World War, Montgomery, Slim, Mountbatten and their imitators, Horrocks was aware that there was something sadly amiss with Wavell's style of command. It was all the more extraordinary because Wavell was a man of great personal sensitivity and sensibility. Horrocks was never likely to be anything but an extrovert and a soldiers' general, but if he had ever contemplated the alternative the memory of Wavell would have been enough warning of the consequences of aloofness. However, like Auchinleck, Wavell suffered by being asked to do the impossible. After his successes against the Italians he was pressed to attack in the Middle East before he was ready and to send troops to Greece for a forlorn hope when he could have made good use of them in the desert. His final attempt at the impossible was to defeat the Japanese in Malaya and Burma in 1942, when he was Commander in Chief South East Asia. The last produced yet another of his 'public relations failures'. When visiting troops in a camp in northern Malaya, he looked at their pale faces – if not under a canopy of rubber trees they were in deep jungle – and said: 'You've been here too long' and departed forthwith to Singapore.

However, he must have been impressed by Horrocks, for at the end of his Aldershot tour Horrocks was greatly surprised to be chosen as DS at the Staff College. DS is the abbreviation for Directing Staff and means a senior instructor. This was 1938. Horrocks was gratified but slightly appalled to find himself graded among the intellectuals, the up-and-coming men of the Army. To have been selected to be a student had been a compliment, but to be chosen as one of the intellectual spearhead who would instruct the brighter members of the Army worried him. He became even more worried as he tried to cope with the barrage of questions and problems they produced. Staff College DS observe their students in lectures, syndicate work and exercises: they also correct their essays. Staff College 'essays' take a standard form and must be logical, clear and grammatically expressed. Mistakes of fact are less frequent than mistakes in syntax or grammar. All errors are underlined in red ink and it is not uncommon for an essay to be returned to the owner with almost as much writing in red ink as appeared in the original blue. However, as many a newly-joined instructor learnt, it is one thing to know that a piece of written expression is wrong and it is another to know why it is wrong. Even more troublesome is *explaining* why it is wrong. It is not unknown for instructors to look around their possessions for an old school grammar book which may have previously had little use; the first few months will often see the DS working harder than the students.

The DS is not merely looking for military knowledge; he is looking for the abilities which may make the student suitable for higher command – or not. DS are very much on the alert for the pushful type who has passed the entrance exam after ingenious cramming courses. Once in, that sort of student likes to draw attention to his merits by asking endless questions. However long the lecture and however tedious the subsequent questioning, the pushful type is always there waiting, even though his may be the very last, and least essential question. Sometimes DS and students are united in loathing a particular person, or even a group, but everyone goes to such extremes to be fair that the 'pushers' often go unchecked to conduct their campaign of personal self-seeking in even higher realms.

The Commandant of the Staff College was now General Sir Bernard Paget. Paget was an intellectual from a strong clerical family. His father was Bishop of Oxford and his mother the daughter of the Dean of St Paul's. He had won a DSO and an MC in the First War and would later become C-in-C South Eastern Command (in the dark days after Dunkirk), C-in-C Home Forces, and C-in-C 21st

Army Group. After the war he became Principal of Ashridge College. He thought well of Horrocks and employed him as his chief staff officer. Horrocks described Paget as 'a very strong character and one of the most honourable men I have ever met'. However in his autobiography Horrocks wrote, 'By the middle of 1938 it became clear to most of us that war against Hitler was almost inevitable and this added an edge to our labours,' which suggests that he, Paget and the rest of the Staff College were living in a world apart. Many people had already concluded that another European war was inevitable when Hitler reoccupied the Rhineland in 1936 and followed it by arming Germany to the teeth.

In September 1939 speculation came to an end. Staff College courses changed suddenly: they had never been easy but now became six months' hard labour. Horrocks was now involved with the organisation of short courses adapted to the needs of wartime intake. The new brand of students and the old guard of staff were, happily, impressed with each other. The first course included many who would make their names in various walks of life later: two of them became Cabinet Ministers and one (Selwyn Lloyd) Speaker of the House of Commons. Horrocks found their presence a great stimulus and rose to the occasion; unlike most of his fellow instructors he had learnt something of civilian viewpoints in his time as a TA adjutant. They, for their part, found Horrocks an impressive teacher, energetic, enquiring and imaginative. It was, perhaps one should recall, the period of the 'phoney war', the 'Great Bore War'. Although Hitler had invaded Poland and crushed its armies in a matter of weeks, and although he had also acquired a powerful and dangerous ally in Russia, military and political thinkers in the West still clung obstinately to the belief that Hitler probably realised he had now gone too far, and must sooner or later back down. There was, of course, no reason for this belief apart from wishful thinking, and illusions were rudely shattered on 9 April 1940 when Hitler invaded Norway and Denmark. (Even so, a few optimists believed he would now stop; it took the invasion of Holland, Belgium and France in the following month to convince them.) General Paget was sent to Norway to command British forces there; his observation of their state of training served him well when he was C-in-C Home Forces later.

Horrocks was due to leave the Staff College in May 1940, to take over command of the 2nd Battalion of the Middlesex Regiment. He was clearly doing well and had caught up and passed most of his contemporaries in the regular army. The prospect of more pay and less entertaining was one of the benefits of his new posting. At the Staff College he had been a keen member of the Drag Hunt and had been involved in endless entertaining. He had never had enough money for his needs, for he was involved in many activities and generous as well. He had taken on external examining in order to try to narrow the gap between expenditure and income. Even when his memory of other events had faded, he had a strong recollection of years when financial worries had never been absent.

The 2nd Battalion was already in France and Horrocks was preparing for a leisurely handover to his successor at the Staff College when the news of the invasion of 10 May reached him. It hardly seems surprising that the British were caught napping in France if Horrocks, the Chief Instructor at the Staff College, was unaware of impending events. And, on his own statement, he only learned of the news from the telephone switchboard operator who thought he might be interested to know.

The plans for another German invasion of France – if it came – had been discussed frequently at the Staff College. There were good reasons for advancing and stopping the Germans as soon as possible, but almost equally good reasons for staying back and cutting them off by flanking attacks. In the event it was decided to move forward, although in practice this was the prelude to an almost equally fast move backwards. Three days after the invasion Horrocks was taking over his new command in Louvain. It was part of 3rd Division, commanded by Major-General B.L. Montgomery.

When Horrocks arrived in the 2nd Battalion he did not like what he saw. It had already been mauled and was tired. As Horrocks knew, the first casualty of war is sleep. When an army is advancing, lack of sleep is partly overcome by high morale; when it is retreating the fact that there is no chance to rest and recuperate is an added burden. The 2nd Battalion was economising on effort by omitting to shave and Horrocks, with a long history of preserving morale under depressing conditions, was well aware that this was a dangerous factor. He believed that the cleaner and smarter the soldier the better. Nowadays when soldiers are often smothered in camouflage paint their appearance in battle may seem less important, but experience proves that a man who had shaved feels fresher and more alert, and if trained to keep himself as clean as possible he will do the same for his weapons. Horrocks' insistence on the battalion being clean and tidy, whatever the conditions, initially gave the impression that this was some unrealistic base-wallah who would soon learn sense. But soon first impressions were corrected.

Less than two hours after Horrocks arrived he was told that the divisional commander wished to see him. He did not look forward to the meeting for, from what he had heard, General Montgomery was unpredictable, unorthodox, demanding, ruthless and a show-off. But the meeting produced nothing except the usual courtesies. Both men would have been astonished if they had realised the length of time they would serve together.

The battalion was in action the following day. They were machine-gunners and their task was to prevent any German infantry break-through by standing their ground and then, if possible, counter-attacking. The battalion was well trained. Contrary to the general view, Horrocks considered that this and the other regular battalions were extremely efficient. At this moment he himself learnt something about preserving morale in battle. The commanding officer of the Ulster Rifles had seen some of his men running to the rear at Louvain. He stopped them. They turned to go back to the front again but he checked them, insisted they should smoke a cigarette, and finish it (although their position was now being heavily shelled) and then walk back to the front. Horrocks never forgot that.

In France, he began as he intended to go on. He found out as much as he could about the general military situation and as he toured the platoons he briefed each of them on what was happening. This, of course, was what Montgomery liked to do, but it is interesting to note that Horrocks was doing it of his own volition long before he had close contact with Montgomery. Montgomery developed this practice as a result of fighting in the First World War when no one, least of all battalion officers, knew what was happening. He often stated that his habit of telling the soldiers under his command as much as he could without breaching security was a result of the total ignorance of events in which he had fought during part of the First World War. Horrocks, of course, who had only been in action for a few weeks in early 1914, would not have been expected to know what was going on generally.

But the information he imparted began to be disquieting. Although they were holding their sector there were reports that the Germans had penetrated deeply into the French positions. At first Horrocks reacted philosophically. During the First World War the French had shown great resilience and tactical skill. He felt that if the Germans had been allowed to penetrate they were probably regret-ting it by now. Disillusion came when three days later the 2nd Middlesex were told to take part in a general withdrawal; the French, on their right, had disintegrated. Subsequently when he reviewed the campaign his sympathies went to Viscount Gort, the British Commander-in-Chief. Gort was a general of impressive appearance and military record; he was a VC, but his intellectual limits were well known. Horrocks thought Gort was in an impossible situation in that he was under the command of the French Commander-in-Chief whose army was falling to pieces and who was suffering from a form of mental disorder; and on Gort's left was the Belgian army which suddenly capitulated without reference to the Allies. Horrocks considered that Gort displayed remarkable fortitude in the circumstances, but this must have been the view of hindsight for he had no opportunity of observing Gort personally.

One man he did meet, and whom he was to see often later, was Alan Brooke, then a lieutenant-general. Brooke, as it is now realised, was probably the best potential general of the Second World War. In France he was the commander of 2 Corps and had the onerous task of trying to maintain the British Expeditionary Force as a coherent organisation. The measure of his achievement was the number of British soldiers who eventually reached Dunkirk and were evacuated. Brooke was never again able to demonstrate his abilities as a field commander as he became C-in-C Home Forces and then Chief of the Imperial General Staff. In both posts he worked closely with Churchill, often restraining the Prime Minister's wilder flights of fancy. Brooke was a military genius and undoubtedly contributed greatly to the eventual Allied victory, but was too important to be given the commands he would have liked: C-in-C Middle East, and Commander 21st Army Group. Horrocks noted in France that Alan Brooke behaved as if nothing was amiss, or not proceeding to plan: only later did he learn that Brooke was near despair.

One sign of coming events was the behaviour of the future Field Marshal Montgomery. Whatever the crisis Montgomery insisted on regular meals and a full night's sleep. Horrocks noted ruefully that he was the only person in the entire Army who enjoyed those privileges. Everyone else was completely exhausted. However, on one night Montgomery had to forgo most of his night's sleep, for his division had to withdraw to close the gap created by the surrender of the Belgian Army. In spite of roads being heavily congested with transport, abandoned vehicles and refugees, the move was accomplished successfully, as Montgomery had confidently predicted it would be.

Although the 1940 campaign had been a disaster for the British Army, it was of considerable benefit to certain people. Brooke was promoted to being C-in-C Home Forces, Montgomery replaced him as Commander of 2 Corps, and Horrocks became a brigadier. Although Horrocks had been a battalion commander for a mere seventeen days, it had been an eventful period and he was deemed to have acquitted himself well. His official promotion to brigadier did not come till he took over 9th Brigade in 3rd Division, but he did serve for a short time in that rank while still in France. Unfortunately for him, by the time he received the news that he was to take over command of 11th Brigade (whose previous commander had now been appointed to command 3rd Division) the brigade had already received orders to move to Dunkirk. Horrocks visited a few units on the day he arrived, and then stayed at the control point at Coxyde as the brigade moved towards the beach.

When all the identifiable troops had passed through Coxyde, Horrocks followed them to La Panne. There to his surprise he found the beaches swarming with troops, and no sign of any evacuation having begun. La Panne was being shelled and bombed and some of the houses were burning. A number of soldiers had found their way into cellars and his first task was to get these out, get them to the beach and supervise their evacuation. He did not notice any breakdown of discipline although some soldiers were so eager to get into the smaller boats that they overturned them. Horrocks dealt with the situation by himself wading out, with a torch, having previously arranged with one of his officers on the beach to despatch twenty men at a time. Each time Horrocks flashed the torch, another twenty waded out and no more boats were overturned. After doing this for some time, standing in water up to his chest, Horrocks got cramp and returned to the beach. There were troops everywhere and he set about finding those who belonged to his brigade. There were none to be seen: the rest of the division had gone on to Dunkirk. He set off after them, 'a very wet, very tired, and very temporary brigadier with no staff and no troops'.

Although the Navy was doing its utmost to get people away, and the RAF often came over to tackle the German bombers, the Army had clearly shot its bolt. The beaches and the surrounding land were packed with men who now only had rifles; all heavier weapons had been abandoned, destroyed when possible. Horrocks pondered gloomily on the prospects if the German tanks now appeared, for nothing could have stopped the holocaust if they had. The fact that they did not so intrigued Horrocks that subsequently he went to considerable trouble to find out why they did not.

It is still widely believed that the orders for the Panzer commanders to halt outside Dunkirk came from Hitler who was still hoping to make peace with Britain and felt that mass destruction by the Panzers at Dunkirk would do nothing to assist this. However, as Horrocks later discovered, the original order came from von Rundstedt. Von Rundstedt had good reasons for his decision. The first was that he had heard that Britain was sending fresh divisions to Calais and Boulogne and that there would be a counter-attack by these and the French who were said to be moving new divisions up from the south. In view of this expected double attack it was necessary to have the German tanks in readiness, and as they had now been in action continuously for two weeks most of them urgently needed maintenance. Many of them had strayed far from their original path in the 'expanding torrent' theory of armoured warfare and unless they could be concentrated quickly the Germans would be at a considerable disadvantage in an Allied counter-attack. Finally, von Rundstedt felt that the tanks had done their job. They were not suited to operations on soft sandy beaches and the German infantry should now take over. Having made this decision, he explained the reasons for it to Hitler, who agreed without demur. Hitler made an additional point that if the tanks went closer to the beaches they would inhibit the Luftwaffe which was enjoying itself strafing and bombing soldiers with virtually no anti-aircraft weapons. As the evacuation reached its final stages, Horrocks noted that men were now so tired with walking, and numb through lack of sleep, that the noise of naval guns and falling bombs caused no reaction at all. Eventually his own turn to embark came and he was shepherded on to a destroyer.

But his troubles were not over. He had just time to enjoy some rum and hot milk when the destroyer was hit and began to capsize. Fortunately there were two other smaller boats alongside and he managed to scramble on to one of them. It was a tug, crammed with troops, and was, like any other ship in the area, under attack from German aircraft. A call was made for someone to man a Lewis anti-aircraft gun and Horrocks promptly came forward. It was, he said, his happiest moment of the last fortnight. He rattled off drum after drum, though without appearing to affect their German adversaries.

But the ship survived. On arrival at Ramsgate Horrocks was astonished to be met by cheering crowds; he would have been less surprised in view of the results of the recent battles if they had been met with hisses and jeers. But for some unaccountable British reason they found themselves heroes.

It was a time of surprises. At Ramsgate he was sent to a train which he understood was going to Reading. From Reading to Camberley, where his home still was, would be a mere sixteen miles. He dropped off to sleep.

He was very tired and did not wake up until someone shook him and said he had to get out of the train. 'Is this Reading?' he asked. 'No,' came the reply, 'it's Darlington.' Here, at a transit camp he had time to have a much needed hot bath before being despatched to Lyme Regis. There he decided to have an enormous meal. As he started to order the manager suggested he should leave choosing the items to him and appalled Horrocks (ever hard-up) by adding a bottle of champagne. When Horrocks nervously asked for the bill he was told there was nothing to pay.

So the first phase of action in the Second World War had come to an end and left Horrocks with plenty to think about. He was impressed with Montgomery who had proved himself very cool, decisive, and reliable in a desperate situation, and he had been impressed with the potential of the troops though not with their training and equipment. His battalion of the Middlesex, in the time he had been with it, had performed well, a fact he put down to the vigorous training programme of his predecessor in command. These were first thoughts; clearly there would be much more hard pondering to be done before British and French troops could confront the Panzers with any hope of success. And the hard thinking might have to be done quickly, for Hitler, enraged at the huge numbers of troops who had escaped (over 300,000), had every intention of carrying the war to Britain at the first opportune moment.

Chapter 5

A Variety of Experiences

Although his own career seemed to be leaping ahead, Horrocks was much too concerned with the general situation to take much satisfaction in it. Forty-four years later it is difficult even for those who experienced the atmosphere after Dunkirk to understand their feelings at the time: for those born afterwards it must be impossible. In spite of the general euphoria at having rescued so many men from Dunkirk there was soon a grim realisation that what had happened in France could quite easily happen in Britain too. German bombers were seen more frequently over British towns, and ominous rumours of a German invasion fleet being massed on the French coast suggested that matters would get much worse before, if ever, they grew better. The country seethed with rumours, but there were plenty of hard facts to be observed too. The latter included the intensive training of soldiers, and the hasty, almost frenzied, attention to coastal defence. Life was a mixture of grim reality and fantasy. The account of German military prowess given with considerable emphasis by those who had returned via Dunkirk did not make the average citizen rate our chances very highly if the Panzers ever landed on British soil. On the other hand, there were the inspiring though grim messages from Churchill, the comforting thought that twenty-one miles of sea still separated Britain from the German Army, and lastly the extraordinary dulling effect that rampant bureaucracy had on people's minds. For the war had set loose hordes of petty tyrants; air raid wardens, food rationing officials, tradespeople who had always resented being at the service of the public and were now determined to show the boot was on the other foot. There were notices advising people not to travel when their journeys were not vital, not to spread rumours, and not to do anything except comply with a constant stream of bureaucratic instructions.

Horrocks' brigade (which he took over on 17 June 1940) had been allotted the stretch of the coast between Rottingdean and Shoreham. If his brigade had been stretched out in a thin khaki line, it would have given him less than ten men to every hundred yards. But the real problem was not so much numbers as mobility. The area was very densely populated and if an attack had taken place the difficulties of moving through a built-up area would have been increased by the numbers of people blocking the roads. Yet compared with other areas it was quite stoutly defended. Horrocks viewed the situation with equanimity because he did not believe that a German invasion could take place in the near future. Equanimity was necessary for another problem with which he was soon confronted. Montgomery used to visit him, inspect his dispositions, then note that a certain house was obstructing the line of fire. 'Have them out, Horrocks. Blow up the house. Defence must come first!' Horrocks was well aware that Montgomery was right in theory but felt that such drastic action might, at that moment, be somewhat premature.

Churchill paid a secret visit and stayed to watch an exercise. But, he was soon recognised and large numbers of people collected to see him. Horrocks found the occasion slightly disturbing. The enthusiastic crowds trusted implicitly in Churchill to save them, and were sure that he could: Horrocks, knowing the military situation, hoped that their trust would be justified. While rumours abounded among the civilian population, there was some hard-core fact for Horrocks to digest in the information he received from the Higher Command. Aerial reconnaissance had established that the Germans were assembling barges on the French coast, and practising invasion moves. Other information was coming from 'Ultra' although this, as yet, was far from the complete service it would provide later. To keep his troops alert and mobile, Horrocks arranged a number of exercises in which they were switched from point to point. As the autumn approached and the possibility of invasion seemed more likely, Horrocks established an early-warning system in which his own part was to sleep next door to the brigade operations room. A major problem was to avoid giving a false alarm. If that happened, the resultant confusion in Brighton would take days to sort out. Horrocks had signallers at the end of each pier, and the officer in charge of each detachment had orders to let him know the moment he saw anything which looked like the real thing. If he did, he was to send Brigade HQ a message by both wireless and line and to fire a white signal rocket. Once that happened Horrocks would pass on the message and the whole of southern England would be on the alert. One memorable night his brigade major came in and announced that a white rocket had just gone up at the end of the pier. This looked like the real thing but, oddly enough, there was no confirmatory message on either telephone or radio. Why not? Investigations were hastily begun. There had indeed been a white rocket, but it had come from a ship which at that moment happened to be passing the end of the pier. A less experienced commander might have decided there was no time to lose and set off the alarm. Had Horrocks done so, whatever the extenuating circumstances his subsequent career might have been very different.

There was at this time, although Horrocks makes no mention of it in his autobiography, a considerable clash of opinion about how invasion – if it took place – should be dealt with. Auchinleck, who was successively commander of 5 Corps and then GOC-in-C Southern Command, had ordered that the invasion should be met on the beaches, assuming that the invaders, after a sea crossing, would be at their most vulnerable. Montgomery disagreed and stated that the best policy would be to allow the Germans to land and then attack them and destroy them with a concentrated force. Montgomery had no scruples about attempting to undermine his superior's authority and, although Horrocks was aware of this and personally held Auchinleck in high esteem, he did not let it influence his loyalty to Montgomery. Montgomery's view of the correct tactics for dealing with invasion caused 3rd Division to be withdrawn from the coast to positions from which it might launch counter-attacks. Those positions were in Gloucestershire, Dorset and Somerset. Training in these areas brought Horrocks into contact with the Home Guard, which had a store of local knowledge and a wealth of experience in the shape of members who had served in the First World War (though some of them were not as fit as they used to be). The experience of working with local units was not as much a novelty for Horrocks as it would have been for some people for, of course, he had learnt the ropes when adjutant of the 9th Middlesex.

But his command did not last beyond the end of the year in any case. In January 1941 he became BGS (Brigadier, General Staff) in Eastern Command, a position he held till the following June. The job of BGS consisted principally of organising training exercises at brigade level or above. As every soldier knows, it is not difficult to organise exercises on a small scale, and perfection is not impossible. Once the numbers increase, and many units are involved, the entire exercise may become a tangle and quite useless as training. In such situations the acronym SNAFU or MFU ('Situation normal – all fouled up' or 'Military foul up'; 'foul' is not of course the word most commonly employed) tend to be used. It was valuable experience for Horrocks, and would serve him in good stead in later, real battles, for as BGS he could see weak points where mistakes were most likely to occur. To have the opportunity to observe the results of planning at this stage in his career suggested that he was going to be a 'lucky' general. Success in war depends on many factors: surprise, planning, logistics – the list is lengthy but one of the most important is whether the commanding general has good luck. To some extent a man makes his own luck by foresight but in war there are occasions when success depends almost entirely on luck. At sea, battleships may be observed and sunk because of a break in cloud cover, bad weather can disrupt the most carefully laid plans (as it nearly did the D-Day landings) and an accident can delay the delivery of an important message and cause disaster. Some people avoid misfortunes: others do not. Some generals have been proved to be lucky: others not. Almost everything in Horrocks' career seemed to have given him the right experience at the right time. He had been wounded and captured early in the First World War, thus avoiding the slaughter which overtook his regiment later; had he remained with it he would almost certainly have been killed. He gained unusual and interesting experience in Russia, he was at the Staff College as a student at the right time, he was there again as an instructor, equally fortuitously. He had commanded a battalion in action. He had met and made a favourable impression on many of the senior officers who were going to be very important in the future. And not least he had a happy disposition.

On 25 June 1941 he was appointed Commander of 44 (Home Counties) Division, with the acting rank of major-general. The division was made up of three TA brigades – 131st (The Queens), 132nd (The Buffs and West Kents), and 133rd (The Sussex). It was stationed in what was potentially the hottest spot on the entire English coastline, the area stretching from the Isle of Thanet to Folkestone. It was not necessarily the most likely spot for invasion, for that could well have been the Hastings area, but it was certainly the area which experienced most of the German softening-up tactics. Dover had already had this experience in the First World War. The area, with some accuracy, had been christened 'Hellfire Corner' by American journalists. Bombs fell wherever the Germans thought they should, and in many other places when they were jettisoned in order to assist the raiders to get away. The air above was often the scene of desperate aerial 'dog fights'. Out in the Channel were brisk activities by motor gun boats, motor torpedo boats, minelayers, and other craft. Most of the Channel naval battles took place at night and Horrocks used to go to Admiral Ramsay's HQ in Dover Castle and listen to the reports as they came in minute by minute. Needless to say he got on very well with Admiral Ramsay, whom he would encounter often later in combined operations.

By this time Montgomery had succeeded Auchinleck as GOC South Eastern Command and was determined to make his mark. No one in the command had the slightest doubt that the troops in his area would be brought to the peak of efficiency at the earliest possible moment. It suited Horrocks, whose recent experience in France had made him only too well aware of the need for constant and vigorous training, but it did not suit many others. Montgomery was totally ruthless. He considered, doubtless rightly, that there were far too many people doing sedentary jobs who were unfit and probably overweight. Every officer in his command was ordered to carry out two cross-country runs a week. Protests were ignored. Anyone who produced a medical certificate to say that cross-country running would be too dangerous for him automatically ruled himself out of any interesting appointment, including the one he was currently in. Montgomery's theory was that as battle is a physical strain, everyone taking part should be physically fit. Some people thought that the stress on certain physical standards was absurd and was detrimental to mental activity but they did not convey their views to the GOC, although there was ample opportunity. Montgomery toured his command tirelessly. He was quick to spot efficiency, and even quicker at spotting potential failure. He did a lot of 'weeding-out', leaving in his wake a number of embittered senior officers. Some of his decrees were so arbitrary that it seems astonishing that there was not more reaction. The most remarkable was the one concerning wives and families. After September 1940 when the weather had made a German invasion impossible until the spring, many of those serving in South Eastern Command had made themselves reasonably comfortable. Wives had joined them as many soldiers, both officers and other ranks, were able to live in accommodation close to their stations. After the disaster of France and the tension of summer and autumn, a more relaxed attitude was beginning to prevail. This, however, was no good for Montgomery. Although well aware that the German invasion of Russia (22 June 1941) had ruled out any invasion of Britain for a long time to come, if ever, he continued to prepare for it as it if were imminent. For maximum efficiency he decreed that the South Eastern Command area would be rid of all domestic encumbrances, that is, wives or families. If an invasion occurred, men would be unable to do their allotted jobs properly because they would be worrying about the possible fate of their wives or families who might be in the immediate path of the invader. Those who suggested that there were advantages in having the refreshing influence of domestic bliss to help maintain morale received short shrift. Horrocks recalled many occasions when wives were still in the district after they had been presumed to have gone further inland, but his best story concerned the young officer who told his landlady (for he was living in a billet) that his wife was coming to visit him but, as Montgomery had ordered that no wives should visit the area, she had to travel and spend the weekend under the name of Miss Smith. The landlady was sympathetic and agreed to co-operate in every way. Of course, the lady concerned really was a Miss Smith.

Horrocks enjoyed Montgomery's energetic approach and thoroughness, and appreciated the value of these qualities in training. Whatever else Dunkirk did or did not do, it certainly instilled in the survivors a fervent desire to ensure that such a débâcle did not happen again. Many of the less intelligent officers followed the Montgomery line and assumed that our defeats before Dunkirk had largely been due to inferior training and lack of physical fitness. Certainly the BEF in 1940 had become stagnant. But the assumption that hard training would be the sole solution to British problems was a jejune one. Fortunately there were large number of scientists, inventors, and unorthodox thinkers who were pressing ahead with developments which would prove better battle-winners than PT and celibacy.

But there is a happy medium, as Horrocks decided when he was transferred to his next command, 9th Armoured Division. The move took place on 20 March 1942.

The appointment of Horrocks to the command of an armoured division was unexpected. As an infantryman Horrocks would not understand the techniques of armoured warfare, still less the niceties of cavalry tradition. There has always been, and still is, a degree of constraint between members of the different arms. Senior officers who have come up through the more technical units – engineers, signallers, gunners – are thought not to understand the problems of handling infantry; likewise the infantry regards cavalry generals with suspicion, 'block-headed donkey wallopers'. The attitude of other units towards the infantry, the footsloggers (as they used to be) tends to be patronising, 'nice chaps but quite out of touch with technical problems'.

9th Division was made up of the 15th/19th Hussars, the 5th (Inniskilling) Dragoon Guards, the 4th/7th Dragoon Guards, the 13th/18th Hussars, the East Riding Yeomanry and the Fife and Forfar Yeomanry. It would not occur to any of the members of those regiments that there could be a better cavalry regiment than their own, and of course no regiments in any other arm could be compared with cavalry regiments anyway.

Horrocks' arrival caused a mild stir, but he proved to be a sound choice. Major N. Denny, MC, who became his ADC, believes he was the first infantryman to command an armoured division. Horrocks took two days to look around, then summoned the officers to a cinema and addressed them. He informed them he had just had a look at the vehicles parade state and it informed him that only about half of the vehicles were capable of moving at all. 'You,' he said, 'know all about mechanical things. As an infantryman, I don't. However, in the infantry division I have just come from, almost all the vehicles are serviceable. Perhaps you would care to explain why so many of yours are not.' A REME (Royal Electrical and Mechanical Engineers) officer got up to answer this rhetorical question and was, according to Denny, promptly shut up in a very firm but polite way, by the suggestion that perhaps the officer would be better employed in making sure vehicles would perform than in making explanations why they could not.

Denny said that before the address everyone was asking why they, a cavalry division, should have got 'a bloody infantryman whom they had never heard of'. Half an hour later they were telling each other how lucky they were to have got such a spirited personality as a commander. 'He was one of the few commanders,' said Denny, 'who could really address troops and make it stick. Most who attempted to do so were an absolute disaster.' Denny thought that Horrocks was better than Montgomery because Horrocks' approach was modest, whereas Montgomery's constant self-justification tended to be irritating.

But Horrocks brought in some of the Montgomery methods. The regiments in the division were well trained, and apart from the standard of maintenance, he had little fault to find with performance. All the ancillary units, such as gunners and signallers, were extremely efficient. They were not, however, properly co-ordinated, they were not a coherent fighting unit, and they were living far too comfortably. The division was at this time in Northamptonshire, with headquarters at Guilsborough; wives, families, and other peacetime comforts had softened the rigours of war so much that it hardly seemed a concern of the division at all. Horrocks decided a move from Northampton was urgently necessary and so took them off to Newmarket to live under canvas during the winter. The flat, bleak countryside around Newmarket was ideal for exercises with armoured vehicles and Horrocks saw that they made good use of it. As soon as an exercise was completed, another was ready to follow. Happily, the harder he worked them the more they seemed to like it.

Wartime cavalry regiments included a good number of officers and men who had come from county yeomanry regiments. These seemed to Horrocks to embody the very qualities he was looking for: dash, fearlessness, self-reliance and a strong desire to be as competent professionally as their more experienced regular companions. Curiously enough, some three hundred years earlier, Oliver Cromwell had looked for precisely those same qualities for his cavalry squadrons. He demanded young men of spirit who did not believe that rank and wealth entitled them to command.

Horrocks understood the outlook of the young cavalryman – who was now in a squadron of tanks rather than a squadron of horses – and they found him an inspiring leader. He would, of course, have made a very suitable cavalryman himself; he was a courageous and skilled horseman, a good shot, and a man who drove cars with a speed and abandon which made passengers catch their breath. Denny noted that not only was Horrocks known to all the soldiers in his division but he also gave them confidence. They felt that with Horrocks in command everything would be all right in the uncertain future. Denny lost contact with Horrocks when the latter was posted to the Middle East but met him again in Normandy and served with him to the end of the war.

Horrocks was not only teaching 9th Division; he was also learning. Armoured warfare is essentially mobile and the commander operates from a command tank. Horrocks felt at home in a tank. A small Command HQ, the ability to move rapidly, see everything for himself and be at the front, suited him perfectly.

His last exercise with 9th Armoured Division was up in the Northumberland/Durham area. Although it was only August the weather was so unpleasant that most of the division remembered this as one of their least enjoyable experiences of the war. But from the point of view of being made welcome it was also outstanding; the friendliness and hospitality of the Geordies, none too well off themselves, was almost embarrassing.

On 14 August 1942 Horrocks received marching orders once more. He was to take over 13 Corps in North Africa. It meant promotion. He, who a mere three years earlier had been a major, acting lt-colonel, would be a lt-general. Everything seemed to be happening a little too quickly. He had been enjoying himself with 9th Armoured, and was looking forward to taking them into action. Commanding an armoured division in battle would be an exacting task; the contemplated command of a corps which would contain two, perhaps three, divisions was a daunting prospect. Secretly he wondered whether he had not been over-promoted, as all his recent rises in rank had been in units which, though officially on active service, had not been in action. He doubted whether a newcomer and novice from home would be readily accepted by the old hands of the Eighth Army who had seen it all. For while Horrocks had been practising war in the United Kingdom the reality had been occurring in the Middle East in which he had no experience. There had been Wavell's campaign against the Italians, the arrival of Rommel, the failure of Wavell's 'Battleaxe' offensive, Wavell's replacement by Auchinleck, Auchinleck's gains and losses against Rommel, culminating in the desperate battles at Alamein the previous July, the abrupt dismissal of Auchinleck and his replacement by Alexander.

Montgomery had now taken over Eighth Army. Montgomery suffered from no lack of confidence, although just as inexperienced as Horrocks in desert warfare and even less experienced than Horrocks in the art of armoured warfare. The Eighth Army had taken some severe blows: Rommel had always been quick to exploit any weakness, and it had not been a lucky army in that its Australian components had been withdrawn, it had been ill-supplied with suitable equipment, and its highly promising General 'Strafer' Gott had been killed. Montgomery scented a possible crisis in morale. Above all, he realised he must have an enthusiastic supporter. His own presence was due to the death of Gott two days before. Gott had been commanding 13 Corps since the previous February and had just been chosen to command Eighth Army when the aircraft he was travelling in was shot down. Since 25 June Auchinleck had been commanding Eighth Army himself (Ritchie had been dismissed and there was no one else with the requisite ability and experience). Montgomery should have taken over Eighth Army from Auchinleck on 15 August but did so on the twelfth in the latter's absence on his C-in-C duties. Montgomery therefore sent for Horrocks before he was officially in a position to do so. None of this was appreciated by Horrocks who undoubtedly owed this particular promotion to Montgomery's need for a loyal and reliable aide whom he knew well, rather than Horrocks' immediate qualifications for the appointment of corps commander. Nevertheless Horrocks quickly adapted himself. This was lucky for everyone, for Horrocks' previous experience of commanding troops in battle had been minimal: three weeks as a second lieutenant in 1914 and slightly less than three weeks as a lt-colonel in 1940. His period as a brigadier in France in 1940 had not involved commanding the brigade in action.

On the way out the aircraft refuelled at Gibraltar. The Rock had happy memories for him and he reflected how lucky he had been to have such understanding and devoted parents to provide him with stability and security. Stability and security seemed rather absent from his life at this moment. It had already been gently conveyed to him that the Middle East was a stern taskmaster and that several promising generals had met an abrupt end to their careers there: Cunningham, Ritchie and Corbett were among the more notable.

Chapter 6

The Reality

With Auchinleck's departure the new Commander-in-Chief Middle East was General the Hon. Sir Harold Alexander, better known as 'Alex'. Alexander was a popular general, much loved by his men, and somewhat in the Montgomery mould in that he took special care to learn the names of troops he was visiting or revisiting. This gave an impression of omniscience, and undoubtedly he was a staunch and capable general. However, there were those who said that his abilities were somewhat overrated and that he owed some of his advancement to charm and luck rather than professional skill. Perhaps his luckiest moment had been in evading capture in Burma. Had that occurred, when he was conducting the withdrawal, his name would have been bracketed with that of Percival, to whom the fall of Singapore is often exclusively and quite unjustly attributed. Horrocks had some slight doubts about Alexander's capabilities, finding him slightly withdrawn although of impeccable courtesy.

On arrival at Montgomery's Eighth Army Headquarters, Horrocks was put 'straight into the picture' as Montgomery liked to describe it. Montgomery's custom, as is now well known, was to travel with a map caravan. At this briefing Horrocks was immensely impressed by Montgomery's grasp of the essentials of the situation. Horrocks was unaware that Montgomery had already been briefed by Auchinleck, an occasion of which he had subsequently given a distorted account, and had a good selection of 'Ultra' messages to provide him with 'insight'. The author recalls hearing Montgomery say that he would put photographs of opposing commanders on the walls of his caravan and by looking at them try to imagine what they were likely to do next. This was before the 'Ultra' story was revealed. There was, of course, no need to look at photographs and wonder what the enemy would do next if you had an 'Ultra' decrypt of his plans lying on the table in front of you.

Horrocks said later that he had never previously heard of Alamein. This seems surprising because in pre-war Staff College discussions on the strategic importance of the Middle East it had always been assumed that if an enemy attacked Egypt from the west the Alamein position would be the place to check it. The position was of strategic importance because it was only thirty-five miles wide and had the sea on one flank and the Qattara depression on the other. Montgomery went on to say that if attacked again the Eighth Army would not retreat but would die where it stood. This, of course, was all part of the 'things have changed for the better now that I am in command and Auchinleck has gone' theme, and it convinced Horrocks at the time, though he had second thoughts later. Ruthless and dishonest though these tactics of Montgomery were, it must be acknowledged that they did act as a morale-booster to an army which had been sadly battered through no fault of its own. Curiously enough, although Churchill had been urging Auchinleck to launch an offensive on Rommel before the end of September, he put no similar pressure on Montgomery. Montgomery was therefore able to amass a supply of modern arms and equipment which made victory virtually inevitable.

The immediate prospect, however, was not a new offensive by the Eighth Army but a fresh attack from Rommel. The essential need for understanding of the three battles which took place between June and November 1942 is that they were all based on the Alamein line. First were the July battles when Auchinleck had stopped Rommel with tactics which, in the words of the latter, 'nearly made him weep with frustration'. The second battle in the area took place in the southern sector of the line towards what was known as the Alam Halfa position. The Alam Halfa ridge was some fifteen miles behind the middle point of the Alamein line from El Alamein to Qaret and Himeimat. The third battle took place in October and ended with the withdrawal of Rommel from the Alamein area.

From 'Ultra' Montgomery was aware that Rommel intended attacking again in the near future and also knew where that attack would take place. 'Ultra' was now providing a steady service of reliable information about future German plans. Where it was less effective was in assessing some of the information. Thus when Rommel had complained piteously to the German High Command about his shortage of war material, Allied Intelligence had believed every word he said. However his complaints about his parlous state were treated with scepticism by his German superiors and by our units confronting him who realised that his hard-luck stories were meant to induce the German High Command to allow him more supplies. Every general believes that he needs more supplies of some items; some believe they need further supplies of everything.

Horrocks believed every word which Montgomery spoke when the latter briefed him but later developed doubts about the accuracy of Montgomery's claims. According to Montgomery. Auchinleck had informed him that he was planning to withdraw to the Upper Nile if there was any chance that the Eighth Army might be destroyed in a further German attack. As a 'fall-back' proviso this would have made tactical sense, for an intact Allied army based in the Upper Nile area could threaten German communications if the latter reached Cairo. Montgomery told Horrocks that Auchinleck had *definite* plans to withdraw, and made the same statements later in his *Memoirs*. Auchinleck, of course, denied this slur and some years after the war Montgomery retracted it. Horrocks had considerable sympathy for Auchinleck who, he thought, had performed magnificently with limited resources; he considered Auchinleck's victory in the July battles to be one of the most important in the war. Horrocks' appreciation of Auchinleck's abilities was sharpened by the knowledge that 'the Auk' had survived military disasters on more than one occasion: Norway and the 'Crusader' battles spring to mind.

In his own autobiography Horrocks gave a long and detailed tribute to Auchinleck. He wrote: 'As we now know the Prime Minister was moving heaven and earth to get the commander of the Eighth Army to launch an immediate offensive. It says much for Auchinleck's moral courage that, at this time, when he was convinced that such an offensive would have little chance of success, and he was under a cloud, he refused to attack until he was satisfied that his troops were trained and reorganised. The 44th (Home Counties) Division straight from the United Kingdom without any desert experience would inevitably have been in the attack. They might well erect a monument to Auchinleck who unquestionably saved them from very heavy casualties.'

As Horrocks had commanded 44th Division in the recent past he knew very well how unfitted they were to be flung into a desert battle against the Panzers. He too had good reason to feel grateful to Auchinleck.

In view of the fact that Horrocks worked so closely with Montgomery, and was virtually his right-hand man, it is often assumed that he was blind to Montgomery's faults. This was not so: he was well aware of them. He could also see very clearly where Montgomery's virtues lay. Montgomery gave Horrocks opportunities and backing that Horrocks might not have received from anyone else, and Monty, a good picker of men, was certainly justified in doing so. As a member of his new team Horrocks did very well. At Alam Halfa he was probably the only person exercising initiative.

Nevertheless, grateful though he was to Montgomery for affording him opportunities personally, he was never happy about the denigration of Auchinleck's character. Rather than conclude that the whole episode smacked of sharp practice by Montgomery, he assumed that the conversation between Auchinleck and Montgomery had been

Brian Horrocks, aged nine, with his sister Jean at Gibraltar in 1904. 'I had an extremely happy childhood'

2nd Lt Brian Horrocks as a prisoner of war in Germany. His uniform, after three years of captivity, is none the better for the experience

Horrocks on the Russian train on which he travelled 3,000 miles. He is in the centre, hands behind his back

The British Modern Pentathlon Championship in 1924 was won by Horrocks, here sitting second from the left. Subsequently he represented Great Britain in the 1924 Olympic Games

With 9th Armoured Division, taking a close look into armoured warfare

George VI and Horrocks look on with astonishment as Montgomery demonstrates his fly switch, North Africa, 1943

Probably the greatest moment of Horrocks' career. At the end of the Battle of Mareth, largely won by his efforts, he enters El Hamma, a genuine conquering hero

1943. Dangerously wounded, with his military career apparently at an end, Horrocks tries to look cheerful

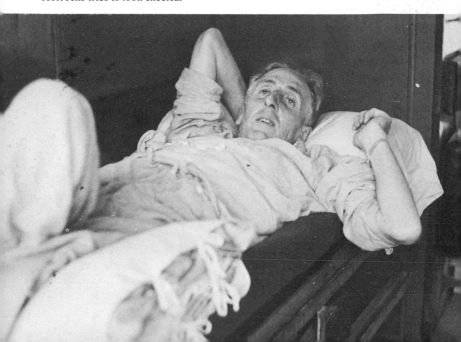

Horrocks and Eisenhower in 1944

King George VI meets the regimental commander of 82nd US
Airborne Division in September 1944. *Left to right:* Horrocks,
King George VI, General James Gavin (the Divisional Commander),
General A. March (82nd Division Artillery), Col Roy Lindquist, Col Reuben
Tucker, Col William Eichman, Col Charles Billingslea

5 May 1945: Horrocks receives the surrender of the German forces in the Corps Ems sector

Horrocks and Montgomery taking a somewhat informal lunch during the Battle of the Reichwald, 1945

As Black Rod in the Garter ceremony at Windsor in 1957

Outside the cottage at
Emsworth with Lady Horrocks
and their boxer, Maxie

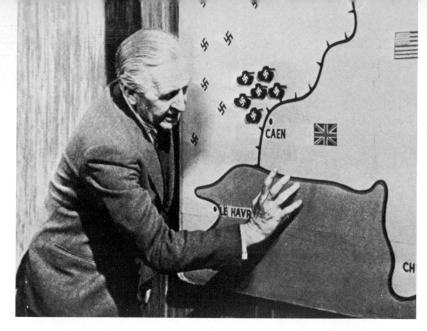

Horrocks describing the D-Day landings in one of his television programmes

A civilian at last; at heart still an old soldier

brief and that the latter had leapt to unjustified conclusions. He did not realise that this was not the first time Montgomery had tried to undermine his superior's authority. However, the presence of a bright, brisk, entirely confident Montgomery on the desert scene undoubtedly had a good effect on morale. Fortunately for those whose morale was now being boosted, Montgomery proved as good as his words.

Although Horrocks had learnt a lot about armoured warfare in his time with 9th Division he soon realised that armoured warfare in the desert was something quite different from domestic theory. Out here, he learnt, the conventional pattern of tanks and infantry co-operating in an advance needed to be adjusted. The desert was not merely shifting sand: as often as not it was rock. Furthermore, cover was minimal. This led to the saying, 'The tank is the queen of the battlefield.'

The only way in which victory could be gained was by the successful use of armoured fighting vehicles. Under normal circumstances cavalry would gain ground by skilful attacking and infantry would then hold it. But these were not normal circumstances. The desert battleground stretched over a distance of some seven hundred miles east to west and on occasion several hundred miles north to south. The most important areas were along the North African coast and a resourceful commander, provided he did not run out of fuel or water, could proceed in wide hook movements designed to cut off his opponent's forward units from their supply columns. A method used by both sides was to operate with self-contained armoured units which would settle for the night in 'leaguers' or 'laagers'. 'Laagers' were defensive positions where tanks would be given vital maintenance, while the infantry and gunners protected the flanks of the laager. Most of the tanks used by British forces had been designed and tested for the conditions normally found on Salisbury Plain: the desert conditions were so totally different that they suffered from numerous unexpected breakdowns. The Matilda tank was powered by two London bus engines which were inadequate for the heavy task they had to perform; suspension arms snapped 'like carrots' in the Crusader tanks; water pumps leaked on all tanks; and cooling fans were made useless by sand which clogged the driving chains. Horrocks, unaware of these problems when he first took over 13 Corps, was quickly made familiar with them. Later tanks, particularly the Shermans, were eventually designed and manufactured to minimise mechanical problems.

As Rommel had been frustrated when he tried to break through north of Himeimat during the previous July, there seemed a distinct possibility that his next try would be in the south, particularly as the

Allied dispositions were thinner there. This assumption proved to be correct when Rommel's signals were intercepted and read by Intelligence. Rommel was too experienced and crafty a warrior to communicate all his plans to his superiors and therefore the 'Ultra' intercepts did not give the entire picture. Nevertheless they gave enough for an alert field commander to be able to deduce the rest. It was therefore assumed that Rommel would produce a feint move in which he would appear to be advancing in the sector north of Ruweisat Ridge but once he had drawn the British defence to that area would rapidly move south and east, executing one of the flanking movements in which he was known to specialise. Intelligence could not do more than produce the options open to Rommel; his final choice would probably not be made until the battle was well under way. In the event the battle turned out to be shorter and sharper than expected: it began on the night of 30 August 1942 and was over by 7 September, apart from some harassing of the Germans by the RAF. Rommel's options had been between making a very wide encircling movement well to the south and then coming up behind the Alam Halfa ridge, and making a shorter encircling move ending in a drive to and over the Alam Halfa ridge itself. It was felt by Horrocks and his staff that Rommel was almost certain to try the latter, as it was suspected he did not have sufficient fuel to enable him to make a very wide sweep. Furthermore, if Rommel had taken the first option (the wide sweep) he would have left himself wide open to a flank attack from the forces on the ridge and could have found it very difficult to extricate himself if that had not been quickly beaten off. But he must have looked at the prospects at Alam Halfa with some confidence. Less than three months earlier he had run rings round the British units who now opposed him and had only been checked by the dour defensive tactics of Auchinleck in the Alamein line. Horrocks, who was new to desert warfare, now opposed him in a thinly held position. Horrocks suspected that Rommel would be pleased to find an inexperienced corps commander confronting him, and Rommel was not the only person who failed to take Horrocks seriously to begin with. There was an instant, obvious barrier, in the fact that all the old desert hands were deeply sunburnt and made a startling contrast to the newcomers whose skins, particularly when they wore shorts, looked pallid and unacclimatised; and this may have contributed to the misgivings of some of Horrocks' commanders about his dispositions. They had suggestions of their own based on personal experience, and though Horrocks knew that his ideas rested on a better knowledge of Rommel's intentions than even the most experienced guesswork could provide, he was in no position to explain why he was overruling ideas which, on the known facts, seemed sound.* At times he had to remind subordinates who was the Corps Commander and who was not.

Horrocks also appreciated that the tanks in the British forces were invariably inferior to those opposing them. The Germans had Panzer III and Panzer IV Specials and a variety of powerful guns, including the 88-mm. The British had a few Matildas, which were now obsolete, Crusaders which were unreliable and whose armour did not give protection against 50-mm shells, Stuarts, which were light tanks suitable for reconnaissance, and Grants. Grants lacked speed and had a restricted arc of fire but in general were well-made, well-armoured, reliable tanks. 7th Armoured Brigade initially had sixty Grants to oppose an attack by marginally superior German tanks which would outnumber them four to one.

Horrocks decided that the only way to deal with Rommel was by fighting a defensive battle. As Horrocks knew, Rommel, although always ready to mount disconcerting attacks, was also an expert at defensive tactics. A ploy which had cost British forces dear had been to advance, exchange some shots, appear to be mauled, and then retreat. This little exercise gave the opposing British tanks confidence and they hastily rushed off in pursuit. Two unpleasant experiences then occurred. The first was to be caught by 88-mm guns which had been sited for this very eventuality; the second was to be counter-attacked by the tanks they thought they were pursuing. Horrocks had no 88s but he had a selection of artillery, including 5.5 gun-hows, and 4.5 guns, though not enough of either. The Grant tanks were his most precious asset and it would have been madness to have risked them in battle against superior numbers. Their time would come but the ratio of numbers must be adjusted by other means first.

However, the idea of a defensive battle did not suit Churchill, who paid a surprise visit to 13 Corps HQ before Horrocks had been there a week. He was briefed on Horrocks' plan and told how the forward units planned to give the illusion that a German breakthrough had occurred, and how minefields would direct the German moves along the expected direction. Horrocks explained that when the Germans had buried their noses in the areas where opposition was severe, his own units would get in behind and destroy the German supply lines. Churchill did not like it. 'You are too defensive-minded,' he said. 'Why don't you attack? That's the way to win battles, not sitting down in defence.' This, Horrocks had tried to explain, was a case of rabbit and dog. The German dog would go after the supposed rabbit then, at the critical point when the dog was exhausted, the rabbit

* In order to preserve the secrecy of 'Ultra', its existence was disclosed to a very small number of top-level Commanders only.

would turn and eat the dog. (This story became famous but unfortunately tended to get turned round so that it was put out as 'Dog eats rabbit' – a version which Horrocks eventually accepted himself.)

The phrase impressed Churchill, though he did not approve of its implications. He muttered it at intervals as he walked around. Clearly he thought Horrocks was too young and inexperienced, as well as being the wrong type for the job. As he returned to Cairo he said to Montgomery: 'That chap Horrocks is no good. Get rid of him.' Montgomery stood his ground firmly. Horrocks' self-confidence was temporarily battered by the Churchillian scowl, but he was pleased to see that everyone else's in the corps was raised by the visit.

Not least of the problems of the desert commanders was that the war had taken on something of the atmosphere of a private game. It was dangerous, it was boring and uncomfortable, the flies, the heat and the sand were a constant drain on patience and health, but it was a 'clean' war in that the two armies respected, almost liked each other. Rommel was better known and more admired than most of the British commanders. At times the armies seemed curiously alike. Owing to the number of occasions each side had overrun the other's positions, much captured equipment was being used by both sides. Germans and British were as familiar with the enemy's rations as their own. Both had adopted 'Lili Marlene' as their theme song.

Montgomery and Horrocks set about diminishing the Rommel image by creating one of their own. Long before this, standard issue uniforms had been found to be unsuitable for desert conditions. Slacks were found to be more suitable than shorts, and a scarf worn loosely round the neck helped to keep the sand out and the warrior comfortable. Once the 'uniform' went, some colourful variations were to be seen. Montgomery did not discourage this; he capitalised on it by wearing an Australian hat and later a tank beret with two badges, and was almost always, unconventionally dressed. Horrocks, though a firm believer in cleanness and efficiency, had never been noted for the tidiness of his appearance, and he took to less formal dress with relish.

Brigadier C.E. Lucas-Phillips in his book *Alamein* described Horrocks as 'a man whose physical appearance very much belied his military qualities. Silver-haired, clean shaven, classically featured, one would take him for a judge, a bishop, or a don. He was, however, very much a fighting soldier. Eisenhower, when lunching with the author in Venice, said he thought Horrocks the outstanding British general under Montgomery.

'Not all his junior generals liked him, but nearly all acknowledged the extraordinary quality "Jorrocks" had of radiating confidence wherever he went, and his great gift of "putting things over" lucidly. Pip Roberts, who commanded the celebrated 22nd Armoured Brigade, testifies that merely to see Horrocks drive by gave an immense stimulus to the troops.'

Roberts was well qualified to know what men thought of Horrocks. 22nd Armoured Brigade was the formation chosen by Horrocks to blunt the teeth of the German attack in front of the Alam El Halfa ridge. Fortunately for 22nd Brigade the thought of Rommel's impending attack – which had been expected in August but arrived a few days later than anticipated – had spurred the repair shops to exceptional efforts, and in consequence there were now ninety-two Grants, instead of sixty, available to Horrocks.

While waiting for Rommel's arrival Horrocks held two exercises which were virtually rehearsals for the battle. At one of them he briefed the war correspondents and apparently gave them a very clear indication of his plans. Montgomery was not pleased when he heard of it for he felt that this was giving too much of the game away. Horrocks' excuse for what certainly seems a rash action was that an adequate briefing of correspondents before a battle leads to accurate reporting of it later, and more particularly, giving credit where credit is due. Montgomery knew very well that battles are often wrongly reported because a correspondent, not realising who is doing the hard work, tends to obtain reports from the most easily accessible units. These are usually accessible because they are taking little, if any, part in the battle. On the Horrocks principle the right people received the credit and he never found that his pre-battle briefings were 'leaked'.

13 Corps consisted of two infantry divisions (one New Zealand and one British) and two armoured divisions, plus supporting troops. The New Zealand Division consisted of 5th and 6th New Zealand Infantry Brigades and 131st (British) Brigade which was temporarily replacing 4th New Zealand Brigade. The other infantry division was Horrocks' old command 44th (Home Counties). It was their first experience in the desert and their first taste of action, but they did well. As 131st Brigade had been lent temporarily to the New Zealanders, 44th Division was a brigade short of its full complement. The New Zealand Division was commanded by the redoubtable General Sir Bernard Freyberg, VC. The armoured divisions were 7th and 10th, both already distinguished in desert warfare. The air forces on each side were fairly evenly matched. Not least of the factors influencing the Allied determination to win this battle was the desire to be rid of Stuka dive bomber attacks. Although the Stukas rarely did much material damage, they were very daring and persistent.

In spite of the natural impression that Alam Halfa was a battle entirely planned by Montgomery and his staff, it should be remembered that this battle had already been foreseen by Auchinleck who, months before, had flown over the area frequently and personally chosen the sites where the minefields should be positioned. Auchinleck had a high regard for the unorthodox – too high a regard, some said – and had therefore sanctioned various deception plans. These were developed after he left Egypt and one of them was employed at Alam Halfa. The Alam Halfa deception was to allow a map to be 'captured'. The map showed the state of the ground behind the British forward positions and indicated which parts were suitable for tanks and which were not. The map was duly 'captured' by the Germans and taken to Rommel's headquarters. It is not known how much effect it had on his plans because in the event all the ground seemed particularly unsuitable for fast mobile warfare when put to the test.

Horrocks had to hold himself firmly in check once the opening moves were made. He was tempted to stay in the operations room and watch the battle develop as the situation reports came in. But he had learnt from Montgomery that one essential in battle is for the commander to display complete confidence in his battle plan and also to ensure that he, even if he is the only person to do so, should have a good night's rest. The following days, when decisions must be taken, will require the highest degree of mental alertness; lack of sleep would preclude that.

The battle began in accordance with forecasts. It soon became clear that small attacks which had been mounted against 30 Corps in the northern areas were not serious; the main thrust was clearly in the south. A prediction of when and where Rommel's tanks would turn had been made by Brigadier F. de Butts, and the prediction turned out to be correct. Of de Butts' views on Horrocks, more later.

To the south-west of the Alam Halfa ridge was trig point numbered 102. Around this were the 22nd Armoured Brigade tanks, well dug in. The Germans penetrated a short distance into the position but Roberts then counter-attacked with the Greys (now, after amalgamation, the Royal Scots Dragoon Guards) and pushed them out again.

On the second day Rommel tried another probe. This time he tried to pass to the west of the ridge but again was checked and driven back. As he paused to regroup, his forces were given a relentless pounding by the Desert Air Force. Horrocks was tempted to send out his Grants and take advantage of the very difficult circumstances in which the Germans now found themselves, but dared not risk losing these precious assets. The Germans, he knew, were very good at fighting back from desperate positions and he suspected that in the circumstances the Panzers might still be more than a match for the Grants. He had, he recalled, been expressly told not to get mauled.

For the next two days the Panzer armies had the unusual and unpleasant experience of being pounded by bomb and shell while Rommel tried various ploys to prise the British tanks out of their well prepared positions. He himself had already lost 100 tanks and the rough going meant that those remaining had used up far more fuel than had been anticipated. A wider flanking movement was now out of the question; his only hope was that the inexperienced corps commander blocking his path would now venture out and try to clinch his victory in a final slogging tank battle. But it was not to be.

Instead, an attack was launched on Rommel's communication line by the New Zealand Division, which had moved down from the Ruweisat ridge for this purpose. Unfortunately this attack was not as successful as had been hoped. Horrocks reluctantly confessed that the weakest link in it was 132nd Brigade which had been taken out of its own division (the British 44th) and was now in action for the first time in the confusing conditions of desert fighting in an unfamiliar division. (Both now and in the October battle 44th Division had a difficult time. This was the division which Churchill thought should be launched straight into the desert battle, but which Auchinleck had insisted must be desert-trained first. Montgomery sent it up to Alam Halfa. It also took part in hard fighting in the October battle later and was badly mauled. At El Agheila 44th Division was disbanded and used for reinforcements within the Eighth Army. In spite of its misfortune it took an important part in the Alamein victory of October.)

The attack on his rear areas, though not very effective, convinced Rommel that it was time to go. He withdrew, but stayed in the area. Montgomery described these events as follows: 'They began to pull back quickly to the area of our minefield through which they had originally come. We left them there and called off the battle. Moreover, it suited me to have their forces in strength on the southern flank since I was considering making my main blow, later on, on the northern part of the front. I remember Horrocks protesting to me that the enemy remained in possession not only of our original minefield but also of some good view points to observe his corps area. I replied that he should get busy and make some new minefields for his corps. As regards the observation points, such as Himeimat, it suited me that Rommel should be able to have a good look at all the preparations for attack we were making on our southern flank; they were a feint.'

Horrocks was not entirely convinced by this argument, but was not in a position to complain. Montgomery was pleased with his corps commander. He said: 'Horrocks fought his battle in full accord with the master plan and he deserves great credit for his action on that day [sic]. He tells a story of how I congratulated him when it was all over, and then proceeded to tell him what he had done wrong and to give him a talk on how to command a corps in battle.'

Horrocks said that Monty 'was, as usual quite right'. The preparations for attack on the southern flank, to which Montgomery referred, were a series of dummy pipe lines, dumps and vehicles. Many of these ingenious devices were inflatable. An entire dummy brigade headquarters could be packed in the back of a truck!

At the end of the battle Horrocks rang up Montgomery and asked him if he could send a telegram to Churchill, saying 'Rabbit ate dog'. Montgomery refused permission. In view of the fact that Churchill had probably by this time forgotten the phrase and would only wonder whether Horrocks had gone mad, Montgomery was probably right.

Freddie de Butts, whom I have talked about earlier, later became Brigadier F.M. de Butts. Of Horrocks he had this to say: 'Horrocks was always one of my war heroes, and one of those top generals under whom I was privileged to serve in the Wavell/Monty class.

'I was GSO2 Intelligence, 13 Corps behind the Alamein line in August '42 when Horrocks arrived out of the blue to take over. We were still reeling from the shock of Strafer Gott's death when his aircraft was shot down, and morale was low. There was a dangerous feeling abroad that Rommel was invincible. We had withdrawn 500 miles in three months and there was even talk of further withdrawal up the Nile or into Palestine.

'Monty's arrival to take over Eighth Army had an electrical effect, and history has given full justice to the occasion. Horrocks appeared as one of Monty's lieutenants about a fortnight later to take over 13 Corps, the oldest established corps in the desert army. I well remember his first day. The entire staff were immediately assembled and he gave us a taste of what became the famous Horrocks oratory. Enormous confidence, a dynamic and forceful delivery and great charm of manner. The message was personal from Churchill. . . . We are going to win – Important reinforcements and vast quantities of war material are arriving – You've done a great job. . . . Monty has got Rommel taped. We lapped it up and I for one went away feeling a lot better.

'That evening in the Mess he told a story about World War One which I can remember today as clearly as if he had just spoken. It was about his treatment as a wounded p.o.w. in a German hospital. I went to bed hating the Germans which was exactly what Horrocks intended.

'Alam Halfa was Horrocks' battle as much as Monty's. The strategy may have been Monty's but the man who directed the battle was Horrocks. We were lucky that the Intelligence appreciation was spot on, and to a large extent Rommel played into our hands.

'Horrocks and Monty seemed to understand each other perfectly and it was perhaps a measure of their quality as leaders that both were accepted almost without question by desert rats who had been at it for two years and seen senior generals come and go: men like Cunningham, Ritchie, Willoughby-Norrie, Godwin-Austen, Ramsden and finally Auchinleck; all of them corps or army commanders.

'I have heard the view expressed that had he not been so badly wounded at Bizerta, Horrocks might well have made CIGS after the war. I would agree with this view; he was certainly in the top class and should rank with the big names: Monty, Alex, Slim, Wavell, Alanbrooke and Harding, all of whom became field marshals.

'It may not have been only the tragedy at Bizerta which finished his military career. He was after all badly wounded in World War One. I remember him suffering acutely from gippy tummy just after arriving at 13 Corps and don't think he was completely fit when Alam Halfa started.'

General Sir John Hackett, however, felt that Horrocks was always too much on the optimistic side 'which was clearly evident in Market Garden' (the Arnhem operation).

'I recall, rather oddly, the first time I came across him. It was immediately after the battle of Alam Halfa, in which I had been second in command of the 4th/8th Hussars in mobile operations at the extreme southern end of Eighth Army, in 7th Armoured Division. We had had a very brisk battle and were now enjoying a little peace and quiet on a sunny morning. A cloud of dust appeared and out of it a staff car emerged. There then got out a staff officer who set up a blackboard and a tallish, willowy, white-haired figure dressed as a general set about explaining to a somewhat puzzled group of officers how the battle had been won by the corps it appeared this white-haired character (whose name we did not know) had been commanding. Not only did we not know who he was, few of us even knew what corps we were in, though we all knew we were part of 7th Armoured Division because of the desert rats on our sleeves and vehicles. After what, by general consent, we thought was an incomprehensible piece of self-congratulation, the blackboard was restored to the staff car and the party drove off. That was my first introduction to Horrocks.

'I saw quite a lot of him later. In spite of the ballyhoo he seemed to generate he was really quite a modest man and not really ambitious. He would have made a reasonable CIGS I believe, but to tell you the truth, I do not really believe that that is a post which makes demands too heavy to be met by the average competent senior officer. The Hardings and Templers could do that job on their heads, and I believe Horrocks would have done it well enough.'

Horrocks' military career was not, of course, completely finished at Bizerta, as we see later. However, Freddie de Butts implies that the seriousness of the injury interrupted a career which had not reached its potential peak. Horrocks was not present at D-Day and although he commanded 30 Corps in Europe later he was never again fully fit.

It is interesting that neither Montgomery nor Horrocks himself made any mention of the 'gippy tummy'. Although the phrase suggests a very minor affliction, 'gippy tummy' was often a serious, debilitating illness. At best it was embarrassing diarrhoea; at worst it was a fever with high temperature, severe intestinal pains and vomiting as well as diarrhoea. The presence of flies everywhere ensured that few if any soldiers ever avoided 'gippy tummy'. Horrocks may have regarded it as all part of the scene and something to be endured, but it must have increased his difficulties enormously. Rommel, of course, was racked by stomach pains intermittently throughout his campaign, although his were said to be due more to nerves than to germs.

De Butts went on to say: 'You ask what sort of intelligence he had. As Chief Instructor at Camberley in 1940 he must have been very highly thought of, even in those early days. Standards at the Staff College were high. As a field commander in World War Two he had great flair and tremendous energy; it is no exaggeration to say he could inspire men. As Black Rod and particularly as a TV star he became known to millions. Like Monty he could reduce a complicated military problem to certain basic essentials and put them across clearly and simply.

'One last thought is that like Monty he could be ruthless. After he had been in command of 13 Corps for only a few weeks one brigade commander was sacked. Woe betide those who crossed him. But that was war.

'To attempt to sum up, he was in my view one of the really great generals of the war, and it was a privilege to have served under him.'

Not everyone was quite so enthusiastic. There were those who felt that Horrocks was too much of a Monty man, that he faithfully echoed the principles of a not over-principled superior, that much of the celebrated charm was synthetic. That, in short, he was not perhaps as sincere as he seemed.

It had taken him seven years to rise from captain to corps commander; it was a meteoric career. He does not appear to have been criticised by private soldiers, as Montgomery often was. In fact soldiers were often wary of Monty's democratic approach, his gifts of cigarettes which when examined had the words 'A present from the – Red Cross' on the packet. On the other hand, it is difficult to believe that Horrocks could have replaced Montgomery.

Alban Coventry was GSO3 (Intelligence) in the desert battles. He said: 'The outstanding quality which has remained in my mind is one of disinterested warmth and acute observation and interest in all those around him. A fair example of this came one day when he called me to his caravan to interrogate an Italian prisoner. He made me sit there with the man, a simple soldier, seated beside me whilst he stood at the door, on a lower plane, looking on, listening, and asking a question from time to time. Flies were something of a plague then. Horrocks was particularly struck to note that the poor Italian, like some Egyptian infant, seemed unable to react to their persistent crawling over his face and round his eyes; this showed, better than any answer, how low morale had sunk.

'Though not fitted to comment on Horrocks as a military commander it seems to me that whereas Monty was interested in men as being fit or unfit for his purpose, Horrocks was also interested in them by nature as human beings. This is no way diminished, and indeed perhaps increased his efficiency as a leader, at least with such as I ... one is struck by the difference in tone in the account Horrocks gives of the situation he found in Egypt, at Alam Halfa, and Alamein, and that given by Monty. There is a certain natural generosity in Horrocks which will not be belied and transpires all his judgements.'

Undoubtedly Horrocks was lucky to arrive in the desert in time to play a major part in the first real victory. The July battles had represented a victory for Auchinleck in that they had checked Rommel in his drive to Cairo, but they came at the end of such a long series of setbacks that they seemed to many to be the Axis war machines grinding to a halt rather than a clear-cut battle (although in fact they were greater and more important than Alam Halfa). But the battle of Alam Halfa had been no minor skirmish either. In that week the Germans had sustained 1,859 casualties and the Italians 1,051. The British had had nearly as many casualties as the Germans – 1,750. The Germans had lost thirty-eight tanks, the Italians eleven. The British had lost sixty-seven tanks, thirty-one of them being the precious Grants.

Alam Halfa seemed to be the end of Rommel's hopes of reaching Cairo and thus represented a tremendous boost for Allied morale.

But of course Rommel was still on the other side of the Alamein line, still an unpredictable menace. Everyone, not least the German High Command, realised that the balance of power was now being affected by supplies; his were becoming fewer because of the success of the Allies in intercepting them. On the other hand Montgomery's arsenal was swelling every day.

Chapter 7

Alamein and After

During the weeks which followed Alam Halfa the talk in Eighth Army – apart from the usual conversational subjects of soldiers deprived of normal comforts – was of the next and final stage in the Benghazi stakes. This time it looked as if Rommel could really be pushed back and held back. This was the attack which Churchill, since the previous March, had been pressing Auchinleck to make. When Auchinleck, at the end of the July battles, had said he could not manage it until September, he was replaced by Montgomery who did not make it until the end of October.

By 22 October 1942 Montgomery had 220,000 men and just over 1,000 tanks. More significantly, over a third of those tanks were Shermans. The Axis had 108,000 men, of whom half were German, and 600 tanks. Although disparaging remarks have been made about Italian soldiers – based mainly on the record of those who had been defeated by Wavell and O'Connor – those in the desert army were now as good as most of the Germans, and better than many. Of artillery Montgomery had approximately 1,000 pieces, outnumbering the enemy by two to one, though not necessarily qualitatively. In the air the Allies had a superiority of roughly two to one.

However, as many a general has found to his cost, numbers are not everything. Furthermore, for a successful attack the military equation is three to one, not two to one.

Montgomery was a very suitable opponent for Rommel, for if the latter made a rash move Montgomery would undoubtedly make him pay for it. Rommel was given to the quick, bold move; Montgomery to the counter-measure. However, on this occasion Rommel was not present at all and the Germans were well positioned behind a screen of minefields on a narrow front on which they had already fought a succession of battles. Whichever way the battle developed the Axis would be difficult and unpredictable opponents.

Rommel, who was due to be replaced in September, left North Africa in September for health reasons. His command was taken over by von Stumme who died of a heart attack in the opening hours of the October battle at Alamein (at which point von Thoma took over). The Axis dispositions in front of the Allies were therefore von

Stumme's. Rommel was recalled from Italy on 26 October to fight a battle which had already been lost, despite his achievement in extricating a large proportion of the Axis forces and making Eighth Army's subsequent progress more difficult. As Sir David Hunt points out in that admirable book *A Don at War*, which analyses the entire campaign, most people appeared to think that the third Alamein battle was almost a private bout between Montgomery and Rommel.

Rommel's abilities have been discussed at great length by numerous people well-qualified to judge. He has been praised and criticised with equal vigour. Undoubtedly he had a genius for armoured warfare and his eventual defeat was caused as much by inadequate supplies as by Montgomery. Yet in the early days he had had superior equipment and numbers but failed to win the campaign. It has been said of him that he was a first-class divisional commander but not really a corps or an army commander. The same comment might be made on Horrocks' abilities.

Montgomery was well aware that he lacked a tank general of the quality of Rommel in the Eighth Army, that he needed one and that the only person with ability approaching the required level was Horrocks. In consequence, as soon as Alam Halfa was over Montgomery decided to transfer Horrocks to 10 Corps.

10 Corps was a new creation. Montgomery had begun to form this unit as soon as he assumed command of Eighth Army, for he realised that he needed a mobile 'strike force' which would be as dangerously effective as the group under Rommel's command. The other corps would be mixed armour and infantry, or infantry alone; 13th would come into the former category, 30th in the latter. The new 10 Corps was to consist of two armoured divisions, 1st and 10th, 2nd Armoured Brigade and the New Zealand Lorried Infantry Division. Horrocks had been told privately by General Alexander, the C-in-C, that when it had been formed he was to command it. There were, not surprisingly, one or two changes in the original plans for the new corps, but what finally emerged was a very brisk-looking élite formation. Horrocks had been happy to command 13 Corps, which included infantry, and in which the tanks had had a fairly static role at Alam Halfa, but the thought of commanding 10 Corps gave him a flutter of alarm. Apart from the fact that the component units were all seasoned old desert warriors who would resent a novice from the infantry, there was the inner conviction that he was simply not qualified for the post. Horrocks tended to take the cavalry at their own valuation, which could be somewhat daunting for a person of conventional outlook. He therefore asked to stay with 13 Corps which was now used to him, and where he was popular, and

suggested that Major-General Herbert Lumsden would be much more suitable for the 10 Corps appointment than he would. Lumsden was a 12th Lancer with an admirable record; he was also in the tradition of the better cavalry officers: well-mannered, quick-thinking, a first-class horseman, and extremely brave. Montgomery listened to Horrocks' view of the matter and decided that there was substance in it. Lumsden was therefore appointed.

Montgomery's attention was totally concentrated on the forth-coming 'third Alamein', which the Germans had been persuaded by 'leaked information, would be starting on 7 November or there-abouts: it was really due to start on 23 October. Horrocks would have a minor role only, for 13 Corps would still remain in the southern sector.

An advance by Eighth Army at Alamein would only be possible if the Axis forces had first of all been pounded and confused by a massive sustained artillery barrage: arrangements for this were made. The Desert Air Force would also have a considerable effect on the enemy. But even with these advantages, there were so many minefields that progress into the Axis positions would only be possible if the sappers from the Royal Engineers could clear paths through them. It may seem strange to many people today who have been brought up on a diet of war films which show tanks or infantry crashing through to their objectives to realise that such progress is rarely possible until the sappers have cleared and marked the paths. They did so at Alamein and again on the D-Day beaches. The courage and coolness of people who carefully dig out and immobilise mines of diabolical ingenuity is almost beyond praise. If they make a mistake, and sometimes they do, they are at best killed, at worst horribly maimed for life. 30 Corps' task was to create the lanes through the minefields, 10 Corps' was to drive through and make a large gap in the middle of the enemy position. 13 Corps would take part in the general attack but it was unlikely to get very far on its own; its task was to appear to be the main thrust and thus induce von Stumme to deploy an important part of his force ahead of them. There was, of course, the appropriate volume of completely spurious signals traffic over wireless and line to create the impression that last-minute orders were being issued and so on.

In his autobiography Horrocks makes an interesting point about the Sherman tank which everyone believes was a purely American design. As it was named after an American general, this was a natural supposition. However, Horrocks emphasises that the Sherman design was largely British. The Grant, which was entirely American, was a good tank but had faults. The Americans were very sensitive about the criticisms and refused to accept them. Britain therefore paid (in dollars) for the construction of 300 tanks to be made in the USA, whose design eliminated the faults which the Grant possessed (limited arc of fire, high silhouette, etc.) At the time America was still neutral. However, in December 1941 America came into the war and the new tanks, instead of being sent to the Middle East, were handed over to the American Army. However, the events of 1942 convinced Roosevelt that they would be better employed by Britain in the Middle East than retained in American forces which were not committed to any form of action at that time. He therefore arranged that they should be sent to the Western Desert where, of course, they made the vital difference to the later Alamein battles. Horrocks felt that the Sherman tank was a fine example of Anglo-American co-operation and mutual goodwill.

In view of the fact that Churchill had pressed Auchinleck to use troops before the latter felt that they were acclimatised and trained, and had been very angry on receiving a refusal, it seems ironic that (according to Horrocks) Montgomery modified his plan for the October battle because he felt that the troops were neither fit enough nor adequately trained for it. It was not, of course, easy to maintain a high standard of physical fitness when troops were holding static positions. The original plan had been to drive straight towards the Axis armoured units and destroy them. This, Montgomery felt, was beyond the capabilities of his troops; it does not seem a surprising conclusion in view of the long history of the Germans foiling British thrusts and then counter-attacking themselves. Had Montgomery adhered to his original plan, he could have lost the battle in the opening stages and left a gap in his own position which would have been difficult to plug. The second option, which was adopted, was to attack the Axis infantry and then, when the German armour came in to help their infantry, to tackle them with our own armour.

Montgomery briefed his officers down to and including the rank of lieutenant-colonel on 19 and 20 October. Horrocks, who had heard him many times before, found this 'electrifying'. Most of what he said was then passed on by the unit commanders to the soldiers who would be involved. It was a far cry from Montgomery's own experience in the First World War when quite senior officers had been unaware of the general situation, let alone of any particular battle plan. The spearhead of the attack was formidable. It would consist of 9th Australian, 51st Highland, 2nd New Zealand and 1st South African Divisions, an awesome quartet. Montgomery had hammered in the point that everyone must kill Germans and these words did not fall on deaf ears. The 51st Highland Division was commanded by the indefatigable Douglas Wimberley. The division had been recreated after the original 51st had been captured at St

Valéry, after Dunkirk, and Wimberley had every intention of wiping out the insult in the way that Scottish chieftains had wiped out insults since time immemorial.

Horrocks found the battle somewhat frustrating. 13 Corps did not advance very far before becoming entangled in unsuspected minefields. These took time to negotiate but Horrocks felt there was still an excellent prospect of making substantial headway when he brought his armour into use. Unfortunately for his hopes, Montgomery rang him up and said that under no circumstances was he to do anything which might involve the loss of tanks. He was, however, allowed to make minor raids and look generally menacing. It was absolutely impossible to move far without using his tanks, but Horrocks, who owed his position as corps commander to the fact that Montgomery had sent to England for him, could not and did not complain. At Alam Halfa he had been able to fight the battle as he wished (apart from avoiding getting 'mauled'); less than two months later he was being held on a very tight rein indeed. However, he also saw the justification; 21st Panzer Division, which was one of the Germans' most experienced and successful armoured units, stayed facing 13 Corps until the battle was four days old, then it was withdrawn, to strengthen the Axis in the north. 13 Corps was gradually thinned down as Montgomery took units to use in the northern sector, but the crisis point of the battle did not occur until the early hours of 25 October. By that time, in spite of adroitly switching Allied units to counter German thrusts, Montgomery became aware that the battle had bogged down. His forward units were not yet through the planned northern corridor and the southern corridor probe, which went over the Miteiriya ridge, had been completely checked by an unsuspected minefield. Fighting had now been going on for two days and nights and, although a commander can continue a drive, if successful, for sixty hours, he has much less time at his disposal if the drive loses impetus or stops altogether. The drive *had* stopped. In the heat and the dust and the confusion, it was everyone else's fault. Horrocks, as an infantryman turned cavalry commander, saw the points of view of both arms only too clearly. The tanks had expected the sappers to clear a lane through the minefield and the infantry to knock out enemy anti-tank guns which were all carefully sited to catch the tanks as they picked their way through the tunnels. When the tanks found that to press on simply meant the loss of more tanks they suggested that there were uncleared mines and unlocated anti-tank guns. The sappers and infantry, who felt they had done all and more than could have been expected, retorted that the tanks gave up the struggle too easily.

At one end of the scale were the commanders – Montgomery,

Leese, Horrocks – at the other the infantryman and the tank driver. A lieutenant in the Buffs wrote later: 'The inferno that was the great battle of Alamein continued unabated. The appalling din of guns firing and shells bursting, the grim sights of mangled men and twisted corpses, the nauseating smell that was a mixture of sulphur and rotting human flesh, the mental strain from sleeplessness and responsibility, the fear of breaking down in front of the men: all these became everyday things. I suppose that we grew accustomed to them, for as time went on we noticed them less.'

And a member of a tank crew: 'As the light became full day, the sky overhead became black with fighter planes and bombers trying to shoot each other down. This was indeed war with a vengeance. I remember jumping on top of the turret on my tank and asking Major Everleigh, who was trying to shoot down a plane with a .5 machine gun, to let me have a go.

'Then as the day wore on the sight of sappers lining up and going over the ridge to probe for mines with bayonets was terrible and awe-inspiring to watch. Every one of them deserved a medal, as they seemed to go to certain death. They no sooner "went over" than bursts of enemy machine-gun fire seemed to wipe them out; then another line would form up, stub out their cigarettes, and move over the top. It was a privilege to be in the company of such men.

'The Alamein battle was a sheer slogging match over open sights, brutal and horrifying. I can remember dust churned to a fine powder moving back and forth like liquid away from the tank tracks as it swirled over the bodies of men. If I remember rightly we were left with seventeen tanks in the whole brigade and ceased to exist as a brigade. The Germans broke and ran.'

Correlli Barnett, in his penetrating analysis of Alamein, *The Desert Generals*, considered that the crisis of the night of 25 October had been brought about by Montgomery's own decision to direct the battle himself rather than delegate some of the decisions to the divisional commanders. By the twenty-fifth his drive had stopped, and it was fortunate for him that Rommel was absent from the battlefield, leaving a much inferior general in control. When Rommel retired he was not deceived by the 13 Corps ploy in the south and promptly brought 21st Panzer north. By then the Axis forces were running short of fuel. Even so, the Eighth Army breakthrough was slow in coming, with Rommel's forces contesting every yard. The final victory owed much to the Desert Air Force (commanded by a New Zealander) and the 9th Australian Division which had seemed both tireless and unstoppable. Horrocks felt that Montgomery proved himself when he insisted the attack should continue although losses had already been so severe that there were good reasons for halting, calling the battle a draw, and regrouping for another assault later. Horrocks was very guarded in his comments but appreciated the enormous difficulties of commanding an army over 200,000 strong, and felt that Montgomery had done well to persevere. Montgomery, in proposing to accept enormous sacrifice of armour and men in the final stages, had been ruthless and determined. Had the last drive petered out, he would never have recovered from this defeat in his first major battle, for all the brave words. It would have been the end of the Monty legend before it had properly begun. Horrocks never criticized Montgomery's handling of the battle, whatever his private thoughts.

The pursuit after Rommel had begun to retreat started slowly; Horrocks thought that in the circumstances this was understandable though regrettable. As is well known, once the pursuit did begin it was impeded by heavy rainstorms. Horrocks took no part in this exciting experience, for what remained of the now depleted 13 Corps was left on the battlefield. Horrocks felt very much out of it until in December 1942 he was told that he was to take over command of 10 Corps from Lumsden, who had returned to Britain. He took over on 9 December. 10 Corps had now been withdrawn from the pursuit and was in reserve fifty miles west of Tobruk.

This appointment meant future action, though not immediately. The fact that Horrocks had been allotted such a passive role at Alamein seemed to indicate that Montgomery was not entirely sure of his overall capabilities. He could see the quick-thinking Horrocks as a satisfactory leader of an armoured unit, but perhaps felt that a confused situation, such as the one in which 30 Corps found itself, would not have suited his talents. Montgomery also had doubts about whether Horrocks would be ruthless enough. These seemed to be supported by the fact that after the battle was over Horrocks had not adopted a ruthless attitude to the few pockets of Axis troops who were still trying to make a fight of it. Instead of crashing into them with a heavy attack, as some might have done, he tried a mild bombardment and an appeal to surrender. Neither produced much result.

With the appointment to 10 Corps, Horrocks' tail was very much up again. Since the previous August his ADC had been Captain Harold Young of the 12th Lancers. Young noted that Horrocks had been given considerable freedom before the battle of Alam Halfa; he had been allotted his task but not given precise instructions as to how it should be performed. Young stressed that the entire plan for the battle of Alam Halfa was Auchinleck's plan; this makes Montgomery's claim to have identified the importance of the ridge by studying a map seem a little fanciful. Young felt that Horrocks was essentially a field commander. He disliked politicians and tried to avoid them as much as possible.

(Young's own war had begun with the 6th Cavalry Training Regiment at Maidstone; he was moved to Shorncliffe during the autumn of 1940 when the invasion was a strong possibility and given the task of patrolling the cliffs of Dover on a horse, armed with a sword. After attending the Horsed-Cavalry Officer Cadet Training Unit at Weedon, Young was commissioned and asked in what regiment he would like to serve. Thinking rightly that there was no future for horsed cavalry, and not being inspired by tanks, he asked if he could join the Fleet Air Arm. He was told there was such an enormous waiting list there was no point in adding his name to it. He was then sent on a cavalry mechanisation course and afterwards posted, voluntarily, to the 12th Lancers. While on patrol in the desert he was caught in a Stuka attack and wounded. Although the wound was not serious, it made it impossible for him to sit in a tank for long periods, so he became a liaison officer. Horrocks had arrived in the Middle East with an ADC named Spooner, an infantryman. Spooner was an excellent ADC but had no desert experience, and therefore suggested that someone used to the desert should replace him as ADC. Horrocks therefore chose Young, and retained him till the end of the war, except for short periods when illness intervened. In Europe Young shared the post of ADC with the late Lord Rupert Nevill. Nevill, although an excellent ADC, was an indifferent map-reader and easily got lost. Horrocks used to watch him staring anxiously at a map and would take it over from him, laughing, not unpleasantly, at his discomfiture. Young himself had no trouble with maps.)

By this time the pincers were beginning to close on the Axis forces in North Africa. On 8 November 1942 another large Allied force had landed, aiming to seize the ports of Casablanca, Oran, and Algiers. The force, which included British First Army, was commanded by Lt-General Dwight D. Eisenhower. The objectives were duly captured and the Allies turned their attention to Tunis. They captured Bône but the Germans, well aware of the importance of retaining their last foothold on the African continent, continued to fly in troops and supplies, both of which were supplemented by sea. There was thus a stalemate. The Axis had by no means abandoned hope; Rommel, who had remained in command in spite of differences of opinion with both Hitler and Mussolini, not to mention his own German army superiors, had every intention of making the Allies pay for any gains, or even lose them again.

Meanwhile Montgomery was making his own move forward. The Eighth Army made steady progress until it reached what was known as the Mareth line, a former French defensive position. The successes of First Army in Tunisia had been impressive but it was felt that, compared with Eighth Army, the Americans and British were comparative novices. It was therefore decided that Montgomery should give a series of lectures to the senior officers in the western sector; this would also enable leaders to 'get together' and develop friendships and mutual understanding.

Those who visualised a happy liaison may have underestimated some of the difficulties. One of those on whom Montgomery's speeches had a very limited effect was General George Patton; it was a forecast of other clashes of will later. Horrocks was surprised and not over-pleased, in a subsequent conversation, to learn Patton's reaction. Though not caring greatly for Patton's personality, he had a grudging admiration for the American's versatility: Montgomery was always Montgomery, on active service or away from it, but Patton could act the part he found himself playing at any given time.

Experience of working with him increased Horrocks' admiration for Montgomery's style of command. He believed that the troops shared this feeling of affection. According to the late Lt-Colonel Esmond Warner of the Coldstream Guards, who was on Montgomery's staff, Montgomery never missed an opportunity to underline the fact that he was a victorious general. He believed in showing himself to the troops as much as possible, even though driving in an open vehicle under a hot sun could make him somewhat uncomfortable. Had Horrocks ever served in the ranks, he might have been more sceptical when he observed Montgomery being given rapturous cheers. Horrocks had gone from a public school to Sandhurst, from Sandhurst to the Officers' Mess, from there to officer prison camps, and from there on, always served well away from the salty comments of the barrack room. He was totally devoted to the soldiers under his command, interested in them, felt almost like a father to them, but probably never had the slightest idea of what they said about him, good or bad, when he was out of earshot. Undoubtedly they appreciated his courage, his loyalty to them, and his goodwill, but they may well have thought him a benign being from another planet rather than a fellow soldier. Montgomery, though coming from an identically sheltered background, was more cynical and calculating than Horrocks could ever be; he knew how to build up his public image, just how far he could go. Most people who saw or knew Horrocks liked him; the same was not true for Montgomery.

Horrocks compared Montgomery with Napoleon and Slim. After a lapse of nearly two hundred years it is impossible to say whether he was right or wrong about Napoleon but it is certainly appropriate to say something about Slim. Slim was honest and indomitable, and modest. Slim knew the ordinary soldier: though not for long, he had been one himself. Slim was a brilliant general who was trusted. Montgomery was probably a better general, but his fame did not rest on that fact alone. It rested on a sustained and well thought-out public relations campaign. It is interesting to see that when he gave Horrocks a copy of his book *The Path to Leadership* he wrote on the flyleaf: 'To Jorrocks, who knew how to win the hearts and minds of his men.' In fact Horrocks had no idea of *how* to win the hearts and minds of his men: the fact that he did so depended entirely on his own personality and integrity.

However, it should also be realised that Montgomery's technique was exactly what was required at the time. He came to prominence in the very worst period of the war. There was faith in Churchill but in no one else, especially in the army after Dunkirk. Montgomery was ahead of his time (in Britain at least) in appreciating that people need heroes; if they are not provided with authentic ones they will create them from film stars, pop music singers, boxers or footballers. As G.K. Chesterton put it: 'When people cease to believe in God they do not believe in nothing, they believe in anything.' God had failed the Germans in the First World War, therefore the Germans accepted Hitler and Nordic mythology. But behind Hitler there was also a very efficient propaganda machine. It has been said that if Goebbels had had television the Allies would never have won the war. Montgomery restored faith in British generalship which, sadly, Wavell and Auchinleck, though brilliant generals, had failed to do. Horrocks, with his unusual record, his gestures, the expressive use of his hands, and a genuine interest in people, had much to help him although his full potential was never realised until he became a sought-after television personality. In the latter role he far outshone Montgomery, yet always with the feeling that he was much inferior to Montgomery, that he lacked his power of ruthless decision, and that he could never have stood the strain of supreme command as Montgomery did.

Horrocks had plenty of opportunity to observe Montgomery on the chase up to El Agheila. Headed by units of 7th Armoured Division, Eighth Army reached Tobruk on 13 November, Benghazi on the twentieth and Agheila a week later. Rommel was clearly prepared to make a stand at Agheila, which Eighth Army had previously reached twice in the past, only to withdraw. The countryside here was broken and difficult and thus the attack took some time to prepare. In the event it proved less difficult than expected. A month later there was another brisk action at Buerat. Progress was now much slower: the Eighth Army was operating at the end of a long difficult line of communications and Rommel was operating from closer, interior lines.

On 23 January 1943 the Eighth Army was in Tripoli. At the beginning of February it crossed the frontier of Tunisia, in mid-month captured Ben Gardane and Medenine. The Mareth line, which runs north-south due south of Gabes, was undoubtedly going to be a serious obstacle. The French had originally fortified it against possible Italian attack from Libya; the Germans had improved on the French defences and were still working on them. Behind the line was a range known as the Matmata hills, and here, it was learnt, Rommel had concentrated three armoured divisions. Long acquaintanceship with the Axis skills at battle suggested that this was a prelude to a powerful offensive. So when it began 7th Armoured Division plus an impressive array of anti-tank guns was ready for it. This proved adequate and the Germans lost fifty-two tanks (about half the total number) before abandoning the attack. Eighth Army lost none.

Although weakness was showing in the Axis' offensive capability, there was no doubt that in the Mareth line they had a formidable obstacle. On its left flank was a deep heavily-fortified wadi which made the use of tanks impossible (the Wadi Zigzaou), on the right was a portion of the Matmata hills; and beyond that lay barren desert. By the time the battle for the Mareth line began Rommel, now a very sick man, had retired from the scene and gone back to Germany. He had handed over to General von Arnim. Although Intelligence was aware of the change of command, Montgomery contrived to talk (to the Army and to the Press) as if Rommel was still there.

All this time Horrocks, with 10 Corps, had been kept in reserve, ready to deal with any Axis breakthrough or flank attack. The news that he would once again be in the thick of the action was exciting and welcome although Horrocks was always at pains to assert that he was not warlike by nature.

There was however no prospect of his making a flank attack around either end of the Mareth line. And even if, by some unexpected good fortune, anyone made a breakthrough, the successful unit would be confronted by 15th Panzer Division, which the Axis had in reserve.

Montgomery therefore decided that the most suitable place to attack would be at the northern end, through the formidable Wadi Zigzaou. For this 50th, a very stout-hearted Northumbrian division, 51st Highland Division, and 4th Indian Division were to provide the infantry attack and two armoured divisions from 10 Corps the metal punch.

The battle began on 20 March in heavy rain which made a difficult situation even worse. 50th Division fought magnificently and secured all its objectives, but its losses were horrific. Even worse, when the infantry had reached the far side of the wadi neither tanks nor anti-tank units could get through to give them necessary support. In consequence the unfortunate infantry were attacked by 15th Panzer and 90th Light Division and pushed back. These two veterans of the desert were all too familiar to Eighth Army, and it was obvious that no further progress was likely in that area. Montgomery therefore summoned his commanders and told them that the northern assault had now been abandoned, though the infantry in that area should continue fighting in order to tie down the two German divisions. The attack would now be switched to the left flank. This gave Horrocks his chance, which he took very well.

The new approach was to be by a flanking movement using the combined efforts of 10 Corps and the New Zealand Division. General Bernard Freyberg, VC, commanding the New Zealand Division, was not at all pleased at being put under the command of Horrocks, who was six years younger, had been a general for five months less, and was vastly less experienced in fighting Axis forces. Horrocks took good care to explain that his function was to co-ordinate rather than to direct the activities of the New Zealand Division; he was himself annoyed at being given such an awkward assignment, with insufficient time for preparation.

The advance involved a 150-mile sweep and then an approach through a difficult gap in the mountains. After this there would be a desperate attack through well-defended German and Italian positions. In the last stages the attack would have to run the gauntlet of the combined power of 21st Panzer, 15th Panzer, and 164th Light Division.

Mareth was perhaps Horrocks' greatest contribution to the war. He led the attack through what had been thought an almost impossible approach route, when the attack in the north by 30 Corps had failed. If the flank attack had not succeeded the Allies would have been firmly checked, Montgomery's reputation as a tactician would have been shattered, and a long grinding battle would have ensued. But it succeeded. The Desert Air Force supported it by pounding the Germans on a scale hitherto unknown. A French force under General Leclerc secured a vital pass. The New Zealanders fought like tigers. And the British units pressed on with relentless determination, always doing more than anyone, including themselves, would have expected.

The final attack began at 4 p.m. and went on till nightfall. Then there was a pause to allow the moon to rise and give some light. It was vital that once the attack began it should continue successfully: if not the attackers would find themselves trapped in a valley where they would be exterminated the following day. In the later stages the attack was supplemented by 1st Armoured Division. This wide flanking move, pushed through with tremendous drive and tenacity, was one of the most desperate assaults of the war. Assisted by relentless air attacks, it crunched its way through the German division, who had been astonished to find this apparently invincible juggernaut bearing down on their flanks. Not least of its assets were the new 17-pounder anti-tank guns which were the Allied answer to the German 88s. The battle of Mareth lasted a week and led to the capture of El Hamma. It was a tremendous Allied triumph, for it destroyed three Italian divisions and badly mauled 15th Panzer, 21st Panzer, and 164th Light Division.

For Horrocks the battle was a major success, not least because he had been thrown into it with inadequate notice and had therefore been unable to make the advance preparations he would have wished. He was of course enormously pleased to have played a leading part in winning such a brilliant but arduous battle but his feeling of elation was badly punctured by the arrival of a Russian general. 'He was,' said Horrocks, 'as I expected, a Russian general who was paying a courtesy visit to our Eighth Army. Even so, there was something curiously menacing about him with his stubby revolver strapped to his belt.'

The Russian was not even interested in the Mareth battle, still less impressed by it. He described the war on the Russian front, particularly at Stalingrad. Horrocks, with memories of his time in Russia, could visualise the scene only too clearly. He realised that the privations they had suffered in the desert war were as nothing compared to the Russian experiences as they retreated before the advancing Germans. The desert war, Horrocks felt, was a mere sideshow; the real war was elsewhere. But it was not merely the difference between the two fronts which left the strongest impression. It was the realisation – which touched something in his memory – that the Russian viewpoint and the Allies' were poles apart. For the moment they were allies, but in the Russian he could sense something completely inflexible and self-orientated. Horrocks was engaged in a war to defeat the Germans so that everyone could live in peace subsequently. The Russian was engaged in a war against everyone who was not a Russian communist, a war in which the battles of attrition against Germany were but a part. And, Horrocks realised, however long and perhaps impossible was the task the Russians set themselves, and however many blunders they made, nothing would stop them stubbornly pursuing their aim.

Horrocks could not brood too long on that slightly unnerving meeting with the Russian: there was still much work to be done. Germany, which at one time was threatening the whole Middle Eastern oil supply (including the forty-seven million barrels which were sent to Russia), was now penned into the last toehold in Africa. But Germany was not yet finished, even in Africa. Before the Germans gave up there was more hard fighting to be done. The next stage would be at the Gabes Gap which lay in the path of Eighth Army's advance and was strongly defended. The Gabes Gap was a deep wadi surrounded by hills.

On 6 April the Gap, whose proper name was Wadi Akarit, came under attack. It was a 30 Corps operation, in which 51st and 4th Indian Divisions distinguished themselves. By the time the assault began all the Axis airfields had been well pounded by the Desert Air Force, which now gave full support to the Army. However the German and Italian aircraft did not take this meekly and missed no chance to harry the Allied forces.

The plan had been finalised three days before the attack began. When 30 Corps troops had made the initial penetration, the New Zealand Division, which up till the moment of going through the gap had been under 30 Corps command, would, on passing through, come under 10 Corps. As the New Zealanders had learnt to respect Horrocks at the battle of Mareth, this somewhat strange changing of horses in mid-stream did not disconcert them.

These later battles, which, though less important strategically than the earlier ones, were often harder and more complicated, have never caught the attention of the general public. One reason may be that the Arabic place names are difficult to pronounce and spell, and even more difficult to find on the map. With succinct brevity the official history states: 'Administratively, the British forces were well found. Thus for example, 30 Corps fired at the Wadi Akarit some 82,000 shells, field and medium, and large quantities of mortar and small arms. . . . Petrol was plentiful in Tripoli but expenditure had to be carefully controlled very largely because barrels and jerricans were scarce owing to various malpractices by the troops.' Transport was badly in need of maintenance; furthermore, some of the reinforcements sent out for these difficult battles were sadly lacking in training and experience.

The 'last battle', as it was thought to be, did not go as well as had been anticipated in spite of the heavy initial bombardment and the air attack. Exemplary courage was shown by the leading units and everything seemed to be progressing satisfactorily for the first seven hours of the fighting, which had begun at 1 a.m. on 6 April. (In spite of the problems of fighting in the dark the 4th Indian Division had done particularly well.) There is some confusion about what happened after 8.45 a.m. The 4th Indian Division commander, General Tuker, said that at that time Horrocks came to his headquarters and told him that the required breakthrough had now been made and that 10 Corps could now go through and finish off the enemy resistance. Horrocks then telephoned Montgomery asking for permission to use 10 Corps, and received it. At 11.10 a.m. Horrocks took command of the New Zealand Division. However, it appears that an anti-tank ditch had not been cleared and as 10 Corps forward units, the Staffordshire Yeomanry and 3rd Royal Tank Regiment, led the advance they encountered several well-concealed 88-mm guns. This ended the advance for the time being.

Montgomery was by no means pleased to hear of this, for he had already sent a telegram to Alexander at GHQ informing him that 'all main objectives have been captured according to plan'. In fact Eighth Army was now under pressure itself, with the Germans desperately fighting back to regain lost ground. Losses were mounting steadily on both sides. But if there was confusion on the Allied side there was even more among the Axis commanders. Some thought that although the battle appeared to be lost there might be some gain in continuing to fight; others did not. There was also disagreement about how and when the eventual withdrawal should be made. In the event it took place during the night of the eighth.

The British, although left in possession of the battlefield, were by no means happy over the manner of it. Viewing the battle in hindsight, it was not easy to decide whether the fault lay with 30 Corps for not going far enough and leaving some anti-tank defences uncleared. Possibly 30 Corps had done all that could be expected. If so, perhaps 10 Corps should have been more forceful and accepted heavy losses in its leading units. Was it perhaps a general fault of army training that this sort of mishap could occur? Wherever the fault lay, it was glaringly obvious that an opportunity had been lost to destroy the German Army in North Africa for good. Instead that Army had been allowed to slip away and fight another day.

If Horrocks had any doubts about the success of his role in this battle he did not voice them. In his autobiography he states: 'On 6th and 7th April 30 Corps launched a full-scale attack on the Wadi Akarit position, and after some hard fighting, particularly by 51st Highland and 4th Indian Divisions, they smashed their way through. It was now the turn of my mobile 10 Corps to burst out of the bottleneck and sweep forward over the fertile coastal plain of Tunisia towards Tunis.'

Horrocks' reluctance to expand upon the battle was probably due to respect for the feelings of Leese (30 Corps) and Tuker (4th Indian

Division). As the armoured corps commander he no doubt felt that infantry had done very well, but not quite well enough. In one sense he was right. However, one is left with the feeling that if Horrocks had been a Rommel or a Guderian he would have smashed through or around the obstacles and annihilated the rest of the German opposition. In hindsight he would have been right but he may have been well aware that the regiment which would bear the brunt of it was the Staffordshire Yeomanry, who had already suffered heavy losses in previous battles in this war. His decision not to push his corps forward in spite of all obstacles is a tribute to his humane attitude but reflects less well on him as a battle-winning armoured corps commander.

Soon after the battle of the Gabes Gap, Eighth Army liberated Sfax and Sousse. They were now in daily contact with the American forces and First British Army. The battle for North Africa was drawing to a close, but the last stage was likely to be as hard-fought as any of the previous battles. The final phase began on the night of 19/20 April when Enfidaville and Takrouna were captured. Takrouna was a costly triumph for the New Zealanders. Horrocks described it as 'steep slopes half covered by boulders surmounted by a high rock pinnacle with a flat top on which were stone buildings and an Arab tomb, occupied in strength by the enemy. The sides of the pinnacle were almost sheer.' The final assault was led by a Maori sergeant named Manahi. Horrocks, who followed the assault and carefully inspected the ground afterwards, recommended Manahi for a VC. He was not pleased when the intrepid sergeant was merely awarded a DCM (Distinguished Conduct Medal).

This final stage was clearly going to be intense and bitter. Montgomery told Horrocks to organise the attack and then, to Horrocks' surprise, said that he himself was leaving Horrocks in command as he was off to Cairo to discuss the plans for the invasion of Sicily. This gave Horrocks what he later described as the worst few days in his life, although that can hardly have been true. Under Horrocks were the veterans Tuker and Freyberg. Tuker commanded 4th Indian Division, which had already shown itself to be second to none; he had the somewhat unusual nickname of 'Gertie' and would earn greater esteem later. Of Freyberg we have already spoken. Both these divisional commanders knew that to attack along the coastal plain, as Montgomery had ordered, would be a bloody and protracted business; both felt that to have brought their divisions thus far in order to have men unnecessarily slaughtered was out of all reason. Horrocks disliked the prospect of an attack along the coastal plain as much as they did and tried to find an alternative. There did not appear to be one, but he hesitated to launch such a costly enterprise.

Montgomery then reappeared, unwell, in a bad temper from his dislike of the GHQ Sicily invasion plan, and expecting to find Horrocks making progress towards Tunis. To his intense annoyance he found Horrocks filled with doubts and accused him of 'belly-aching'. Horrocks retorted that he could direct the attack all right but there would not be much left of Eighth Army when it was complete. He suggested that First Army should handle the attack from their front which was much more suitable. There was a stalemate for three days while all possible ways of mounting the Eighth Army attack were considered.

But Montgomery had thought again. Lt-General Sir John Crocker, who commanded 9 Corps in First Army, had been wounded. This left his corps without an obvious commander and gave Montgomery a chance to press the claim of Horrocks. In consequence Horrocks was told to detach 4th Indian and 7th Armoured Divisions and 201st Guards Brigade from 10 Corps and take them to 9 Corps, which he would then command for an assault on the First Army front. This move, if successful, would finish the war in the area.

Horrocks found the first days of his new command somewhat disconcerting. First Army was a new army, smart, regimental, clean and tidy. Eighth by contrast looked what it was, an army which had battered its way from Alamein to Tunisia, and gloried in it. Horrocks, though a believer in smartness, felt that the sheer professionalism of Eighth Army outweighed the other defects. He was also very quickly aware that First Army and Eighth Army were not going to like each other; and they did not. He had already had some experience of damaging animosities which tend to arise from minor causes. On this occasion, the fact that Eighth Army were inclined to look upon First Army as complete novices who had yet to obtain a taste of the real thing did not please First Army, who already had plenty of hard fighting to their credit, short though the time they had been in Africa. One of their divisions, 78th, later painted on their trucks 'We have no connection with 8th Army'. Fortunately the First Army commander, General Anderson, was very friendly, which was more than could be said for some of his subordinates.

The forward units of First Army were in the Merjeda valley. Horrocks went up to survey the country ahead. Although soldiers in forward areas are inclined to complain that the 'top brass' never comes near them, they are far from pleased when generals like Horrocks actually do so. The information that a VIP is in the line opposite tends to come to the enemy's attention and after an interval a steady indiscriminate bombardment falls on the area. Horrocks took care to assure the troops in the lines that he would try to look as unimportant as possible but regretted that if they did find themselves shelled subsequently it was one of the inescapable hazards of war.

The attack went in on 6 May. The infantry divisions led; the armour followed up closely. Everything fell into place as the great armada rolled forward. It did not stop till they reached Tunis. The honour of being the first into the town was claimed both by the Derbyshire Yeomanry and the 11th Hussars. They may well have arrived simultaneously: there was more than one road into the town.

But Horrocks never saw this confused though impressive sight. He had been told that numerous Germans were escaping to the east. It was a moment when Alexander demonstrated his ability as Commander-in-Chief. Realising that if the Germans were able to establish themselves in the Cape Bon peninsula they would be able to fight on for a long time, he ordered Horrocks to take steps to prevent them. Horrocks thus sent 6th Armoured Division to drive on to Hammamet (from Hamman Lif), and the powerful thrust completely disorganised German attempts to form another defensive line in that naturally strong area, with the consequence that 250,415 German and Italian troops then surrendered. Horrocks was amazed that such a vast number gave up so tamely after fighting so well for so long; it was one of the larger surrenders of the war, completely dwarfing those on Crete and at Singapore and Stalingrad, though even greater numbers would lay down their arms in following years. Hitler exculpated himself over the desert campaign and ultimate defeat by saying that it was the price Germany had to pay for keeping Italy in the war: without it the Allies would have been able to land in Italy unopposed and reach the Brenner Pass. Owing to the fighting taking place at Stalingrad, Germany would not at the time have been able to spare any troops for Italy.

Horrocks was puzzled by the surrender which he understood was spontaneous and not due to an order from the higher command. He felt that the Axis would have gained much by continuing to fight and, among other benefits, would have delayed the Allied invasion of Sicily. From his knowledge of the German character he decided that the surrender happened because German organisation had broken down. There was plenty of food and ammunition but the will to organise further resistance was absent. His reasoning may be percipient but is not entirely flawless, for later of course, when Germany had been invaded and chaos was everywhere, individual German units fought with ferocity and determination. Perhaps the feeling that they were defending the soil of the fatherland sustained them later.

For Horrocks everything now looked better than he could ever have anticipated. But he had thought for others than himself. Tripoli was a base medical area with twelve hospitals. He noticed that the sisters were out every night, being entertained in various officers' messes. Meanwhile, the troops who had not spoken to a British or American woman for months could only look on enviously. Horrocks thereupon invited all the matrons to lunch, twelve of them, a prospect even he found daunting. The result was twice-weekly dances for 'other ranks' (non-officers) which were, it seems, an enormous success.

There were more serious matters in the offing too. The war was a long way from being over, and for the moment the Middle East was a planner's paradise. Decisions were made and then revoked; generals and unit commanders waited until the final plan should be agreed. Eventually it was decided that 10 Corps would be included in General Mark Clark's 5th Army for the Salerno landing. It meant good-bye to the Eighth Army with whom Horrocks had served so long and happily, but he looked forward to working in this new sphere. However a landing from the sea involved a different set of operational plans from an assault over solid ground. The key to success in a seaborne invasion was to have material in the correct proportion. Although the landing force seemed a veritable armada, every cubic foot of space in every ship was carefully apportioned. One of the items for possible inclusion was a new smoke screen apparatus which was claimed to be extremely effective. (Smoke screens are liable to strange disruptions, drifting or disappearing at the least convenient moment.) In June Horrocks went to Bizerta to watch 46th Infantry Division rehearsing its assault on Salerno. Before long the air raid sirens went. As the notes died away the new smoke screen began billowing out over the town. Much impressed, Horrocks and the divisional commander went down into the street to get a better look.

A single German fighter, lost in the smoke, suddenly broke clear and swooped over the town, using up its ammunition. One bullet hit Horrocks in the chest, went through his lungs and intestines and came out of his spine; another smashed his leg. No one else was hit.

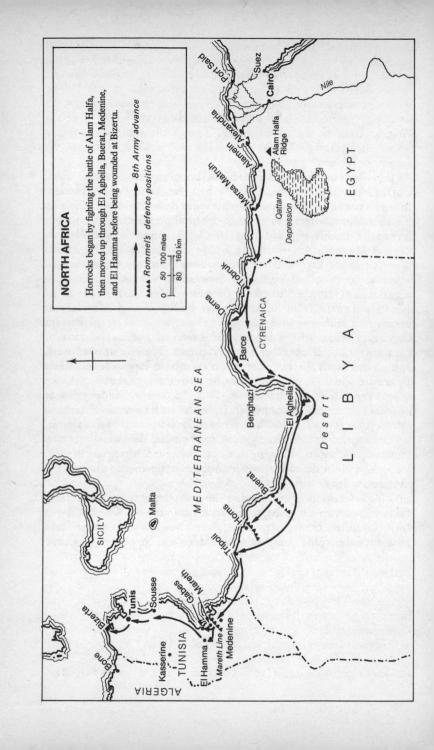

NORTH AFRICA

Horrocks began by fighting the battle of Alam Halfa, then moved up through El Agheila, Buerat, Medenine, and El Hamma before being wounded at Bizerta.

→ 8th Army advance

▲▲▲▲ Rommel's defence positions

0   50   100 miles
0   80   160 km

Chapter 8

The Long Road to Recovery

At this time Harold Young, Horrocks' longest serving ADC, was in Cairo, recovering from jaundice. When the message came through that Horrocks had been wounded, Young promptly hitched a lift to Tunis and stayed close to him. But after Horrocks had spent three months in the American hospital, the head surgeon, Colonel Carter, drew Young on one side and said: 'We can't do any more for him here; complications are building up. You must get him back to England as soon as possible.' Young therefore went straight to Algiers and, through the ADC network (as he put it), got to see Eisenhower's Chief of Staff, General Bedell Smith. Bedell Smith arranged a return journey in an American aircraft with a US nurse, Colonel Carter, and Young, and Horrocks was taken into the Cambridge Military Hospital, Aldershot. Present at the highly complicated operation which then followed was Horrocks' old friend Robert Macintosh, now Professor Robert Macintosh, Chief Anaesthetist for the Royal Air Force.

Although a very sick man, Horrocks was very keen to know exactly how the war was progressing and so for several weeks Young used to travel to the War Office, be briefed, and then return to Horrocks to keep him informed. But the recovery was going to take a long time, so in the meantime Young looked around for a suitable temporary appointment. He found one at Sandhurst as an instructor. This enabled him to see Horrocks regularly. By this time Horrocks had had six major operations, carried out by Mr Edward Muir of King's College Hospital, later to be Surgeon to the Royal Household and HM the Queen. The last of the operations took place sooner than the medical authorities wished, for although Horrocks had had a series of periods of convalescing he was still weak. He was, however, desperately anxious to get fit again, and felt that the sooner all the necessary operating had been completed the sooner he would be able to return to the battle. He spent fourteen months alternating between Cambridge Hospital and the Somerley Convalescent Home at Ringwood in Hampshire.

When Horrocks was first sent to Somerley the Colonel-in-Charge, Colonel Goodwin, told Captain Arthur Edwards, who was also a patient at the hospital, that a distinguished patient was arriving and that he would like Edwards, who had almost fully recovered, to act as an unofficial ADC while the distinguished patient was in residence. Horrocks duly arrived and was given a room at the front of the building where he could rest quietly. It did not take him long to become bored with his solitary confinement and he wandered off into the general common room and started to make friends. Edwards was doubtful as to how the colonel would view this development, particularly as Horrocks was soon sitting in a low armchair answering the questions of a fascinated audience, whom he quickly had completely transfixed by a typical Horrocks stage performance. Edwards was a little uneasy and tentatively suggested he might like to take a rest. Horrocks swept him on one side and continued briskly. Suddenly there was another member of the audience – the colonel. He dismissed the audience, descended on Horrocks, escorted him back to his room and issued strict orders. This was no colonel-to-general situation, but doctor-to-patient. Horrocks meekly bowed to the storm; he knew the value of discipline. Before long, needless to say, the colonel was Horrocks' most enthusiastic listener.

Harold Young, who had listened to Horrocks on many occasions, believed that Horrocks' skill lay in giving the broad picture of any operation with each part in the right proportion. Horrocks would never get bogged down in details. This broad view, Young thought, made Horrocks very good at selecting subordinates. He was quite ruthless, even though he could be kind. If he thought a man was not up to his job, the man went. Equally if Horrocks wanted someone to command a particular unit, he would lobby shamelessly to get him. His time in the Military Secretary's Department had taught him useful lessons about achieving his ends.

Before he had fully recovered Horrocks made several attempts to persuade Montgomery he was now a fit man. Montgomery was not deceived. He took a brief searching look. 'Go away and get really well,' he said, 'then we shall see if there's still a job for you.' But on 31 July 1944, a year after he had been wounded in Bizerta, Horrocks was given the news he had hoped for. Although not fully fit, he was well enough to return to service; Montgomery knew as soon as he did. On 2 August Montgomery sent his private aircraft for Horrocks to transport him to France to take over 30 Corps again. At this time Horrocks had installed his wife and daughter in a small cottage at Compton, Winchester. He persuaded the pilot to circle over the cottage on the way to Normandy, so that he could wave to them. Horrocks was back in action again.

At first he felt hopelessly out of it. Everyone but himself seemed to know exactly what to do and what was going on. For Horrocks

France was vastly different from the England he had known, and the North Africa he had recently fought in. He began to wonder whether he would ever catch up in this new army from which he had been absent fourteen months. As he travelled to 21st Army Group Tactical Headquarters he was held up in one of the numerous traffic jams. To his delight a face looked down from a passing tank and said, 'Glad to see you back, sir.' The welcome lifted his spirits. He was back among friends. What he did not realise at the time was that the man in the tank was his former ADC Denny. Denny, smothered in dust, at first thought that the red hat in the jeep which was pushing its way through belonged to a military policeman. He was about to say something cutting about that sort of behaviour when he suddenly recognised that the man under the 'brass' was Horrocks, and changed his words accordingly. Horrocks would see more of Denny later.

As time passed he noticed many soldiers of all ranks whom he had met before in the desert. He had a theory that where there was fighting to be done you always seemed to find the same people doing it. The rest of his old friends, he was sure, were in the thick of it in Italy.

He was welcomed by both Montgomery and Eisenhower, the latter being particularly warm in his greeting. Montgomery looked at him more irritably, scanning his features for signs of weariness or incipient breakdown. Horrocks was nervous about Montgomery's searching looks, for he knew very well that his recovery was not complete: he still had waves of sickness and periods of high temperature. It never seems to have occurred to him that to take over command of a corps in an important campaign while bluffing about his physical well-being was either dishonest or irresponsible. His confidence in his own ability had now grown to an extent that he felt that even with a few temporary setbacks he could handle a corps as well as, if not better than, anyone else. And, of course, as his subsequent career showed, he could not bear a life of inaction.

Meanwhile he wondered how Montgomery was faring under the long period of unbroken strain. There had been a lot of criticism of Montgomery's manner and methods, not least from the Americans. But Montgomery, whatever his inner thoughts, still appeared as solid as a rock.

The sequence of events since the landings in June had not been entirely satisfactory. Caen had proved a more difficult obstacle than expected; progress had been slow. The pressing need was to capture a major port. Cherbourg was the obvious prize, so while the British and Canadians tied down an equal number of German divisions on the eastern front (fourteen each), the Americans had been able to

103

build up a superiority of nineteen to nine in their sector. Rommel was reported to have been wounded, leaving von Rundstedt in sole charge. There had been conflict of opinion between the two over the way the invasion should be met and von Rundstedt's more cautious, though ultimately unsuccessful, plan had been adopted. Subsequently von Rundstedt blamed the disaster of the successful D-Day landings on the fact that Hitler had interfered with his battle strategy. Hitler was trying to direct both the Russian campaign and the Normandy battle at the same time, from Germany.

Another old friend here was 'Bimbo' Dempsey, now the commander of 2nd Army. Twice in the past he had succeeded Dempsey (as Staff Captain in the War Office and as Brigade Major in 5th Infantry Brigade) and once been succeeded by him (in 13 Corps); now, after the fourteen months' interval, Dempsey was ahead again and would stay ahead for the rest of the war. Dempsey briefed him on the general situation. (In his description of recent events Dempsey did not bother to tell him that his own aircraft had crashed and turned over on landing that morning. He had not been injured and he gave no sign of the traumatic experience.)

30 Corps was an élite formation. It contained 7th Armoured Division, 43rd Wessex and 50th Northumberland Division, and 8th Armoured Brigade. Since landing at 'Gold' Beach, at Arromanches, 2nd Army had pushed inland through the hard going of the difficult 'bocage' country. Bocage was a natural defence against tanks, for over the centuries the Norman farmers had separated their fields by throwing up stones and loose soil into the hedgerows. This process resulted in a succession of earth walls, with hedges on top of them. The Germans had made full use of them. And now 30 Corps' advance looked like being delayed again by a feature named Mont Pinçon. It lay approximately midway between Villers Bocage and Condé, was 1200 feet high, and completely dominated the countryside. Whoever held it could observe the enemy's dispositions and note every movement they made.

As they approached this vital feature the weather was hot and sultry, the Germans were apparently immovable and casualties were mounting alarmingly quickly. Horrocks began to feel that if the army was bogged down for long here morale would begin to suffer. He had already noted that certain veteran units appeared to have run out of steam. Many of their best officers had been killed and some of their replacements lacked the necessary experience. Battle-scarred units are liable to develop internal problems if the soldiers are more experienced than many of the officers. Good officers are always at a premium and the problem had been worsened not merely by casualties but also by departures to specialist units such as parachutists, gliders, SAS, and Phantom.

But one man who had the right qualities had stayed with his regiment and that was Captain R. Denny of 13th/18th Hussars. This was the Denny who had been Horrocks' ADC when he commanded 9th Armoured Division, and the man who had greeted him after his arrival in France. Denny, leading two troops of tanks, had discovered a narrow track, apparently leading to the top of the hill. Furthermore it seemed to be undefended, probably because it was thought to be unsuitable for tanks. Shades of the capture of Quebec in 1759. . . . It was indeed a very narrow track and one of the tanks fell off it into a gravel pit. The rest, a mere half-dozen, got through. The tanks would not have lasted long without support once the Germans realised they were there, but they were soon joined by the 4th Wiltshires, who fought their way to the top in the dark, in spite of having been in action for forty-eight hours already. Denny was awarded a Military Cross for his remarkable piece of initiative. He had certainly earned it: his feat had transformed the entire strategic scene in Normandy.

As Denny had ample opportunity to observe Horrocks from close quarters and to gauge the reactions of the men towards him, his opinions are of considerable interest. He emphasised that Horrocks was greatly admired by the average trooper. When, for a short time in 1944, the 13th/18th were loaned to another corps, the troopers used to ask Denny: 'When are we going to get back to Jorrocks, sir?' Denny also doubted whether any other general had ever been so amiably disposed to his ADC. If the day's programme seemed particularly boring – in the days in 9th Division – Horrocks would ask: 'Do you want to bother to come along?' Another memory was Horrocks' obsession with punctuality, and his perfectly timed arrivals. Yet his idea of driving a car was to see how fast it would go. The only general in the British Army to drive faster and more dangerously than Horrocks was Oliver Leese.

Denny also considered that Horrocks' great gift was to be able to praise or admonish without making the recipient over- or under-confident. He was never unkind or sarcastic, but always firm and decisive. An officer would leave his presence not so much feeling humble as wishing to do better in the future. The fact that Horrocks had gone grey early in life gave him a patriarchal air.

Denny recalled that in 1944 when the 13th/18th were concluding a reconnaissance his tank, like many others, had become somewhat domesticated. The weather was appalling, cold and wet, and the tank crews had adapted themselves to brewing mugs of tea even when the tank was moving. It was said that they could even fry eggs.

Suspended at the back of the tank was a sack of coal, in case they came to a billet where there was a fireplace. On this occasion they also had two geese hanging on the back. None of these things affected the operational ability of the tank but they certainly did much for morale. Suddenly they encountered Horrocks, concluding his own recce right at the front. Horrocks approved of their adaptability but said: 'Look, you are just going to pass by an American division and if they see those geese they'll wonder whether we are fighting a war or not. Put them inside.'

So the geese went inside. Soon afterwards a full-scale battle began and the geese, after being stood on for about a week, were none the better for it. 'So we never were able to eat those geese,' said Denny philosophically, 'but if that was the way Horrocks wanted it, we had to abide by the letter of the law.'

30 Corps made full use of their vantage on Mont Pinçon. Every German movement was monitored and greeted with appropriate shelling. Then they moved on. Gradually the German forces were caught in the Falaise pocket, hemmed in by Allied forces. By the time the Normandy battles were over the Germans had had nearly 300,000 casualties and lost another 200,000 taken prisoner. Losses in equipment, tanks and guns had been on an equivalent scale. Even so, one third of the German 7th Army had escaped east, although without equipment.

As there were now several Allied armies in close proximity, planning had to be very careful in order to prevent them tangling with each other or blocking each other's paths. Horrocks decided to cross the Seine at Vernon, using 43rd Division as the spearhead. Everything was going splendidly. Unfortunately for Horrocks, hubris was just around the corner. Hardly had he issued the appropriate orders than he felt sick and feverish. He returned hastily to his caravan, hoping that nobody had noticed. He had just reached it and crawled onto his bed when the ADC appeared. 'Field Marshal Montgomery will visit your HQ early tomorrow.' Realising that if Montgomery saw him in his present state he was almost certain to be invalided home and replaced, Horrocks told the ADC to send Montgomery a message requesting him to postpone the visit for two days 'as he was very busy inspecting units away from HQ'. This despatched, he lay back to sweat out the fever.

Alas for hopes. A mere two hours later the caravan door opened and Montgomery himself appeared. 'Ah yes, Jorrocks,' he said. 'I guessed something was wrong as soon as I got your message. But don't worry. I shan't invalid you home. Your caravan is now going to be moved up to my Tactical HQ and you won't be allowed to leave it until I tell you you can. There's nothing you could do for a day or two anyway. The divisional commander has got his orders and he doesn't want the corps commander breathing down his neck.'

Montgomery was as good as his word and every day that Horrocks was ill came to see him and talk to him. It probably suited Montgomery to have someone to talk to at that time, as he was very frustrated by seeing his plans overruled by Eisenhower. The fateful decision at this time was on how the European war should continue. Montgomery wanted to make a swift thrust along the northern coastal area, believing this would catch the Germans off balance. Most people felt that this seemed an unlikely project for Montgomery, for in previous battles he had insisted on long preparation and steam-roller tactics. Eisenhower felt that such a thrust could be too vulnerable, thinking that the Germans might be able to maul an advance on such a narrow front. Furthermore, Montgomery's thrust could not have been organised without the assistance of most of the transport from the American divisions. Militarily this would be unwise; politically, especially if the thrust were not a success, it would be disastrous. Eisenhower therefore decided on the 'broad front' policy of a steady advance all along the front. This, of course, meant that nearly all the Allied forces were committed all the time though in certain areas the 'broad front' was perilously thin. The last fact was made all too clear when the Germans broke through it in the Ardennes offensive in December 1944.

Montgomery was not pleased to be overruled, but had to make the best of it. He decided to make his thrust just the same, but to do it on his existing resources. He would use 30 Corps as the spearhead, and Horrocks, now recovered, left Tactical Headquarters on 26 August to prepare for his part in it. Life had suddenly become exciting and full of optimism again. It was, of course, a rash gamble on the part of Montgomery to put a person in Horrocks' state of health in charge of what must at the best be a gruelling and testing enterprise. But Montgomery realised that there was no one else with Horrocks' dash and experience, no one whom he felt he could trust to carry out his orders to the letter and in the spirit of the letter.

The essence of the new move was speed. In Horrocks' absence 43rd Division had crossed the Seine at Vernon as planned. On his left was 12 Corps, on his right the American 19 Corps. He went over to see the commander of 19 Corps to iron out any problems that might arise from their having a mutual boundary line. The meeting went well. However, soon after the next move began, 19 Corps swung left and were blocking the advance of 30 Corps right – a difficult situation which Horrocks resolved with a friendly telegram. From then on it was plain sailing. 30 Corps had a fifty-mile frontage and crunched through the German defences, none of which was on a large scale, without difficulty. Once again everything was going to plan, welcome to 'les libérateurs', assistance by the Resistance, minimal breakdowns. Horrocks was now living in a mobile HQ, a tank as his command post. He loved that tank, that way of life. When in 1982 the Falklands War began, he said to the author: 'I'm glad I'm not trying to command in this war. In a tank you knew where you were and what you were doing. I don't know how you'd begin to control operations in the Falklands.' But small though his HQ was, he was able to maintain close contact by wireless with all his sub units. He did, of course, now have an escort of three tanks. The corps was proceeding at speed through open country and in such circumstances generals are sometimes captured or killed. They were aiming at advancing twenty to thirty miles a day, preferably the latter. They travelled through the night in order to surprise the defence at Amiens, a trek led by 11th Armoured Division in pouring rain. Visibility was almost nil. Crews fell asleep at each halt. To make things worse they occasionally tangled with German vehicles, some of which were proceeding in the same direction as they were.

But it worked. The local resistance had secured the Somme bridges and the division entered the town on time. An infantry brigade was close behind. Everything was going to plan, Montgomery's plan. On from Amiens they were crossing the battlefields of the First World War, through Arras, Douai, on towards the Belgian frontier. On 2 September he was in Douai and took some pleasure in telling the Guards Armoured Division that their objective for the next day was Brussels. Brussels was seventy-five miles away. The Guards looked at him carefully, unruffled but incredulous, and realised he was serious. They made it a race between the various regiments in the leading units. It was not an entirely fair contest, for the Grenadiers, who at one point looked like winning, ran into some stiff opposition and lost twenty-two killed and thirty-one wounded.

Brussels had seen so many tanks during the course of the war; it scarcely looked up when more arrived. Then the citizens suddenly noticed that these were not Panzers. They could scarcely believe it. Then they did, and celebrated on a scale which has probably never been seen before or since. It was as well for Brussels that no one had made a fight for the town during the war, for its appearance might have been different. The Belgians had always been pro-British and recalled vividly such events as the Zeebrugge raid of April 1918 which has been commemorated every year since.

In the middle of the festivities Horrocks had to plan and coordinate the next moves. It was not an easy task but a step towards it was taken when he was invited by the Queen Mother to set up his headquarters in the grounds of the Palace of Laeken, which were secluded. She became very friendly with 30 Corps and presented them with what became a mascot, a small wild boar. (The corps sign was already a wild boar.) Fortunately it was only a baby and was very friendly. They christened it 'Chewing Gum' because its nose felt and looked exactly like that homely article.

On 4 September Horrocks had his second narrow escape of the war. He had been ordered to fly back for a conference in 2nd Army HQ, and set off in a small two-seater Auster. The pilot had the awkward task of flying along a narrow corridor and avoiding German attempts at interference. But it was not the Germans who put Horrocks in jeopardy. The aircraft compass failed and the pilot soon had to confess he was hopelessly lost. Horrocks suggested that the best policy would be to land and make some enquiries. This they did, to find themselves still in Belgium but some fifty miles behind the enemy lines. They took off again promptly but before they reached 2nd Army HQ had to land once more, this time for petrol. Fortunately, on the second occasion they were within their own lines. These mishaps, Horrocks felt, seemed in part to be due to what is called 'pilot error', and he was dubious about travelling back to Brussels in the same plane with the same pilot. In the end, not wishing to hurt the man's feelings, he did.

Chapter 9

The End of the Thrust

The speed at which Montgomery had now moved astonished and confounded his critics. Horrocks' corps had taken a mere six days to cover 250 miles. Admittedly opposition had been light and vital ports had been bypassed rather than captured, but it was an impressive record. Supply was already beginning to be a problem and would only worsen, unless a port could be captured. 11th Armoured Division poised to make a drive for Antwerp, which would clearly be an enormous asset with its extensive docks. But, Antwerp lay fifty miles inland, and the docks continued to be shelled by Germans in Merxem who could not easily be dislodged. Furthermore Walcheren island at the mouth of the estuary blocked the inlet, which was also mined. So although 11th Armoured Division captured the docks, they could not immediately be used. Subsequently Horrocks decided that to have sent this experienced armoured division into the town rather than bypassing it was a tactical error. He confessed that his sights were so clearly on the Rhine that he had given insufficient thought to the problem of Antwerp, and while the 11th was burrowing its nose into the Belgian port, the Germans were busy evacuating the remains of eight German divisions, a total of 82,000 men, who would otherwise have been trapped between Antwerp and Flushing (Vlissingen). By the time Horrocks realised what was happening the resources of 11th Armoured Division were too thinly spread for him to be able to put matters right. He managed to secure a bridgehead on the Albert Canal but was unable to hold it: the division was now too widely dispersed. Horrocks ungrudgingly accepted the blame for this tactical failure. It was, of course, his own decision to go into Antwerp, although it seems remarkable that it should have been left to him to make it.

Unfortunately the official history of British Intelligence covering this phase of the war has not yet been published, so it is not possible to know how much military information about the Scheldt area was available to Intelligence at this time. What does seem blindingly obvious was that Horrocks could not be expected to know that Walcheren was an almost impossible obstacle and that the straits were mined, but somebody with access to 'Ultra' *must* have known.

Montgomery *should* have known and given appropriate advice to Horrocks. If Montgomery did not know there must have been extraordinary confusion in the operations rooms. Antwerp had not suddenly become fifty miles away from the sea up a heavily defended channel; it had been there always and its approaches had been defended even before the Germans captured it. Furthermore, the idea that Antwerp docks, if captured, could be brought into instant use was clearly the most starry-eyed optimism.

Horrocks was, in fact, encouraged to gamble at Antwerp. It was hoped that the Germans were sufficiently on the run to move off without making a fight of it. And the defences of Walcheren had been hopelessly underestimated.

But the damage was done and a series of disasters followed. 30 Corps was ordered to halt and wait for the supply lines to catch up. Everything was coming from the 'Mulberry' harbour at Arromanches or Cherbourg, distances of over 300 miles, and petrol in particular was running very short. Losses en route from pilferage were alarmingly high. Even when Dieppe was opened up on 7 September it was too small to handle the volume of materials needed. Ostend was no better. Dunkirk, Calais, Boulogne and Le Havre were all urgently needed, but thought to contain 'die in the last ditch' German forces. In the event two British divisions captured Le Havre in less than two days and the Canadians made short work of Boulogne and Calais. As these ports had all been mined and 'denied', it was a month before they were in full use but there is no doubt that the failure to insist on the capture of at least one earlier in the thrust, even at high cost, was one of the greater strategic mistakes of the war. Curiously enough, one of the most distant ports, Brest, was one of the most strongly defended but that was because the Germans had been able to adapt the solid medieval earthworks and walls to present-day needs.

Yet even without supplies there was a chance of further great gains if 30 Corps had not been halted. One cannot but think that had Rommel been in command of 30 Corps instead of Horrocks he would have failed to receive the order to halt, and crashed on. Although troops were pouring out of the Scheldt area, there was only a single, low-grade division ahead of Horrocks on 4 September. It was spread over a fifty-mile front along the Albert Canal. Horrocks believed that this could have been brushed on one side and 30 Corps could have gone on to cross the Rhine. But the Germans were quick to react. A battle-experienced German division was in Holland on its way for a refit in Germany. Its commander, aptly named General Chill, hastily deployed the division along the banks of the Canal. He then set about organising a strong fall-back defence. He was soon joined by the Parachute Army under General Student.

Horrocks considered that the gamble would have been justified, although with the Germans concentrating ahead of him it could have been a risky one. The order to continue the advance came through to him on 7 September, the day Dieppe was captured, but by this time the vital chance had slipped away. In the next four days he advanced ten miles on a five-mile front, fighting grimly all the way.

The next stage in the campaign has been the subject of so many books and discussions, not to mention films, that it is superfluous to go into great detail here. But just as one success often leads to another, so does one bad decision often precede another, worse one. Clearly what should have happened was that the broad front should move forward while Antwerp and the estuary were cleared and put to full use. Instead it was decided that the 2nd British Army, which included 30 Corps, should advance to the Zuider Zee, capturing Grave, Nijmegen and Arnhem on the way, and therefore cut off the Germans still in Belgium and the Netherlands from those in Germany. From the position thus gained the Army could make a swift turn and outflank the Ruhr. The operation would be code-named 'Market Garden'. The 'Garden' part of the name referred to the ground operations, the 'Market' to the substantial airborne participation. 1st British Airborne were to seize the Arnhem bridge; 82nd US Airborne were to seize Grave bridge, rail and road bridges at Nijmegen and the ground south-east of Nijmegen; 101st US Airborne were to capture the road between Grave and Eindhoven. 30 Corps would advance, pass through these recently captured positions and seize the area around Arnhem and to the north.

Horrocks was uneasy about the plan. Not least of his worries was that Montgomery's directives seemed either vague or incorrect. Horrocks doubted whether anyone behind him really appreciated how rapidly the Germans were able to tighten their defences in this sort of emergency. 'Market Garden' was scheduled for 17 September, but might be delayed or otherwise varied according to weather conditions. There was no longer any question of advancing on a broad front with all its possibilities of outflanking movements: this would be a toe-to-toe slogging match on a narrow front, in fact one road only, for the adjoining areas were wooded and marshy. The terrain here made the desert battles seem like child's play. In front of them lay three large canals and three broad rivers: the Meuse, the Waal and the Rhine. There were of course bridges but it seemed highly probable that these would have been blown before

30 Corps arrived on the scene, and although 30 Corps had extensive equipment for bridge-building, the time required to erect adequate constructions would delay their advance and enable the Germans to concentrate even more reinforcements.

The attack, perfectly co-ordinated between infantry, artillery, cavalry and airborne units, began well. The Irish Guards led, and although they lost nine tanks against the stubborn German defence, they forced their way along and by the end of the first day were in the Dutch town of Valkenswaard. The Germans counter-attacked that evening but made no headway. So far, so good, but by an unfortunate coincidence General Model, Commander-in-Chief of the German Forces, was lunching in Oosterbek, six miles west of Arnhem. He was surprised to see British parachutes coming out of the sky to land on a dropping zone some two miles away and departed precipitately to HQ 2 SS Panzer Corps, which was only twenty-eight miles from Arnhem. No one on the Allied side at this time realised that 9th and 10th Panzer Divisions were at that moment in Zutphen, on their way back to Germany for a refit. Although both divisions had had heavy losses in Normandy, they still had a number of tanks and self-propelled weapons. These, of course, would be more than a match for anything the British airborne troops could bring in. The two German divisions had been specially trained for anti-parachute duties. Model quickly appreciated that he had little to fear from 1st Airborne on their own: what he needed to guard against was 30 Corps and what would follow. As we saw earlier, 85th German Division was already in the area; he now ordered 59th Division, 15th and 41st Panzer and 10th SS to converge on to the route between Nijmegen and Arnhem. His tactical plan was greatly aided by the fact that the operation order for 'Market Garden' was captured when an Allied glider was forced down, even though he was at first suspicious that this was a 'plant'. It should not, of course, have been in the glider at all. Everything looked very promising from the German point of view, although this was not the way Hitler saw the situation. Convinced that Model had had the narrowest of escapes, and that he himself might be surprised and captured in a similar attack, he ordered the German Air Force to despatch its reserve formations to Holland.

'Market Garden' then became a battle against time. 1st Airborne put up a magnificent fight against increasingly heavy odds. A detachment from 9th SS Panzer reached Arnhem bridge thirty minutes before Colonel J.D. Frost's 2nd Parachute Battalion. However 2nd Para occupied houses north of the town and prevented 10th SS Panzer from using the bridge; the Germans had to find their way across the river by ferry and did not arrive at Nijmegen until after the Allies had captured it. Developments for the Allies were also proceeding well on other parts of the front. The Guards Armoured Division linked up with 101st US Airborne on the eighteenth. 101st Airborne had made the finest drop of their history, landing nearly 7,000 men exactly on target with minimal losses. The Guards soon reached the territory held by 82nd US Airborne at Grave, where they had captured two important bridges. However, they were then held up just short of the Waal river.

There were two vital bridges over the Waal at Nijmegen, neither of which had been demolished. It was essential to capture one or both, enter the town, move on to the lower Rhine, cross, and relieve 1st Airborne. 1st Airborne, a total of 10,000 men outnumbered and outgunned, cut off from further supply, could not possibly hold out unless relieved, however hard they fought. The Germans, knowing every detail of the Allied plans, had concentrated everything they could muster in 30 Corps path. Desperate attempts were made to burst a way through, but so tightly organised was the defence that it was soon clear that further efforts in this area would be useless. The cream of British and US forces hurled themselves into the attack over and over again but without being able to penetrate far.

In consequence Horrocks and General F.A.M. 'Boy' Browning, Commander of the Airborne forces, decided that the only solution was to outflank the bridges by crossing the river 800 yards downstream from the railway bridge. An opposed river crossing is an unpleasant and high-risk enterprise at the best of times and this one, with the Germans fighting with the desperation of the doomed, was a near-suicidal venture. They required the co-operation of 82nd Airborne, commanded by General James Gavin. Gavin had no hesitation in giving his consent, even though it meant engaging in an enterprise new to them, in British assault boats which they had never seen before. The river is fast-flowing and 400 yards wide at this point. Half the paratroopers were lost on the way over, but the remainder reached the bank, some by swimming, climbed the steep embankment, and obtained a foothold which, with reinforcements, they soon extended. By nightfall they had reached Lent, a mile inland, and cut off both the Waal bridges from the rest of the German forces. It was still vital to capture the bridges, which the enemy had not destroyed, for the remainder of 30 Corps and 2nd Army could hardly hope to cross the Waal on assault boats. The Guards Brigade was still in the thick of it; now after the heroic work of the Irish Guards it was the turn of the Grenadiers to distinguish themselves. Nor were they alone: the American parachutists were still fighting tooth and nail. Eventually the Guards crossed the bridge, which was still intact. It had only remained so because a young officer in the

Royal Engineers, Lt A.G.C. Jones, ran with the tanks and cut the wires to the demolition charges. Jones was awarded a Military Cross; later he rose to the rank of major-general. During his career he played Rugby football for the Army; he considered that his feat at Nijmegen was considerably less hazardous than playing in the front row of the scrum against Welsh Rugby teams.

It was 21 September, and the attack had been rolling forward for four days, but it was now slowing up as the Germans resistance became more and more fanatical. Horrocks recalls that some young Germans were sitting on their tanks shouting: 'I want to die for Hitler.' Every assistance was given to gratify their wishes.

The Germans now had substantial air cover and an increasing tide of reinforcements. The line of communication, held by 101st Airborne, was particularly hard pressed, but held. The area which 30 Corps had now reached was nicknamed 'The Island' as it was virtually surrounded by water and in addition was full of dykes. It was no country for tanks. Artillery support was hampered by the difficulty of identifying appropriate targets although that was soon remedied. Horrocks' old stalwarts, 43rd Wessex Division, were now moving up to deal with the problems of 'The Island' in the way that an infantry division could. The Polish parachute brigade had dropped near Driel on the lower Rhine. Prospects of relieving 1st Airborne still seemed reasonable. Some armoured cars of the Household Cavalry reached the Poles and linked up. They were only seven miles from Arnhem; unfortunately they were not in sufficient strength to do much on their own.

43rd Division fought on doggedly but found progress slow and frustrating. To some who wrote with hindsight, 43rd had been slow and unenterprising. Horrocks was concerned at the criticism. He felt that such comments would only have come from people who were not present at the time, nor familiar with the difficulties of fighting in that sort of terrain. In some areas the Germans were counterattacking, using Tiger tanks, all of which were destroyed. The result was that 30 Corps was hard pressed to hold its recent gains, let alone increase them. Another day passed. Every hour was crucial if 1st Airborne, still fighting on but hemmed in on all sides, were to be relieved.

Looking back it is sadly clear that the Arnhem drop had been a little too ambitious, a little too far ahead. Against that sobering thought is the fact that if it had been a success – and it was not far short of one – the war would have been shortened by what could subsequently have been described as a military masterstroke. As everyone knows, the delays in the Allies reaching Berlin radically changed the map of Europe and made the 'Cold War' possible. The fact too that the British were held up at Arnhem enabled the German Army to delude them into the view that they were licking their wounds and preparing further defence, while in fact they were preparing for a massive counter-attack in the Ardennes.

22 September brought the worrying, though expected, news that German armour had cut through 101st Airborne as they were strung out along the approach road, twenty-five miles of it, trying to keep it open. Much of the road had been under continuous shellfire. The road was eventually reopened by the combined efforts of 32nd Guards Brigade from the north and the two American airborne units from the south, but for a day and a night the forward units of 30 Corps had been cut off from the rest of the corps and supplies.

Further attempts were made to get some troops across the river but casualties were high and the supply of assault boats was limited. Horrocks, subsequently, considered that this was the worst time of his life. Had it been himself who had been at risk it would have been unpleasant but tolerable; the thought that it was others who were relying on, or perhaps now merely hoping for, him to get them out of their desperate predicament was worse than personal danger. His solace in this nail-biting time was the presence of Maxwell Taylor and James Gavin, the former commanding 101st and the latter 82nd, whose calm but thoroughgoing support was always there. Horrocks regarded the two élite units with admiration; they were as good as if not better than their reputations.

Horrocks was, of course, right up at the front himself, observing from forward positions, driving along highly dangerous exposed roads to keep himself completely informed of the situation. He was very much on his own: neither Dempsey nor Montgomery were at hand. Presumably they had decided that Horrocks was the man for this battle and he should be left alone to fight it. This is no reflection on their personal courage: that is above criticism. However, as with the Antwerp decision, it does seem to have meant leaving a burden to Horrocks which he was scarcely qualified to carry. However, on 24 September Horrocks was summoned to St Oedenrode to confer with Dempsey (now his Army Commander). When he set out on the return journey to the front he found the road north had been cut again. This time it was not reopened for four days. He managed to overcome the setback by going across country with an escort of carriers from the Durham Light Infantry, and reached his head-quarters at 10 a.m. the next morning, the twenty-fifth. He learnt that the 4th Dorsets had crossed the river during the night but had lost most of their boats: it was thought that they had all been killed or captured. Ammunition was running short. There was no alternative but to suggest that 1st Airborne should try to make its way back across the river. 2,323 of the original 10,000 succeeded in doing so, as the artillery used up their remaining shells giving them cover. After eight days the bold attempts to capture Arnhem had ended in failure.

In future years Horrocks would often write about or lecture on the Arnhem battle and subsequently became completely sated with discussions of it. He felt, probably wrongly, that if anyone was to blame for the failure it was probably himself. He felt that the Guards and the American airborne units achieved everything and more than could have been expected of them. He felt that 43rd Division did remarkably well in the teeth of relentless opposition but that he might perhaps have given them an easier task, and one which might have brought overall success if he had sent them to cross the Rhine further west to come round to Arnhem from behind. But he had the feeling that whatever tactics he had employed, the Germans had so many good troops concentrated in that terrain which so strongly favoured defenders that a successful line-up was not possible in the time available. He felt that alternative tactics might in the end have led to a larger disaster. 30 Corps had already been cut off several times during the battle. Had they ventured across the Rhine elsewhere, they might have put themselves in jeopardy with the rest of the Army trying to relieve 30 Corps.

Horrocks was well aware that Montgomery was considered to have made a major blunder over Arnhem; he felt that the criticism was unjustified. This was a considered view, taken apart from his loyalty to a superior who had done so much to further Horrocks' own career. At that particular moment, with the Germans reeling from the shock of defeat in Russia and being rolled back from Normandy, it was militarily sound to try to tear a further large hole in their defences. By bad luck the Germans at that moment had too many seasoned troops in the vicinity for the Arnhem gamble to succeed. But, as we saw, it nearly did. Luck favoured the Germans in every way. There had perhaps in Allied headquarters been a little too much reliance on the intelligence we were receiving from many sources, principally 'Ultra'. But 'Ultra' could never cope with a fast-moving situation, and the fact that several battered but not fully crippled divisions were moving back to the fatherland was hardly the sort of information to electrify the code-breakers. Coincidence had caused those divisions to be in the right place at the right time.

What the Arnhem battle seems to demonstrate is an astonishing lack of appreciation of the details of military geography among the planning staff. Yet military training in the inter-war years had placed great emphasis on the study of military geography. Far too often in the Second World War the countryside was read wrongly.

117

Jungle was said to be impassable to troops; Malaya and Burma, among other countries, proved this wrong. The desert, until the Long Range Desert Group proved otherwise, was thought to be a trackless sandy waste where men would get lost and die. Sicily was thought to be an easy option. In Norway both weather and terrain were misunderstood. The Siegfried Line was thought to be as ineffective as the Maginot Line: experience again proved otherwise. Sometimes planning errors were made because of lack of up-to-date intelligence, but much of the time it was a matter of not knowing the terrain. Horrocks, hurtling around the world from Alam Halfa to Mareth, then from hospital to Normandy and Arnhem, could scarcely be expected to have a detailed knowledge of all the ground he was approaching, but others should have done and should have briefed him.

Although geography formed part of the pre-1939 syllabus at Sandhurst, it disappeared entirely from the curriculum when Woolwich and Sandhurst combined to form the RMA Sandhurst in 1947. Geography has, of course, never had much prestige as a subject in schools or universities, but if there is one place where it might seem absolutely essential that place is within the military academies.

One can, of course, have too much faith in maps. When the Germans invaded Russia in 1941 they relied on Russian-made maps. These proved less than satisfactory, for many of the roads marked had not yet been made, as the Germans quickly discovered to their disgust.

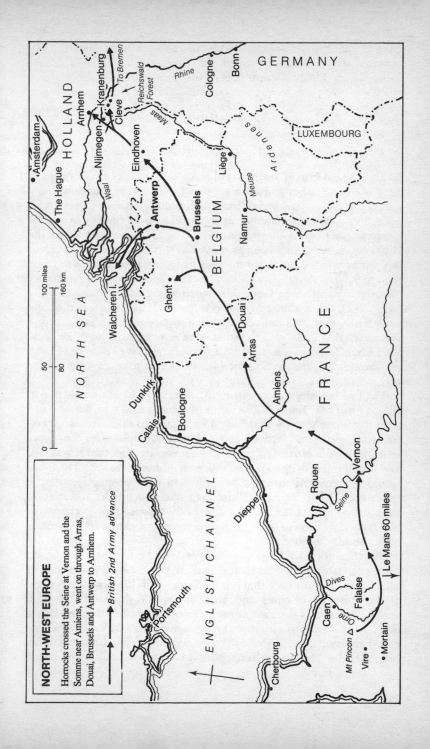

NORTH-WEST EUROPE

Horrocks crossed the Seine at Vernon and the Somme near Amiens, went on through Arras, Douai, Brussels and Antwerp to Arnhem.

——▶ British 2nd Army advance

Chapter 10

The Opposition Stiffens

At the time Arnhem seemed a disastrous setback. In so far as it prevented the Allies finishing off the war in 1944, it undoubtedly was, although in terms of military accountancy it was a very small operation. The broad front strategy could now be continued and 30 Corps would play its allotted part in it. The Canadians took over the Nijmegen sector and 30 Corps moved to the right, near Maastricht in preparation for the drive towards Cologne. Here they were next door to 9th US Army. Horrocks was asked to assist in the American offensive by capturing Geilenkirchen, and for this purpose had the 84th US Division allotted to his command. He was flattered by the confidence that this move showed and hoped that forthcoming events would justify it. The Allies were now approaching the Siegfried Line. To many people the Siegfried Line – 'We're going to hang out the washing on the Siegfried Line' – was a joke: in reality there was nothing at all comic about it.

The line had been begun in 1938, supervised by the construction genius Dr Todt. Eight million tons of cement and a million tons of steel had gone into its building, a barricade packed with bunkers, pillboxes, guns, and tank obstacles. It was 400 miles long, but more important from Horrocks' point of view was the fact that it was two and a half miles deep. To attack this formidable obstacle Horrocks would be required to use a new division with no previous battle experience, 43rd Division which had had too much, and certain supporting units from other parts of 30 Corps. However, on 18 November this mixed force surged forward and captured Geilenkirchen. So far, so good.

But then the rain began – relentlessly. The Germans launched counter-attacks which 30 Corps held off, but forward progress was nil. Horrocks made sure that hot food was available to stave off some of the miseries of mud and wet, but would have preferred to withdraw the new division after its 'blooding' rather than let it bog down in such miserable, frustrating conditions: other more experienced divisions could, he felt, cope with attrition better. Unfortunately with the 'broad front' policy, once a unit was in the line it had to stay in it.

The plan for the next move was for what became known as the battle of the Reichswald, but much would happen before that could take place. While operation orders were being made out for a pincer move to cut off large German forces west of the Rhine, the Allies suddenly found themselves with a totally unexpected crisis on their hands. The assumption that the German forces in the north were being rested and refitted to defend themselves against a further attack in that area was found to be totally misconceived. The Germans, instead of reinforcing their mauled troops in the north, were busy amassing a body of some 250,000 men behind the Ardennes. How they managed to do so unknown to our Intelligence is one of the great mysteries of the war. The Germans knew the Ardennes well. They had enjoyed great success in that area in 1940, much to the Allied surprise and dismay, and now they were aware that the 'broad front' had left four American divisions to hold a front of ninety miles. And there were hardly any reserves on the Allied side, owing to that 'broad front' policy.

Horrocks had retired to Brussels for a brief change of air when he heard the news. Over the telephone came the astonishing information that the Germans had smashed right through the American line well into the Ardennes. The situation was very confused. As Horrocks' corps was the only one available at that particular moment, he was ordered to move it down to protect Brussels. However, an added complication at that moment was a thick fog around Brussels; this effectively prevented him getting back to his headquarters – seventy-five miles away – until it thinned. At first he could hardly believe the Ardennes news. Like everyone else, he thought the Germans were at the end of their resources, physically, mentally and militarily, and in no position to mount a counter-attack on any scale. Yet here they were bounding forward and, if not stopped, a definite threat to Antwerp. Nevertheless, like Patton, he felt that the occasion also offered the Allies a superb opportunity to counter-attack and totally destroy what must surely be the last scrapings of the German barrel of reserves. Everyone except Montgomery decided that the first reports must be exaggerated and that this could not be more than a local attack. Montgomery alone realised how serious it might prove to be.

Eisenhower, in a much criticised decision, divided the troops in the Ardennes sector, placing those in the north under Montgomery, those in the south under Bradley. Montgomery's appointment to command such a large section of American troops was not popular with them. Horrocks noted that it was a situation which called for unlimited tact, a quality with which Montgomery was not liberally endowed.

Not least of Horrocks' frustrations was the difficulty of gathering accurate information. The area abounded with rumours. Otto Skorzeny, renowned for his daring snatch of Mussolini out of Allied hands, was now prominent again. He had organised a force of some fifty jeeps of American-speaking Germans. These, wearing American uniforms quite contrary to the rules of war, had spread alarm and confusion in the American rear areas. The American response had been dramatic. Every visitor to the area, whatever his uniform or story, was treated with the deepest suspicion and the American military police devised a testing system which required knowledge unfamiliar to anyone but Americans and not always familiar to many of them either. It recalled the days of 1940 in France when nuns were suspected of being disguised German parachutists and strange faces were thought to be those of spies or saboteurs. Even Horrocks himself was stopped and interrogated in the Ardennes. He was asked what was the second largest town in Texas. The question completely floored him.

Unfortunately the ultra-sensitivity about spies was not limited to the military police but also seemed to be widespread among more senior ranks too. Montgomery's liaison officers received a very cool reception when they went on fact-finding missions. 'Phantom', with long experience of working with American forces, did much better but even they found conditions difficult at times. A good part of the 'Phantom' success was due to the co-operation given by General Matthew B. Ridgway, commander of the US 18th Airborne Corps. Ridgway later became Commander-in-Chief of the UN Force in the Korean war.

Much to his amazement, on Christmas Day 1944, just when the battle seemed to be reaching its most critical phase, Horrocks was told by Montgomery that he was being sent home. As 30 Corps were holding a vital area between the Meuse and Brussels, the decision seemed to indicate that he was being replaced by a better man. But it was not so. Montgomery had decided that the Ardennes battle was virtually over and that Horrocks should be rested before embarking on offensive battles in the near future. Horrocks protested that the Ardennes battle was still at the crucial stage. It was no use: Montgomery had decided that the turning point of the battle had passed, and he was right. By 11 January the Germans had been pushed back to the Siegfried Line again. (This highly selective description of the battle unfortunately gives no indication of the influence of the Allied Air Forces nor of the stubborn local defence by ground units.)

So Horrocks went off on leave and returned more impressed by Montgomery's foresight than ever before. The next stage was what came to be known as the Reichswald battle, and for this Horrocks had the new experience of himself being under the command of the 1st Canadian Army. The army planned to attack through the Reichswald forest towards Cleve, then to turn south to Goch, from which it would approach the Rhine and Wesel. This would cause the German armies to concentrate their forces in that area and thereby leave a way clear for the US 9th Army to cross the Roer river and come up to join 30 Corps. This move, due to begin on 8 February, was designed to draw the German defences out of position and open up a clear and relatively untroubled route for a Rhine crossing.

This looked a simple task on paper but remarkably less so when examined on the ground. To the immediate front of the Canadians was polder (reclaimed) land which had been flooded again by the Germans and now resembled a huge lake. Between the forest and the polder there was a gap but it had been meticulously planted with mines. Cleve, Goch, and Hochwald were bristling with fortifications. The key point initially was the high ground at Nutterden. At the time the attack began this was held by a single German division but there were five other German divisions in reserve, all of which could be brought into use rapidly when the Germans saw the way the main Allied thrust was leading. Horrocks decided that surprise was vital, and to this end 30 Corps assault troops remained behind the Canadians where their presence would not arouse suspicion, even if noticed at all. Reconnaissance was conducted with the utmost discretion: members of recce parties were issued with Canadian battledress which was slightly greener than the British issue. Horrocks decided that when the moment came he would use five divisions in line: 51st Highland, 53rd Welsh, 15th Scottish, 2nd and 3rd Canadian. Following up were the 43rd Wessex and Guards Armoured, and these, when the time came, would move through to the front and then thrust forward to the Rhineland. Obviously this was not going to be effected without considerable bloodshed, but Horrocks could accept that as the inevitable cost of war. What sickened him was having to agree to the saturation bombing of Cleve. Cleve was a beautiful town with a long history. (Ann of Cleves, Henry VIII's fourth wife, came from here – a sadly unattractive woman who was pensioned off because Henry could not stand the sight of her.) But it was neither the beauty nor the history of Cleve which concerned Horrocks: it was the thought that there were women and children still living there. In a war which had already seen Rotterdam, Coventry, the 'Baedeker' raids on the most beautiful towns in Britain, and the steady toll taken of London's civilians, his hesitation at this late stage may seem remarkable, but

Horrocks had always tried not to let himself be immunised by the necessary slaughter of war.

In some ways the Reichswald battle resembled the slogging battles of the First World War, Passchendaele in particular. 200,000 men were under Horrocks' command, and the air support was also immense. The Germans were overwhelmed but they had a useful ally in the rain and mud. The tanks were quickly bogged down and the infantry had to struggle on without them. Adding to the difficulties was the fact that the mud was full of mines of every description. The Germans then broke a hole in the banks of the Rhine further upstream and the only road forward was under water.

But there was good news. The 15th Scottish were reported to be entering Cleve. Horrocks, much elated, sent forward the 43rd Wessex so that they could move through 15th Scottish and expand on to the plain beyond.

Alas for hopes. The news of the Scottish success was exaggerated: they had not reached Cleve and the arrival of 43 Division merely created a traffic jam of unprecedented dimensions. Horrocks gloomily admitted that this was entirely his fault. However, in time the confusion was sorted out and the combined weight of the two divisions was too much for the Germans trying to hold Cleve. The story was much the same along the whole front, a bitter, slow, First World War type of battle. Against the seven attacking Allied divisions the Germans had now mustered ten, with a formidable array of artillery. But the British artillery, not for the first time in this war, was more than a match for the opposition. Horrocks used to say that of all the arms the gunners probably contributed most to the winning of the war. As an ex-infantryman he had a high regard for any means by which the soldier might capture ground without the suicidal attacks of 1914-18. He used to ponder at some length on the way in which the modern soldier fought. No longer did he see his comrades, or his opposition: much of his fighting took place at night and many of the casualties were the result of impersonal agents – mines, booby traps, long-range gunfire. It was surprising that the modern soldier coped so well with harsh conditions and isolation because everything in civilised life, bright lights, community activity, and emphasis on safety, all conditioned men to an existence vastly different from the modern battlefield. Yet they did it.

The battle ground on for five weeks, with the floods rising steadily. At one stage 30 Corps' only road was several feet under water. But the attack never slackened. Horrocks felt the strain himself, particularly when he heard the names of some of those killed. In his style of leadership he knew many of them personally, and felt their deaths as a great waste and personal loss.

Finally, on 10 February, the 43rd Division in an inspired dash reached the higher ground overlooking Goch. The battle was then finished off by the Scots, notably 51st Highland, 15th Scottish, and 52nd Lowland, and the Scottish Horse.

The next stage, to Hochwald, was mainly a Canadian battle. The opposition consisted largely of German paratroopers who conceded nothing while alive to defend it. At times the Canadians had the utmost difficulty in avoiding being pushed back but eventually, after slogging it out toe-to-toe, they forged ahead and captured the vital German positions. While this struggle was going on the 9th US Division was forcing its way towards the Roer river which it managed to cross by the twenty-third. The pincers could now close. By 10 March the battle of the Reichswald was completed and the west bank of the Rhine was in Allied hands. The Germans, fighting relentlessly and putting up artillery barrages as heavy as any seen in the war, had suffered over 70,000 casualties, of which nearly 17,000 were taken prisoner. British and Canadian losses were just under 16,000. It was not the sort of battle which Horrocks wished to command: a grim, painful, uncomfortable and costly struggle with no scope for brilliant tactics or avoidance of heavy losses. But it had had to be fought. During the battle 30 Corps had swollen to unprecedented size, incorporating nine divisions and a mass of artillery. However, after this gruelling battle 30 Corps reverted to a more normal size and came back from the command of 1st Canadian Army to 2nd British Army. The next stage was to cross the Rhine and drive into the heart of Germany. It would not be easy.

The crossing itself was planned to take place between the two towns Rees and Wesel. 30 Corps' objective was Rees, but the going would be hard, for the way was defended by paratroopers and Panzer grenadiers. Obviously the crossing would be easier if they could deceive the Germans over the exact spot, although any surprise would be far from easy owing to the fact that the east bank was higher than the west and the latter was therefore under fairly constant observation.

Horrocks paid a tribute to the staff work of the then Brigadier of the General Staff, C.B. Jones. 'Splosh' Jones, as he was nicknamed, later became General Sir Charles Jones. He was a Royal Engineer and to that corps fell the task of assembling the necessary assault craft and bridging equipment. The crossing was to be made at night, with a smoke screen to add to the obscurity. Horrocks had vivid memories of the smoke screen he was inspecting in Bizerta when he was so badly wounded. This one demonstrated the unpredictability of smoke screens and gas attacks by blowing back into the faces of 30 Corps' men; the effect of breathing in the smoke was a feeling of nausea which, unwelcome at any time, was particularly annoying at that moment.

The crossing on 23 March was preceded by the normal bombardment. In the dark, smoke, and general obscurity, Horrocks could see very little but just after 9 p.m. heard the welcome news that the Black Watch were across the Rhine. The crossing, from which heavy casualties had been expected, proved less arduous than anticipated and losses were comparatively light. One unexpected difficulty was the speed of the current which took assault craft down river rapidly and thus made landings more difficult.

But worse was to come. Instead of crumbling, German resistance became stiffer as 30 Corps pushed on. The following day, much to everyone's surprise, the 15th Panzer Grenadier Division launched a counter-attack of such ferocity that the Allies were nearly sent spinning backward. Horrocks observed that, although he was constantly hearing of large numbers of Germans surrendering in other areas, there was no similar activity to be seen on his front. In fact the fighting seemed harder than ever. This he attributed to the leadership of experienced German officers and NCOs who had a remarkable ability for taking over second-class recruits, some of them scarcely more than boys, and turning them into high-grade, dour, professional soldiers. Rees, to the south of the Reichswald, was defended with the utmost tenacity. A considerable shock was the death of the commander of 51st Highland Division, Major-General Thomas Rennie. Horrocks called an immediate conference of the three brigade commanders and appointed one of them, Brigadier Oliver, as temporary divisional commander until Rennie's official replacement arrived. Horrocks had warm feelings towards 51st Highland Division. He had known it in France before Dunkirk, then in the desert, and then in Normandy. His confidence in the division's ability was reciprocated by the feeling that if anyone understood and appreciated the 51st it was Horrocks. They forged on.

Resistance still did not slacken. The Germans fought those most difficult of military manoeuvres, rearguard actions, with expert precision. Crossroads and bridges were destroyed in the path of 30 Corps' advance – all but one. That bridge was over the River Ems. Massive demolition material was in position all ready to blow the bridge, and the approach road was covered by a battery of 88-mm guns. Presumably the Germans had arranged this tempting scenario in the hope that the Allies would rush the bridge, suffer heavy casualties as they approached it, and then, if they reached the bridge, have it blown up in their faces. But the bridge would be a godsend to the Allied advance if it could be captured instead.

The task was given to the Coldstream Guards, who moved close up for the purpose. Then came the tightest pieces of timing of the war. First the British artillery hammered the German positions, then it suddenly stopped and the same positions were raked with cross-fire from British tanks which had been brought up for this move. One of the company commanders, Captain Liddell, ran forward in full view of the Germans and cut the wires to the demolition charges. He then ran back, still unwounded, and waved on the tanks. They thereupon hurtled down the road on to the bridge, closely followed by the infantry. In the final assault only one guardsman was killed but the Germans, caught in position, had forty killed and forty taken prisoner. Liddell was recommended for a Victoria Cross but was killed eighteen days later, before it was officially granted. As Horrocks pointed out sadly: 'It is always the best who die in war.'

His old team – Guards Armoured, 43rd Wessex and 51st Highland, supplemented by 3rd Division which had done well from the moment of its first landing on D-Day – continued to probe forward. To Horrocks' surprise, although the German soldiers were fighting stubbornly, a different attitude was seen in the towns; as they approached white sheets were displayed at all the windows. Of the German resistance groups which were said to have been organised behind the Allied lines there was no sign.

In mid-April Horrocks was told that he would have to capture Bremen en route for Hamburg. He was not enthusiastic and hoped to persuade General Neil Ritchie who commanded 12 Corps that the task was one particularly suitable for him. But Ritchie was already on the Elbe, far ahead. He had commanded 12 Corps since D-Day, and had had great success. Those with a memory for the early desert battles will recall that Ritchie had commanded Eighth Army from November 1941 (when he had replaced Cunningham) until June 1942 when, during the disastrous retreat of that month, he had been replaced by Auchinleck himself. Ritchie, incidentally, had played a leading part in the beginnings of the SAS, for when David Stirling had gate-crashed into GHQ Middle East in 1941 he had failed to reach Auchinleck but had encountered Ritchie. Ritchie, amused by the young lieutenant's temerity, agreed to read the papers which were thrust upon him. He liked what he read, took them to Auchinleck who also approved, and the SAS was born.

But with Ritchie well out of reach, Horrocks realised that the ball was in his own court. At this point Montgomery appeared with a large-scale map. He told Horrocks he was far from happy about the idea of getting large numbers of troops entangled in a town such as Bremen, where contact and control could so easily be lost. He asked Horrocks for his views, listened and then told him exactly what to do.

Surprisingly Horrocks did not resent the interference. Others might have done so. But by this time Horrocks had acquired total confidence in Montgomery's judgement, perhaps more than in his own. Horrocks had an uneasy feeling that he had dithered at Antwerp and then taken the wrong decision, and he was not sure that he had pushed 30 Corps hard enough at Arnhem. On both these occasions Montgomery had left him to make his own decisions; on this one Montgomery was taking over.

The capture of Bremen took five days and employed four infantry divisions: 3rd, 43rd, 51st and 52nd. Enemy resistance was stiff though uneven; without the intensive support of the RAF the battle would have taken much longer. The garrison commander was among the 6,000 prisoners taken.

With Bremen now in Allied hands, Montgomery ordered the assault crossing of the Elbe for 28 April.

At this point Eisenhower heard that the Russians had reached the outskirts of Berlin and sent Montgomery a signal asking for all possible speed towards the Baltic. The request must have raised a few cynical eyebrows as the recipients recalled the missed opportunities and poor strategy of earlier years. The American First Army and the Russians had already met at Torgau on 25 April, well to the west of Berlin, and on 6 May the US Ninth Army would also meet the Russians. Meanwhile the British Second Army, which of course included 30 Corps, was heading for Cuxhaven. By now administration was being choken by the fact that large numbers of Allied prisoners were being released from camps in Germany, and far greater numbers of German soldiers were laying down their arms and surrendering. For some time there had been murmurs that the activities of the Tactical Air Forces, in the close support they were giving, should be restricted, for although this was probably the most effective means of assisting the Allied drive across Germany, it was thought that the destruction caused to towns in the path of the armies was no longer justified. However, just when it was felt by everyone that perhaps they ought to start being kinder to the Germans, who had so obviously lost the war by now, they came across the concentration camps. The first was near Bremen. Horrocks was only one of many people to be horrified and nauseated by the sight of these camps: he was physically sick when he saw the inmates at close quarters. He had not cared for the Germans since his harsh treatment in the hospital at Lille in the First World War, but this was something of another dimension. Nausea soon gave way to practical measures. He ordered the surrounding towns and villages to supply a number of German women to clean up the camps and tend to the sick who were still dying rapidly. When he brought the women in the camp he looked closely to see their reaction. He was astonished to see no sign of remorse or pity. It used to be said that the average German had no idea of what went on in the concentration camps. In Horrocks' experience it looked as if it made no difference whether they did or not.

On 3 May he heard confidentially that the Germans were now preparing for total surrender, but that it must be kept secret. It was therefore vital to ensure there should be no more casualties, not even one, but it was not easy to restrain the divisions now poised for the final victorious thrust to defeat the enemy they had fought so hard and so long to conquer. In the event, it was all over not with a bang but a whisper. He heard the news, on the wireless, when he was in the lavatory. The official surrender in his area took place on 5 May. Horrocks sat facing the German general commanding the Corps Ems, who was accompanied by his Chief of Staff. He gave his orders for the surrender and added:

'These orders must be obeyed scrupulously. I warn you I shall have no mercy if they are not. Having seen one of your horror camps my whole attitude to Germans has changed.'

The Chief of Staff protested: 'The Army had nothing to do with those camps.'

Horrocks looked at him coolly: 'There were German soldiers on sentry duty outside those camps and you cannot escape responsibility. The world will never forgive Germany for those camps.'

Surrenders were taking place on all sides that day. The largest number of prisoners was taken by US 18th Airborne: 100,000 on 2 May and 150,000 on 3 May. But a greater feeling of elation was experienced by British 6th Airborne who, having been the first British division to land on D-Day, then became the first to reach the Baltic in 1945, and also were the first to make contact between British and Russian forces.

Montgomery took the surrender of the German forces in Holland, North-west Germany, Schleswig-Holstein, and Denmark at 6.30 on 4 May. According to the official history, Montgomery remarked: 'It looks as if the British Empire part of the German war in Western Europe is over. I was persuaded to drink some champagne at dinner tonight.'

Horrocks needed no such persuasion, although for him victory was tinged with many regrets for the friends he had lost and the destruction of so much which could never be replaced. Two days after the signing he inspected the surrendered troops and congratulated them on having fought so well with so little. But he was uneasily aware that the German military machine had risen from defeat once before and could do so again.

Chapter 11

A New Responsibility

Bitter though Horrocks' feelings were when he contemplated the cruelty and oppression of the Nazis, they were soon submerged by his new task: rehabilitating the conquered. Initially, military administration was on a corps basis and Horrocks was allotted the Hanover district. When he first toured it, it seemed impossible that it could ever be rebuilt; Hanover and Bremen were ruins where the survivors lived in caves under the ruins of their former homes. Besides the heavy casualties of the war, there were still thousands of Germans in Allied prisoner-of-war camps. So in his area Horrocks had the task of clearing up and re-establishing normal life with only the labour of women, of old men, and the disabled at his disposal. Even the boys had gone: they had been sucked into the military machine for the last desperate battles. Horrocks felt that whatever their crimes the Germans had certainly suffered enough to expiate many of them. To his surprise and amusement he found himself acting like a benevolent dictator. Results were quick in coming, a fact he attributed to the efficiency of the 30 Corps staff. This was one of the most experienced in the Allied armies and it turned to the problem of reconstruction as effectively as it had tackled that of destruction. However, Horrocks noticed some resentment on the part of the soldiers who were required to spare no effort in rebuilding the country which had disrupted their own lives, destroyed many of their homes, and been responsible for unspeakable barbarities. Most of them thought the Germans should wallow in their misery and suffer a fraction of the discomfort they had inflicted on others in the long years in which they had been dominant in Europe. The point was put to him by a corporal in the Royal Engineers and Horrocks, realising the man expressed a general view, gathered the man's company around him and explained that their work was vital for both humanitarian and political reasons. If the Allies let the Germans die of starvation, which they surely would if not helped, the ensuing bitterness would outlive their generation. This was Horrocks' first introduction to public relations, an art at which he would become an expert. In the Army so far his listeners, although enthusiastic, had all been captive audiences, believing what they were told or at least having to pretend to do so. With this company of sappers, all called up for the duration of the war and soon to be demobilised, he was addressing a horse of a different colour – and he realised it.

There was at this time a 'no fraternisation' rule which was designed to make the Germans feel guilty without punishing them. Horrocks thought it was completely idiotic. He knew very well that the troops would fraternise with local prostitutes and he felt that their prime objective was not so much sex as contact with women and life outside a military camp. This could have occurred differently if they had been allowed to make friends with ordinary German families, he felt. The British soldier has an extraordinary knack of making friends and conducting a form of conversation with people whose language he cannot speak. In fact there were eleven million 'war widows' in Germany at that time, some genuine widows whose husbands had been killed, and others whose husbands had been taken prisoner at an earlier stage of the war. Many of these had been driven to near-prostitution by hunger and want.

Horrocks could not defy the 'no fraternisation' order but he endeavoured to make it as painless as possible by encouraging everyone in 30 Corps to help German children wherever and whenever possible. They started youth clubs, summer camps and sports meetings. There was a mixture of humanity and expediency in this. Horrocks felt that the Germans would one day be a powerful nation again and it would be as well for them to be imbued with happy memories of the British. Like many in the Allied armies he wondered how long the peace would last and whether next time the Allies would be trying to defend Europe against Russia. His own experience of Russians, not merely after the First World War but for long periods in it when he had shared the same camps, made him feel that, Soviet or not, Russia was an expansionist and restless nation.

But he had reckoned without public opinion in Britain, and more particularly British journalists looking for a story. He had decided that the project was going so well, and not breaking any rules either, that he arranged a party for 150 German children at his headquarters. Unfortunately the party was attended by several journalists who had been sent to find out what Horrocks was doing. Horrocks was used to journalists and got on very well with them, and it did not occur to him that these were a different breed from the wartime variety and were less concerned with benefiting the public than producing a provocative story. The journalists went to work first on the soldiers who were acting as waiters and asked them why they were helping German children when British children could not have similar parties. The next day newspapers in England had headlines such as: 'British General gives Tea Party for German Children.' Horrocks then received a shoal of abusive letters. These he could brush aside but worse was the fact that he was ordered to cease these experiments in social service. He felt the restriction was a mistake in every way and that it transformed the British Army of the Rhine into an army of occupation instead of a forgiving conqueror helping to put a defeated enemy back on its feet.

Not least of his headaches was having to find an occupation for the vast number of men under his command, many of whom were impatiently awaiting demobilisation. Further military training was clearly pointless, so instead he organised rehabilitation courses to re-teach old trades or give an insight into new ones. It was enormously successful and was tackled with such enthusiasm that Horrocks felt it argued very well for the re-establishment and growth of peacetime industry in Britain after the war.

Once 30 Corps got into its stride, its efforts knew no bounds. Holiday and recreational centres were set up and were all run at a profit.

More sobering was their encounter with the Russians to whom, under the post-war settlements, they had to hand over German territory. The transfer involved numerous conferences which went on at boring and interminable length. Horrocks, rapidly regaining his fluency in Russian, needed no interpreter; he was able to make his own decisions. The Russians, in contrast, worked laboriously through interpreters and also had to refer all decisions to their commander-in-chief in Berlin before agreeing anything.

Horrocks, although well aware of Russian unpredictability, had liked many of the Russians he had encountered between 1914 and 1920. But the ones he met now seemed different. He felt that they had been so heavily indoctrinated that they were suspicious of everyone and everything. The fact that Horrocks spoke Russian did not make him a fellow being but an object of deep suspicion. They had no conversation, only stock responses. He remembered the dour Russian general he had met in Tunisia; these staff officers seemed even worse. He noted that at the conferences military generals had no importance. The men with the real power wore no special uniform but their authority was ominously clear from the cautious glances the others occasionally directed toward them. The army had gone a long way from the shambling soldiers he had seen in 1919 and 1920, both militarily and politically. There was no doubt that it was a formidable fighting organisation; it was equally clear that it had become something else too. Ideas of equality had been jettisoned; the organisation of society had been changed but was more rigid now than in the days of the Czars, he felt.

These weeks gave Horrocks much time and reason for pondering on the post-war world. When he saw the Russian Army at close quarters he was impressed by their vast resources of men, all hard and competent, but lacking sophisticated weapons. The question which came to mind was how the German army could have been beaten by such an ill-equipped army. A German who had served on the eastern front gave him the answer. The Russian army was made up of peasants who lived on the steppes in conditions of unvarying harshness and isolation. They were accustomed from childhood to trap and hunt, to live in the open, to expect nothing which they had not obtained by their personal efforts. Army life must have seemed almost luxurious to many of them.

Even so, this view seemed to disregard the fact that those armies had been supplied with vast quantities of war materials by their allies. They had not won the war with peasant armies, but with formidable tanks and aircraft. Much of their equipment had been of Russian design and manufacture, but a greater amount had come from outside. Tough, peasant-type soldiers make excellent fighting armies, as the Japanese had also shown in the war, but eventually the winning cards are held by the men who have a preponderance of machines and metal. The Russians were well aware of their deficiencies in 1945 and forthwith set about remedying them.

But for Horrocks the sight of the Russians reinforced his own view that whatever else happens in a war one ultimately needs infantrymen to occupy the ground. You may bomb and shell a town, besiege it and burn it, but eventually a soldier has to claw his way into the middle and stand up. Such a task can only be achieved by a hard, fit, well-trained man. Horrocks suspected that Western armies were becoming too soft, too fond of their comforts, needing too much support. He himself knew what discomfort and hardship were; he had learned to be tough and enduring and showed these qualities often in battle. As his time in Germany came to an end he gave much thought to the lessons of the past and the requirements of the future.

The Russians of 1945 had come as an unwelcome shock to Horrocks. 'I had always liked the Russians I had met in their country in 1919-20,' he said. 'These men were quite different. They were so suspicious that they hardly dared open their mouths. They were particularly suspicious of me when they found I spoke Russian. The young men were the most frightening because, as a result of the intensive indoctrination to which they had been subjected almost from birth, their brains worked quite differently from any with which I had previously come into contact. They talked in clichés and it was impossible to discuss anything with them at all.'

He enquired whether his old friends, the gipsies, of whose songs and gaiety around the camp fires he had happy memories, still flourished. 'No,' he was told. 'They were bad for the morale of the Russian people.'

Within that year Churchill made a speech at Fulton, Missouri, in which he said: 'From Stettin on the Baltic to Trieste on the Adriatic an Iron Curtain has descended across the continent. Whatever conclusion may be drawn from these facts, and facts they are, this is certainly not the liberated Europe we fought for. Nor is it one which contains the essentials of permanent peace. From what I have seen of our Russian friends and allies during the war, I am convinced that there is nothing they admire so much as strength, and there is nothing for which they have less respect than weakness, especially military weakness.'

Horrocks, with more first-hand knowledge of the Russians than Churchill ever had, endorsed that.

Chapter 12

Home Station

Lieutenant-General (now Sir) Brian Horrocks' next posting was to Western Command. At that time the regional organisation of military districts of Britain was different from that of today and comprised only five commands. These varied considerably in importance; obviously districts which included well-used areas such as Catterick or Aldershot were more prestigious than Eastern or Western Commands. However, at the time Horrocks took up his new appointment National Service had made considerable difference to training requirements; Western Command, which was based on Chester, contained Eaton Hall which was a principal Officer Cadet Training Unit whose products thought they were always as good, and probably better than, those of Sandhurst, a sentiment secretly endorsed by their staff. Western Command extended from Scotland to Wales, from the Isle of Man and Liverpool and Manchester to Birmingham.

Horrocks, fresh from his appointment as corps commander in an army of occupation, found the change to a rigidly peacetime régime somewhat stultifying. A moment of truth was encountered early on. Neither he nor Lady Horrocks liked the look of the official residence of the District Commander. At that particular time the secretary of the Duke of Westminster, on whose estate Eaton Hall lay, was vacating an extremely pleasant house. Horrocks thereupon decided to move in. Having done so he made various arrangements for improvements and proceeded to make the house very comfortable.

However, in due course it was realised by the War Office that the General Officer Commanding Western District, Lt-General Sir Brian Horrocks, had moved his official residence without consultation or permission and had made various alterations subsequently. This was clearly a very serious offence. There was only one man senior enough to give the official reprimand and that man was Montgomery. Horrocks was duly sent for and Montgomery proceeded to give him the strongest dressing-down Horrocks had ever experienced. Not since his Sandhurst days had Horrocks been made to feel so small. Finally Montgomery said: 'Any more of this sort of thing from you and you're out of the Army. Finished. That's all.'

Horrocks, somewhat stunned by the occasion, turned to open the door. 'Yes,' continued Montgomery. 'Just remember that. Of course it's just what *I* would have done myself in your place.'

The story came from General Sir Frank Simpson, who was Vice Chief of the Imperial General Staff at the time, and Deputy to Montgomery, but it had been told to him by Horrocks himself who enjoyed recounting it. Another favourite story of Horrocks at this time, according to General Simpson, was of two Tibetans who had been found serving in the German Army, and been captured by British forces in Germany. The story was that one day Horrocks was visiting one of the camps where captured German prisoners of war were interned. One of his field security officers came up and pointed out two men apart from the rest and said to Horrocks: 'Sir, I think those two chaps aren't Germans at all, but Tibetans. I once worked in Tibet and I believe they are talking in a Tibetan dialect. May I go and talk to them?' Horrocks immediately agreed and the officer went up to the Tibetans and addressed them. They turned to him in astonishment and joy and began speaking rapidly in Tibetan. He was the first person they had met for many months who had been able to speak their language.

The story which then emerged was that the two men lived in northern Tibet. One day they had gone for a walk together in the hills but to their surprise had suddenly been surrounded by men in grey-green uniforms who had taken them away. They were then conveyed by truck and train to a camp where they were given rifles and shown how to fire them. Nobody could speak their language and they could not understand a word of what was said around them: all communication was conducted by signs. After this simple training they were put in more trucks and finally made to walk. Eventually they came to a place where some very nasty noises were being made, bangs and 'wheeshes'. They lay down and then some men in field grey came along, picked them up and took them away. Then the whole performance began again. They were given different kinds of rifles, taught to shoot them, then they were taken off to another place where more loud noises were being made. Here they were surrounded by some men wearing khaki uniforms. Now they were here. Could they please be told what all this was about?

Western Command provided another challenge which suited Horrocks. This was to formulate a practical and interesting training plan for national servicemen, few of whom were willingly embarking on this interruption to their normal routines.

Knowing they would have pre-conceived ideas of what the army was like, i.e. bellowing sergeant-majors and endless drill, he arranged for them to go to the Welsh mountains immediately after arrival and there to practise firing automatics (with blanks). This might seem to some critics like putting the cart before the horse, but it was received with surprise and enthusiasm. Subsequently Horrocks wrote: 'In training I am a great believer in running before you can walk because by finding out how difficult it is to run men take a greater interest in the problem of learning to walk. All training must be done through the brain; the bored man absorbs nothing.'

On this particular exercise there was little time to get bored for as darkness fell the recruits were told that some prisoners had escaped from a nearby gaol and gone into the mountains; it was the job of the recruits to round them up. They were told to choose their own leaders and it was interesting to see whom they chose. They were up all night. The next day they were given their food but told to cook it themselves. Then they marched ten miles back to barracks, immensely pleased with themselves. And Horrocks took care to see that they did not then fall back into a boring routine.

This type of exercise was the forerunner of many later forms of army training, from gruelling endurance tests over the Brecon Beacons to comparatively light escape or evasion exercises. It led to what was known as 'Adventurous Training', often taking place overseas, in which young soldiers were encouraged to embark on expeditions which required courage, initiative, and self-reliance. Sometimes exercises became a little too fanciful, as the cadets were required to travel from Edinburgh to Exeter without spending money, or to obtain signatures or garments from theatrical celebrities, but the underlying idea of developing initiative was good. 'All too much army training,' asserted Horrocks, 'is dull beyond measure.'

He was also embroiled in the 'bedside lamps' furore. Montgomery had decided that the old, austere barrack accommodation should be drastically modernised and when not actually on an exercise the soldier should enjoy some of the comforts he might expect at home; some privacy and a bedside lamp were among the items he listed. Britain at that time was full of camps of decaying Nissen huts, many of which had been hastily built in wartime and seemed to have begun deteriorating rapidly the moment they were erected. Some of the married quarters – of which there are still a few dilapidated unused remnants in Aldershot to this day – were a positive disincentive to anyone wishing to sign for a further period once his National Service was completed. Housing was short everywhere. Temporary accommodation was not intended to last but did. It is an interesting reflection on the building techniques of twenty years later that the wartime expediency hutments have often remained habitable longer than some of the rehousing miracles of the sixties.

Horrocks tried the 'correct channels' at first but as the months passed and there was no sign of action being taken to improve accommodation in his area he decided to launch what he called 'my own offensive'. This, like all unorthodox initiative at the time, produced two results. It obtained the necessary materials without great difficulty and was greeted with howls of rage by incensed bureaucrats. Horrocks, aided by an extremely able administrator, Major-General Holland, had produced many improvements before he was stopped. One of his more successful ventures was to use German prisoners of war for rebuilding and modernising accommodation. Informed that this would enrage the local trade unionists, he invited them to lunch and asked for their views. They advised him to go ahead but not to tell anyone else about it. But eventually pressure from the War Office put a stop to this too.

A few years later, many of the unoccupied camps were used by 'squatters'. Squatters in those days were ordinary people who were driven to desperation waiting for accommodation to replace the bombed or commandeered buildings in which they might otherwise have made homes. Nevertheless the Army was extremely hostile towards these users of empty derelict camps, overlooking the fact that many of the 'squatters' were men who had served with distinction in the armed forces a few years earlier.

Among the frustrations of the time, which included every type of rationing, petrol was severely restricted. As an Army Commander, Horrocks did not need to rely on the meagre civilian rations but nevertheless felt he should set a good example. He therefore obtained bicycles for himself and Lady Horrocks (who still rides hers). Their first outing was rather less than a success for he soon had a puncture and had to send for his official car to get himself home. Lady Horrocks followed on her bicycle.

Horrocks was a satisfied man, but life was not all roses. The sickness which he had fought against for years, the result of a piece of metal which had passed through the length of his body, was now giving him increasing trouble and, although he did not yet suspect it, there would be more operations in the future. Ill-health marred many occasions which he would otherwise have enjoyed. Among his many visitors was Emanuel Shinwell (ex-boxer, ex-conscientious objector, and now Secretary of State for War), and Montgomery himself. He noted with pleasure an occasion when Montgomery gave him a lecture on packing, complete with a demonstration. He showed him how it could be done with ease and simplicity and complete efficiency. The Horrockses watched, were impressed, and the Field Marshal then departed. An hour later Montgomery's ADC rushed back to say that unfortunately the Field Marshal had left all his shirts behind.

After one particularly severe bout of illness, Horrocks went into the Manchester Infirmary for another operation – his seventh. On this occasion the surgeon found a piece of the khaki drill shirt Horrocks had been wearing at Bizerta when the bullet hit him; it was buried deep in his intestines.

The operation was not the end of his troubles. He was far from fit when he was appointed GOC-in-C of the British Army of the Rhine, and in Germany matters came to a head quickly. The succession of fevers had debilitated him more than he had realised, and now his concentration was waning. For a man who had never spared himself and whose whole performance depended on a vigorous, demonstrative approach, there could be no half-measures. When he found himself unable to focus his mind on the material presented to him, he knew that there could be only one decision. He consulted his doctor, knowing well what the answer would be. The doctor confirmed his forebodings: in his state of health he would not be able to continue on active service. He might recover for a time but then he would relapse.

It was not quite the end of his military career, for the Army as a whole, and the Millbank Hospital in particular, made a great effort to get him fit again. He was given a year's leave before facing a Medical Board. But it was, as he suspected, hopeless. The Board pronounced him unfit for further military service and he was invalided out. It was 1949.

Chapter 13

A New Career

When the final blow fell Horrocks regarded it philosophically. He had had thirty-five busy years, and enjoyed the sort of soldiering he liked. Had he been able to stay on he would have had a very different life from anything he had experienced previously. He would, some people thought, have become Chief of the General Staff and eventually a Field Marshal; he thought himself totally unsuited for any higher rank or administrative post. He was a soldier's general, not a political or administrative animal. Some people are happily able to combine the two, but Horrocks was not one of them. On the whole he had no regrets: he was fairly well, he and Lady Horrocks had a little cottage at Compton, near Winchester (the one he had flown over when he took up his appointment to command 30 Corps in France), and he looked forward to seeing more of his family, to fishing and golf and to exploring the Hampshire countryside. He was, in fact, setting off in their ancient Hillman to do the last when the postman came through the gate. He had a letter which looked like all the other bulky, but no longer important, letters Horrocks had so often received. He pushed it into the tray by the steering wheel and forgot it. That evening, Lady Horrocks said, 'Was there anything important in that letter you received this morning?' 'Good Heavens,' said Horrocks. 'I'd completely forgotten it.' He went out and retrieved it. On the envelope were the words 'From the office of the Lord Chamberlain at St James's Palace.' Inside it said:

'You are offered the appointment of Gentleman Usher of the Black Rod in the House of Lords.'

He turned it over in astonishment. He had never heard of Black Rod, nor any other Parliamentary ceremonial or administrative post. But it had a nice romantic ring to it, and even after a fortnight retirement in a small cottage was beginning to seem a little dull. Whatever it was, being Black Rod might offer an interesting change of scene. He accepted.

The history and duties of the appointment of Black Rod are set out very clearly in a bright little publication of Her Majesty's Stationery Office. It is entitled *Black Rod* and costs 60p. Black Rod is described therein as an officer of the Order of the Garter and of the

House of Lords. As the first he takes part in the Garter ceremonies which are held annually at Windsor, and as the second he is required to supervise the administration of the House of Lords and control the admission of visitors.

The first known holder of the appointment appeared in 1261 when one William Whitehorse was granted 12 pence a day for life for bearing the rod in procession on feast days. The processions were of Knights of the Garter, an order founded by Edward III in 1348, and consisting of himself and twenty-five Knights of distinction. The patron saint of the Order was St George, and on 23 April – which is St George's Day – the Order met at Windsor, attended service in the chapel, held discussions, and diverted themselves with feasting. St George's Chapel Windsor is to this day hung with the banners of the present Knights of the Garter. In the early days the Knights were led by an Usher, or doorkeeper, who took them from one point to another, and refused admittance to anyone else when they were engaged in any form of ceremony. The symbol of his authority was a black rod. The holder of the office once used to retain his black rod after departing, but this no longer happens and the present rod dates from 1883. It is three and a half feet long and made of ebony. At the top is a gold lion holding a shield with a crown on it. On this appear the initials E VII R; at the bottom end is a 1904 gold sovereign, so presumably these additions were made in that year in the reign of Edward VII. Black Rod is appropriately dressed in black court dress and carries a sword in a black scabbard. In Parliament the rod is only carried on ceremonial occasions but at Windsor, for the Garter ceremonies, the bearer wears the scarlet mantle of the Order with the Garter badge, a chain of office and a black velvet cap, and carries the rod at all times.

The parliamentary duties seem to have been added to the Garter duties at a later date, probably in early Tudor times. Black Rods of that period seemed to have little work to do and the HMSO booklet records that Sir William Compton, Black Rod in the reign of Henry VIII, managed to combine his duties with fighting in the French campaign and Scottish wars. In the nineteenth century the post became very attractive financially, mainly from the sale of various offices. However, in 1875 Black Rod lost many of his perquisites and was merely rewarded with a straight salary of £2,000 a year. In 1895 that salary was reduced by half; he also lost his official residence. However, £1,000 in 1895 was a not inconsiderable sum, for it was worth perhaps twenty times as much to-day.

In the House of Lords Black Rod has various duties, one of which is the maintenance of order; it is not a responsibility which occasions him much trouble. But he is required to be present when the Lords are sitting, unless the Yeoman Usher relieves him. When there is a division it is Black Rod who sounds the divers bells to summon Lords who are not in the Chamber. He also leads various processions, such as at the introduction of new peers.

His best known ceremonial appearance is to summon the Commons to attend the Queen's Speech at the beginning of each session of Parliament, and on certain other occasions too when the Queen is present. Then Black Rod is told by the Lord Chamberlain to summon the Commons. He then walks to the Commons, preceded by the Superintendent of Customs and a Lords doorkeeper. As he reaches the Members' Lobby, doorkeepers close the western half of the door of the Commons Chamber and prepare the eastern half ready for the Sergeant-at-Arms to slam it in Black Rod's face. Just before Black Rod reaches it, it is slammed shut. He then knocks three times on the door. The Sergeant-at-Arms looks through a grille and then opens the door. Black Rod is announced, advances to the Table and summons the Commons. Then he returns to the Lords with the Commons following.

This ceremony is preserved in order to demonstrate the independence of the Commons from the sovereign, but nobody knows exactly how and when it originated; it was probably 1641. The slamming of the door is an interesting ritual but nothing more, for the Commons does not have a statutory power to refuse admission to Black Rod. When Horrocks first performed the ceremony in 1949 there was a large number of fairly boisterous Labour members in the Commons. As soon as he appeared he was greeted with shouts of 'Go away. Come again to-morrow!' He was temporarily nonplussed, wondering if there had been some mistake, but soon realised what it was – a joke at the expense of the new appointee. Horrocks made an excellent holder of the office, for he had presence, great charm, and experience of ceremonial. In his own account of the appointment he wrote that the term Gentleman Usher of the Black Rod was originally Gentleman Husher. The title, he said, derived from early meetings of the Garter or Parliament when members often became noisy and over-excited. Hence he was the Husher. Horrocks cannot have believed this but the story amused him. (Usher, in fact, comes in a roundabout way from the Latin *ostiarius*, which became *usciere* in Italian and *huissier* in medieval French. Huissier was a well-known word in medieval Britain.)

Although every ceremony was well rehearsed, mistakes did sometimes occur. He recalls one which took place in the Throne Room of Windsor Castle, before King George VI, when three new Knights were to be appointed to the Order of the Garter. The ceremony opened with the command: 'Garter and Black Rod, summon the

Knights.' Horrocks bowed, turned round, walked to the door and rapped on it with his rod. All went well, the door opened, he turned round and marched back, but noticed that the King was looking extremely disturbed. As Horrocks approached, he whispered somewhat crossly, 'Where are the Knights? Bring in the Knights.' Horrocks, appalled, shot a glance over his shoulder and saw that the only Knight behind him was the King of Denmark. Apparently the latter had led the procession and some enthusiast had closed the door in the face of the other two Knights. It was an awkward moment. Horrocks decided to preserve everyone's dignity so, hastily whispering to his companion, the Garter King of Arms, what he intended to do, he bowed once more to George VI, turned round and went through the whole ceremony again. This time the Knights were admitted. All the onlookers imagined that this was correct procedure, and that a member of a royal house should come in alone, but Horrocks, catching the eye of the King, was well aware that he was extremely angry at this unrehearsed piece of ritual.

Horrocks had little reason to demonstrate his authority during the fourteen years he held the office. He had nineteen doorkeepers to assist him and, as they were all either retired petty officers from the Navy or warrant officers from the other two services, the routine was usually untroubled. In cases of serious interruption, whether by members themselves or visitors, Black Rod has to remove the offender. A similar function is exercised by the Sergeant-at-Arms in the House of Commons and there have been occasions when an elderly, frail holder of this office has had to escort out a hulking member half his age. Horrocks' greatest embarrassment was caused by the actress Vivien Leigh who had asked him for a seat so that she could view proceedings. She suddenly rose to her feet and delivered an impassioned plea for the salvation of the St James's Theatre which was scheduled to be demolished. Unfortunately for her, no one took the slightest notice, except Black Rod himself. He moved towards her, said quite firmly: 'Now you will have to go,' and gently took her arm and led her out of the Chamber.

Black Rod sits in a box on the west side of the House, just below the bar (which is a line drawn to include the inside from the outside of the House). Anyone summoned to appear before the Commons or Lords stands at this bar. This enables the House to administer a reprimand to anyone who has offended it; certain journalists have had the experience which tends to intimidate the most blasé.

There was, of course, much standing about and waiting in the exercise of this post but Horrocks' health seemed to be much better and, although he found the long hours tiring and often boring, he had no health problems. He was not interested in politics, so the content of the debates did not greatly engross him. On many days his time would be taken up with endless requests for seats. One piece of wisdom he had remembered from his Sandhurst days was never to trust insider's tips on horses. As many of the lords owned racehorses, he used to receive many tips: eventually he decided that the worst of all tips come from owners, who can so easily misjudge and therefore overrate their horses' chances. Previously, although not in the least snobbish, he had tended to be impressed by high rank and title. As Black Rod he was only too well aware that the noblest and most impressive, whether archbishops, dukes, or marquesses, were very much ordinary human beings. Most of the Lords debates are attended by a small number of members only but occasionally, when a bill comes forward which affects the rights of the landed aristocracy, the House is suddenly crammed with what are known as 'backwoods peers'. Horrocks saw a lot of these, for the beginning of his term of office coincided with the Labour Government of 1945-1951, and the many bills concerning nationalisation. Horrocks was well aware that most of the lords disagreed with the Labour Government measures and were strongly inclined to oppose them. To have done so would have been folly, for the Commons was an elected body and the Lords was largely hereditary. Any large-scale opposition to the will of the Commons would have produced a constitutional crisis which could have culminated in the House of Lords losing its remaining powers.

Most of the time he spent in his box in the Lords would have been boring by anyone's standards. Even the most versatile politician becomes wearied by some of the routine legislation and either does not attend debates, or finds good reason to leave the Chamber for lengthy periods. Horrocks could not do this. Neither could he sit and read a book. His job was to look busy and interested.

His solution was to pass the time doing football pools. Anyone glancing in the direction of Black Rod's box would observe him occasionally looking up and glancing around the Chamber, then looking down and perhaps making a note on a piece of paper. In fact, he was not making notes at all, he was deciding whether Tottenham Hotspur might win away or whether Manchester United would draw at Leeds. An interesting function of football pools is that they give the filler-in of coupons a scholarly, almost mystical air. When the lords were discussing the regulations of the white fish industry, Horrocks would be exuding an air of quiet benevolent interest. Horrocks had arranged for all the leading companies to send him their coupons to the House of Lords. When Parliament was in session he arranged these in various despatch boxes and dealt with them accordingly. His life as Black Rod and the pools punter was kept entirely separate from his ordinary life. He was not secretive about it, but did not make it a topic of conversation either. Before he began he enquired of the Lord Chancellor whether he was not only legally correct but also morally correct in pursuing this pastime. 'Would it,' he enquired, 'be putting too much of a temptation to the company if Black Rod should suddenly win a large sum of money on a football pool? Would the promise implied in the sentence on the form – "Clients wishing to receive no publicity put a cross here" – stand up to the tremendous advertising bonus which would be presented if the eminent figure of Black Rod could be revealed not only as a punter on their pools but also as a winner?' The Lord Chancellor assured him that even if his identity was, inadvertently or purposely, disclosed, this would not be a matter of much consequence.

Horrocks was not content merely with being Black Rod and occupying his mind with football pools forecasts. He also had a yearning for writing. Although he had never claimed to be an intellectual and was never more than a casual reader, he had acquired a liking for clear writing and speech in those long-past days at Uppingham. He had also met many journalists whom he admired for their ability to write clearly, fluently and briskly on almost any subject. As we saw earlier, he had also been an instructor at the Staff College, where the writing of clear, incisive English is given the highest priority. Yet another influence on him was the fact that his father had written cogently on many medical matters, and for many years had been editor of the Royal Army Medical Corps Journal. His father had died during the war when Horrocks was a brigadier. Horrocks said: 'If only he could have lived a little longer till I was a corps commander he would have realised that all his self-sacrifice and unstinting devotion to his most unsatisfactory son had not been in vain.' The last lesson which Horrocks learnt from his father was never to give up. His father had suffered for many years from an intestinal infection which had gradually caused him to abandon all strenuous activities. But, as Horrocks noted, 'he never uttered one word of complaint, and never allowed his physical condition to beat him.' When something had to go he looked for something else to take its place. Horrocks himself, when prevented by ill-health from playing golf (at which he had a handicap of six), cricket and other games, took up sailing which was still within his compass.

Now, in the 1950s, he managed to launch himself on a career of journalism. He began with an article for the now defunct *Daily Despatch*; it was based on a visit he paid to the European battlefields after the war. His professional knowledge and direct, vigorous style soon won him a following among readers. He continued with many more articles, including some for *Picture Post* and also many for the *Sunday Times*. Writing for the latter brought him into contact with a man who became a very close friend and sailing companion, C.D. Hamilton, now Sir Denis Hamilton. Hamilton was over twenty years younger than Horrocks but had had as distinguished a career, though in a different field. He had begun his journalistic life on the *Middlesbrough Evening Gazette* but journalism had been interrupted when he was called up as a Territorial in 1939. He rose to command the 11th Battalion of the Durham Light Infantry and subsequently the 7th Battalion of the Duke of Wellington's Regiment, winning a DSO in 1944. After 1945 he became Editor of the *Sunday Times*. Among many other appointments he became Editor in Chief of Times Newspapers and Chairman of Reuters. He was undoubtedly a great help to Horrocks, who records that once when he was trying to write an article for the *Sunday Times*, Hamilton said: 'Whatever you do, General, don't try to write English.' It was Hamilton who encouraged Horrocks to write his own life story which, according to Hamilton, took much less time and trouble than expected. By the time Horrocks completed it, he had already embarked on another career, as a successful TV presenter and radio broadcaster, as well as being a director of a major industrial company. One might say of Horrocks' career that once one door shut two more opened, but it should be borne in mind that Horrocks himself usually turned the handles of those doors. Nothing – except Black Rod – fell into his lap. Once he had launched himself on a new project, he attracted plenty of good will, but the initial move was his.

This was very clearly shown by his approach to television. In the mid-1950s television was still something of a novelty. Horrocks observed the new medium with interest and decided that he could probably do as well as many of the presenters of programmes. As Sir Huw Wheldon put it, 'He then invented himself as a TV presenter.' His first move was to write to General Sir Ian Jacob, whom he had met during the war. Jacob was at the time Chairman of the BBC and Horrocks wrote him a personal letter, asking for a trial, suggesting he might demonstrate some of the battles in which they had personally fought. The letter was crisp and to the point, though perhaps a little short on diffidence in view of the fact that he had no previous experience in this new and possibly complicated field. Huw Wheldon, a graduate of the London School of Economics, was a leading producer and director in the BBC at the time, and he had also had a distinguished war career. He had originally been commissioned in the Royal Welch Fusiliers but after serving in many theatres and units, including 1st and 6th Airborne Divisions, he had commanded a battalion of the Royal Ulster Rifles. He had been awarded a Military Cross. Obviously Wheldon was the man to look into the Horrocks proposal, for he himself was an experienced producer and writer with a wide military background.

Wheldon, slightly dubious, went down to the House of Lords to see Horrocks. Horrocks met him in his office, and talked for about an hour, vigorously, interestingly, conveying warmth, but not really impressing Wheldon with his potential as a TV presenter. Horrocks spoke with great enthusiasm, rather like an eager schoolboy, but did not seem to Wheldon to have much idea of what might interest or amuse TV viewers, who would be a very different mixture from the former Army audiences. At the end of a sociable but somewhat inconclusive hour, Horrocks suddenly asked Wheldon whether he would be interested in seeing Black Rod's box in the House of Lords. Wheldon was very interested to do this and the occasion produced the first flash of insight that there might be more to Horrocks than an enthusiastic grey-haired general of distinguished appearance but no intellectual depth or originality. The 'flash' came when Horrocks said: 'Good, but first I must get into my romper suit.' The idea that this ancient, stately uniform should be described by the wearer as a romper suit suggested to Wheldon that there might be unconventional traits in Horrocks which could lift his projected talks out of the region of mundane reminiscences.

In the 'box' Wheldon's eye fell on the despatch boxes, one of which Horrocks opened. To Wheldon's astonishment, it was full of football coupons. In another depatch box were postal orders for varying sums. Wheldon felt that this was not the product of an immature schoolboy mind; it was an aspect of sophistication which Wheldon had not suspected in their first hour's conversation. It was, of course, completely out of convention for a retired general in a distinguished ceremonial post to be whiling away his time in this unorthodox but entirely reasonable way. How many other people would have thought of it, Wheldon wondered. Most people would have sat there day after day, infinitely bored and probably showing it.

Wheldon eventually got to know Horrocks very well, for they made about forty programmes together. The programmes used to begin with Horrocks describing the proposed battle to Wheldon. Wheldon would take notes and plan the script outline. Horrocks then spoke into tape recorders, and Wheldon looked for appropriate film. Generally, having seen the available film – of which there was plenty in various archives – he decided only to use it as a supporting element. The main strength in the programmes would be Horrocks talking about the battles. Whenever film was used it affected the programme script, sometimes because it took up time which would otherwise be used for talking, sometimes because it introduced a new aspect which Horrocks then explained. But throughout, the film was subsidiary to Horrocks; it became almost a comment on what he said.

On many occasions Wheldon would collect an audience of perhaps a dozen women; they might be secretaries, producers, young assistants or elderly waitresses, all they needed to be was female. No men were permitted to be present. Horrocks would then address them, using a blackboard. The object of the exercise was not to see whether they were impressed or enchanted with what he said, but whether they completely understood it. When talking on military matters it is all too easy to refer to divisions or companies or AFVs,* and be quite unaware that the listener either does not understand what you are talking about, or, worse still, thinks you are talking of something entirely different because that is the listener's normal concept of the word. Even if they know that a division is an army unit, many might not know whether it comprises ten people or ten thousand. Horrocks and Wheldon then asked questions of the audience to find out exactly how much they had understood. Then he and Wheldon marked the script to take in any necessary points. Both Wheldon and Horrocks seemed clear that both script and presenter had to be in complete harmony. Horrocks then learnt the script word-perfect, and timed his talk to the second. Wheldon recalls that he usually ran through the entire programme as many as three, even on occasion four, times, with separate cameras on the day of presentation (which was always live) without there ever being more than a ten-second variation in timing. And the extraordinary part of it was that it was all – speech, timing, gestures, pauses – from memory. Wheldon felt that this achievement – for achievement it undoubtedly was – showed a thoroughly professional attitude. If Horrocks was going to do something, he was going to do it right. In spite of an air of debonair nonchalance he worked very hard to get everything right. Even when teleprompters were pressed upon him in later productions he continued to work without them. Wheldon was not an enthusiast for teleprompters, considering that they make people look slightly glazed and not thinking about what they are saying. He recalls that in a twenty-nine-minute script not one line would go out of place, not a single word. Horrocks never became at all neurotic about his perfectionism; it was just what he had to do to perform the job properly and he did it.

Wheldon felt that Horrocks had an ability for lateral thinking. This enabled him to stand aside and see his own faults as they might

---

* Armoured Fighting Vehicles.

appear to others. Wheldon used to find occasionally that clichés or slight distortions of the truth would sometimes creep in, e.g. 'We all felt pretty cheerful about our prospects in this battle.' Wheldon would say, 'That does not sound very true,' and Horrocks would say, 'Of course, you're right. I make that sort of mistake sometimes but when it's pointed out to me I understand the logic of the correction immediately.'

Army officers are used to having their mistakes pointed out to them. Whatever their rank there is always someone above them who will put them right. Even if they rise to the highest possible rank they are still under the shadow of correction, for then it is the politician or the journalist who will mercilessly expose any errors. On the way up Army officers become very skilled at public relations. This is not so much the external form of public relations but the variety for internal consumption. In every well-organised headquarters there is a list of all the special attributes of the members of that unit. On each officer and soldier there are details of his interests and problems. Captain Smith may be a bayonet fencer of international class but his wife, bored with his frequent and long absences, may be giving him a little trouble. Brown, a very conscientious company commander, has a promising daughter but a rather tiresome son who has twice run away from his boarding school. When going round the unit the senior officer will have been told about these problems, and even been informed of any nicknames his officers are known by. It is thought that an officer will appreciate being addressed by his nickname; it makes the meeting seem informal. Experienced officers often carry a clipboard with photographs discreetly concealed; this enables them to recognise people whom they may have forgotten but who will be very pleased to be recognised, complete with personal information as outlined above. Horrocks was an early exponent of this art, which he had probably learnt from Montgomery. It may seem a somewhat artificial process but it is essentially worthwhile; it facilitates conversation, produces goodwill, and enables a commander to know the men serving under him. Many of those concerned know that it is a stage performance but it is appreciated none the less. The Army has an admiration for long memories. Warrant officers and non-commissioned officers often have a remarkable facility for recalling the army numbers of people who pass through their hands. In Welsh or Irish regiments it may be the custom to address a soldier as Jones 329 (the last three letters of his eight figure army number) or O'Reilly 216.

When Horrocks had used up the battles in which he had been engaged personally, he moved on to battles in other theatres or other periods of history. This was by no means as easy, but was necessary as he was now a very popular television figure. The new subjects required even more practice than the former ones and he learnt his lines and rehearsed them meticulously. He would walk in London, often in St James's Park, saying the words to himself. However he was aware that an elderly man of distinguished appearance, walking about apparently muttering to himself, might well seem somewhat ludicrous. He therefore took his dog, a boxer named Maxie, with him as often as possible and talked to it. There is, of course, nothing unusual about a man delivering a monologue to his dog in a low voice. If his own dog was for some reason not available he used to borrow a dog from a regimental sergeant-major at the House of Lords. In this way he produced a perfect word-for-word script. He never, never improvised, and some people who knew about his methods tended to be a little scornful. Wheldon was not among them; he respected Horrocks' ability to rehearse to perfection and then perform without deviating a fraction.

Horrocks never appeared nervous before, nor especially relieved after, his programmes. He took an occasional drink, but not in order to brace himself up, nor to celebrate a successful performance. He enjoyed wine, although with advancing years he gave up alcohol altogether. He smoked but not excessively; after he had given it up in old age he found the smell of tobacco nauseating.

In his broadcasts Horrocks gave a clear exposition of the subject he was concerned with but he never ventured into the realms of military philosophy or abstract truth. He was never concerned to promote any cause. Later, when he did lend his name to certain causes his value lay in his reputation, not in an ability to make impassioned pleas. His performances were always warm-blooded; he never made cool clinical analyses.

Wheldon was interested to observe that when Montgomery and Horrocks were together, Montgomery tended to be rather critical and patronising. Horrocks was always polite, almost deferential when Montgomery would say 'I didn't think much of that' or 'I think you over-emphasised the importance of....' Montgomery seemed perhaps a little jealous of Horrocks' ability in this immensely important new medium. When questioned about his feelings towards Montgomery, Horrocks would say, 'I wouldn't choose him for a close friend or neighbour, but if I had to go to war again I'd rather go with Monty than with anyone else.' Horrocks' recollection of Montgomery's wartime ability, his strength, his iron determination, and the fact that he could ponder on a dozen complicated problems at once, was a constant reminder to him that Montgomery was the better soldier. It was therefore impossible for Montgomery to offend Horrocks. Horrocks, whatever he did, was conscious not only of his much inferior rank but even more of his lesser intelligence. The fact that he had been an international pentathlete, the hero of a dozen escapades in Germany, had survived experiences in Russia which might have finished off Montgomery, never came to the forefront of his mind. He was simply convinced by one fact: Montgomery was a field marshal and he himself was a lieutenant-general. The same deference to rank was observable when he was in the presence of other senior military officers, Eisenhower, Alexander, and Slim. *They* may have seen him as an equal and in fact, as he was more of an all-rounder, as a superior, but he never felt that way himself.

Equally, Horrocks acknowledged the expert. He realised he had everything to learn about television, about journalism, and about business, and he set about doing so humbly and without any ideas that he knew better than his teachers on account of his experience in other fields.

A very large contribution to the success of the programmes was made by the late Therese Denny. Therese Denny was an Australian who had come over to Britain and become assistant to Chester Wilmot, the author of *The Struggle for Europe*. After Chester Wilmot had been killed in an aeroplane crash, Therese Denny joined the BBC as a research assistant. Subsequently she became research assistant to Huw Wheldon. Her contribution was invaluable, for she undertook the research for the battles in which Horrocks had not taken part personally. Eventually she became the producer for some of the later programmes. Therese Denny would never have described herself as a great beauty, but Horrocks always behaved to her as if she was. He realised he owed her a debt for helping him to success and even after the programmes ended he always remained very kind and courteous to her. What he perhaps recognised more clearly than anyone was that Therese Denny had summed him up and knew how to make him make the best of himself.

The BBC employed Horrocks to make various sound broadcasts, such as when he gave a talk to Australia on the office of Black Rod. He was much in demand to say a few words – or more – on certain special occasions, dedications in churches or chapels and unveiling of memorials in military cemeteries in Britain and overseas. He was now in his sixties but not lacking in energy and ambition in spite of his legacy of wounds and illness. He was fascinated by the stresses, rivalries and demands of television and broadcasting. He was soon aware of the ferocious rivalries which existed not merely between BBC and ITV, but also within the television units themselves, and between sound and vision. He noted with admiration the precision, professionalism and unsparing effort which went into television production. There, the only standard was perfection, no matter how long that took. The contents of many of the programmes (though not his) might be poor, but the production was beyond criticism. He did not ponder on whether much of the time and talent might be wasted.

In spite of his nonchalant manner he found both broadcasting and television intimidating. He felt, as many do, very conscious of his isolation when presenting a programme. In other jobs he always had staff or assistants at his elbow. They were here too, but he could not turn to them. He was isolated, alone, with cameras watching every move, every gesture.

But he enjoyed it. He enjoyed the bustle and immediacy of the programmes, he enjoyed being with people many years younger than he was and being treated by them as a contemporary. And he enjoyed the fame. He was shocked, appalled, and delighted when his face appeared on the cover of the *Radio Times*. Soon, however, his fame became an embarrassment. Often when walking along the street he would be stopped by complete strangers who would tell him how much they had enjoyed his programmes, which ones they liked best and so on. He was also rung up by admirers, a process that drove him to becoming ex-directory. He has remained ex-directory to the present day, and in later years this has probably robbed him of contacts with former friends. Equally, neither his club nor the BBC would disclose his private address, though letters sent to him were forwarded. He saw himself partly as a TV star and partly as a retired general who had strayed into an unfamiliar and hazardous world. His friends were pleased to see him looking so well on his programmes, not realising that some of the colour in his cheeks came from the make-up department.

His 'fan-mail' varied considerably. The best letters came from his former soldiers or their wives, but he also had letters from people who tried to enlist him in various causes, from others who hated everything he represented; some which were abusive for no apparent reason. All this was going on when he was also discharging the duties of Black Rod with dignity and efficiency and also making a small profit on the football pools.

But after fourteen years, the routine of Black Rod began to pall. He had become bored with the elaborate ceremonial: previously he had enjoyed that ceremonial but disliked the waiting, now he had become wearied by the ritual duties which he had performed so often. He hesitated to resign because that would simply mean inactive retirement and he felt that after all his recent excitements humdrum routine would be too dull. The television programmes were ending: it was felt that they had run their course and he was now being over-exposed. But he was still writing for the *Sunday Times*, which provided both interest and financial reward.

At that moment, his flair for falling on his feet showed itself again, and he was asked if he would like to become a director of Bovis, the building contractors. Some time earlier he had met Neville Vincent, a barrister who was a director of Bovis. Vincent's brother, Harry Vincent, was the Chairman of the Group, and together they had wondered whether Horrocks might like to join the Board.

When offered the post Horrocks did not accept immediately. As he had had no experience of building and property management, he wondered whether he would be a fish out of water. He was aware that other distinguished military and naval figures had joined Boards of large companies but had done little except add prestige by allowing their names to be used on the list of directors. He was also aware that since 1945 there had been numerous property and construction companies whose activities had been both illegal and immoral. He knew that Bovis was not one of them but he wished to learn more about this new world before he took the plunge. With the help of an architect and a quantity surveyor he arranged a little course for himself on how building was organised. He was pleased to learn that Bovis enjoyed a high reputation. With his mind at rest, he accepted the offer, having first resigned his appointment as Black Rod.

There is much in common between the Army and the building trade. Both depend on middle managers, who in the Army are warrant officers and non-commissioned officers, and in the building trade foremen and site agents. Both provide a solid body of common sense based on experience; the 'officers' are soon judged as to whether they know their job, and whether their technical qualifications are at their finger tips. The fact that practically every man in the company had seen or heard of Horrocks through his television, radio, or wartime activities, proved a considerable advantage. Bovis, in fact, was very much a family business which had grown big. However, in growing it had never lost the original personality of the small firm. In this way it was like the old-fashioned firms which had been created by a man of drive and vision and which still retained a family feeling after he had retired. What happens when the founder dies, and his heirs cannot replace him or are not interested, is all too well known. Someone has to be the boss, and if power is not retained by management, it can fall into groups with sectional interests. In Bovis Horrocks found an agreeable sense of loyalty to employers. This was all the easier because the directors spent much time on the sites and learned to know the men and be known by them.

Bovis was expanding rapidly when Horrocks joined and he found this link with thrusting commerce extremely stimulating. At first he proceeded cautiously, well aware that ex-generals who appear on the boards of public companies tend to attract cynical comment. Horrocks realised that some people would dislike him for being what he was, or be jealous of his luck; but he reflected that it was by no means the first time he had been unpopular, and if that had to be lived down he would do it. He did not dispel all the criticism, but the fact of walking over the sites regularly made him a familiar figure. Many of those he chatted to had served under him in the war.

There was a close connection between Bovis and Marks and Spencer. Bovis had either built or altered almost every Marks and Spencer shop in the country. Marks and Spencer was also a revelation to Horrocks. From his Army background he had imagined that welfare was merely a token word in industry, particularly in the retail trades. In many areas it *is* no more than that. But Marks and Spencer knew that happy and regular customers can only be attracted if contented and motivated staff can be retained to serve them. The facilities for staff in Marks and Spencer would have done credit to a first-class hotel. When Bovis worked on Marks and Spencer buildings the same facilities were made available for Bovis employees. Bovis were impressed and decided to provide equally satisfactory facilities for their own employees on the sites. This was a revolutionary concept, for building contractors, for the most part, did not trouble themselves much with welfare, understandably since most of their labour was transient. There was also a feeling that too much molly-coddling would result in slackness and time-wasting. However, Bovis decided that they would install facilities which would enable their employees to leave the site clean and dry. The decision turned out to be sound policy, for they attracted employees when employees were in great demand and not easy to recruit.

Now that Horrocks was a nationally-known public figure, he found himself in constant demand from a variety of organisations who felt that in him they had that *rara avis*, a respected public figure with an impeccable record and an astute business sense. Horrocks did not feel that he possessed the latter. However his presence and advice was sought by St Dunstans, the Forces Help Society, the Queen Alexandra Home for Disabled Sailors, Soldiers and Airmen, and many others. He also became President of the Electronic Rentals Association (later the National Television Rental Association). The Association was made up of all the major television rental firms, and was clearly a pressure group, although Horrocks did not appear to realise it. The purpose of the Association was to obtain a favourable attitude to television rental from Members of Parliament or civil servants who might feel that television rental, like hire purchase, needed an eye kept on it. Horrocks was a good front man, for he was eminently respectable and could obtain a hearing for any delegation which he led.

He himself believed firmly in the virtues of rented television sets, but found some MPs sceptical. Eventually, he found that this particular post made too many demands on his time and resigned it in 1973. It is difficult to know whether he was naive or not over television rentals. At the time he was President, sets were less reliable than to-day and hiring could have had advantages over ownership. It is certainly a popular and widespread way of possessing a set. On the other hand a set has to be hired for a minimum period of one year, which costs about one-third of its new price. Subsequently the hirer may make enough payments to buy the set many times over without ever acquiring ownership.

At this time his principal recreation was sailing. He had taken up this hobby at the age of sixty-one and had become quite skilled. They now had a cottage at Emsworth and a house in Caroline Terrace, near Sloane Square. He was enormously busy. But when Denis Hamilton suggested he should write his reminiscences he decided he could find time for that too. A few enquiries were made for possible publishers and among others Collins were interested. He had doubts whether Collins, with so many authors on their list, would push the book hard enough for it to justify the trouble and expense he would be put to in writing it. Perhaps he should go for a smaller publisher who would be inclined to take more trouble over a new author. Collins assured him that all would be well, as indeed it was. This involved him in another wave of publicity for he attended signing sessions and literary luncheons. But it was a self-inflicted injury.

The book was dedicated to Nancy, his wife who had backed him and supported him steadily, though not uncritically, throughout his life. She was, as he freely acknowledged, far more artistic than he could ever be. All their furniture was her inheritance, he used to say. She had been an above-average painter, too, although when her eyesight began to fail had to give that up. Politically, their outlooks were different as well. He was always a traditional, unthinking Tory, she is a Liberal and in later years a sympathizer with the SDP. Although artistic she was also practical; he could drive but she could run a house without help, which she often preferred to do, and could keep the garden and pets well cared for and in order. They both adored their daughter, who shared her mother's temperament in many ways.

The first edition of *A Full Life* concluded with his TV broadcasts. He was under the impression when he wrote it in 1959 that his life really was over, that the future would hold little but quiet potterings round the waters of the south coast, and perhaps a few chats with old friends. He was wrong.

Chapter 14

Sunset

Although continuing with various employments, and greatly enjoying his work for Bovis, Horrocks began to hanker for a quieter, more rural setting. Their house in Caroline Place was very pleasant, and they could spend weekends at Emsworth, but London was noisy, and travelling to get away from it was beginning to be a strain. In all his life, apart from spells in hospital, Horrocks had never relaxed for long, but had gone from one strenuous activity to another. Now, in his late 70s, he was beginning to feel that he must slow down. The choice was between living by the sea or living in the country. If he went to live by the sea he would be cutting himself off from many of the interests which stimulated him. In particular he did not want to resign from Bovis.

The solution was to move to Somerset. Bovis, and their associate company Gilbert Ash, had offices in Bristol and if the Horrockses could find a house they liked which was not too far away, he himself could keep in close touch through the Bristol offices.

Finding a house they liked seemed almost impossible, so they bought a near-derelict farmhouse at Shepton Mallet. This was then converted into the house they wanted. The rebuilding – for that was what it required – was supervised by Lady Horrocks who earned the title of 'the working foreman'. Eventually the interior was brought to such a pitch of perfection that it gained a reputation as being one of the most attractive small houses in the country. Horrocks cheerfully left all this to his wife; he made no claims to creative talent or artistic ability. His only contribution was to buy four Hereford steers to graze in the six acres of paddock. Jokingly he used to refer to himself as the smallest farmer in Somerset. The possession of four white-faced dignified Herefords was an asset in more ways than one. Having a few cattle, almost as pets, was not of course farming, and he did not pretend it was, but it gave him a feeling of fellowship with the local farmers and enabled him to attend farming dinners and functions without feeling a complete outsider.

And, of course, the desire to own some form of animal, bird or fish, is a very strong instinct in human beings. Owning a few cattle, having a productive garden and doing some fly-fishing, creates a happy illusion of being a son of the soil. He was entitled to feel some pride in his stake in the countryside; he had fought long, and endured hardship and wounds in order to reach this little haven. Intensive farming has brought many changes to rural life but here there was something of the old tradition of English farming. Looking around him, Horrocks felt he had a thin tie of kinship with ancient warriors who had eventually put down the sword and begun to raise crops and cattle in the lands they had formerly fought over.

But Horrocks' mental sword was not quite at rest. He was soon signed up to do thirteen television programmes on the subject of 'The Peace Keepers'. These would not be about the wars of the past and their great battles, but about the employment of the British Army in the present day. Unnoticed by him, and by many, the Army had been engaged on what later became known as 'internal security' or counter-revolutionary warfare (CRW). There had been one moderate-sized war in the post-1945 period, in Korea, but most of the Army's time had been taken up with preventing the eruption of large-scale conflict. Malaya had seen the Army for years on end, so had Aden, the Oman, Cyprus, Palestine, and a dozen other places. Horrocks did not have to visit these trouble spots but he did interview many of the people who had served there. Army public relations regarded these programmes benevolently, as it was thought they would be an aid to recruiting, so all the pain was taken out of travelling to various areas for interviews by the fact that the Army provided helicopters for the purpose. (Fortunately for Horrocks Ireland had not then leapt to prominence on TV screens. As he was half-Irish, he would doubtless have been thought too partisan by both sides in the conflict.)

In the event the programmes received less attention than they deserved. The original series contractors had been Television West and Wales. Halfway through the showing, and just when the last programme had been made, TWW lost its contract to Harlech. As Horrocks realised, Harlech were unlikely to enthuse over a series made by the company they had displaced, but they did not drop it entirely: instead they moved it from 6 p.m. to midnight.

He was not quite out of the limelight. First he was approached by commercial firms to speak about their products on television. Financially the offers were very tempting but his conscience told him that the men who had served under him in wartime might have felt disillusioned if they saw their former hero plugging dog food or patent medicines. Having felt the financial pinch for so many years he was reluctant to let slip such an obvious chance of easy money, but he felt that he would not only be destroying the memories of those who had formerly looked up to him; he would be forfeiting his own self-respect too. He refused.

He did, however, make a film for Bovis, in which he explained the group's aims and methods, and he made a last appearance on television in a commercial for Texaco. In the former he knew from his experience with Bovis that what he was saying was the truth; in the second he had no reason to doubt the virtue of Texaco's product but was more particularly influenced by the fact that Texaco were giving regimental badges to everyone buying four gallons of petrol. They also gave a large sum of money to Army charities. It seemed a fitting way to end his television career.

But it was not the end of his public life. In 1966 Leo Cooper, who at that time was with Hamish Hamilton, had conceived the idea of a series of brief regimental histories. He suggested that Horrocks might care to write the introductions and assist in editing the texts. Horrocks agreed that this was a worthwhile and interesting project and welcomed the chance to leave for posterity a record of many regiments which had given great service to Britain in the past but which now no longer existed. His own former regiment was due to disappear in the next round of amalgamations, though he did not know this at the time. He responded with a typical military appreciation. It begins:

Object: This is a military operation so I suppose we must start by getting our object clear. It seems we are trying to attract two different sorts of people: (a) those who will read anything which is written about military matters or regimental history, provided it is served up in a suitable manner – there are not many of these about. I would call them the lunatic fringe and it does not matter what regiments we include, they will read about them anyhow; (b) the second category comprises people who are vitally concerned with a particular regiment, who have served in it, whose relations have been killed in it, who have grown up in close touch with it, and what we want is to find one of these books on the bookshelf of every officer, NCO, man and a good many of their relatives throughout the country. Now this particular category is very much concerned with one individual regiment and at the present moment throughout the country there is a feeling of acute nostalgia about amalgamation and disappearance of county regiments and also their territorial army links. We want to take advantage of this.

The view, one might feel, could have been expressed a little more tastefully.

He went on to deplore the lack of county feeling in the large towns,

London and Manchester in particular. The appraisal was undoubtedly shrewd. 'I suggest that what we are looking for is a regiment with a glamorous past which can be told in outline only, but with some very good stories about incidents which have occurred within living memory, i.e. in the Great War 1914–18, the last war, and above all, and I emphasise this, a regiment which has had an interesting time during the COLD WAR, because this is something which nobody knows.'

On this basis he eliminated many regiments from the list which the publishers submitted. Strangely enough they included the Manchester Regiment, the Grenadier Guards, the Royal Welch Fusiliers, the 11th Hussars, the Kings Royal Rifle Corps. (Greenjackets), and even his own regiment the Middlesex.

His approach to this 'campaign' was as determined and practical as to any of his former military ventures. He had taken it on, and he was going to make a success of it. He suggested a huge publicity campaign and was certain he could get the Thomson Press (notably the *Sunday Times*) behind it.

'Now as regards the form of the book, I very much liked the cover which you produced and also your suggestion about the Regimental March. Why not, in each book, instead of an introduction start with Reveille followed by the Regimental March and then on the last page have Last Post as they pass away – after all everyone loves a nice bit of slop!'

This comment on the use of the Last Post was followed by a paragraph on the choice of the right author. 'I was delighted to hear you have people at your disposal because what we obviously want is somebody who can write with a light and lively touch without making it cheap.'

Having made these somewhat Macchiavellian remarks he went on to comment on some of the proposed texts. Here he showed greater sensitivity and more shrewdness. On one author he comments:

'I agree with practically everything he says, that regimental histories are dull and far too laudatory in the silliest possible way, but I don't think he wants to laugh too much at these regiments. I doubt whether he himself has had much experience of active service because if he had he would realise it is not so much the danger that counts, but the capacity to stand up to really unpleasant conditions day after day and week after week and then for the soldier to give of his best. This is the quality which makes British infantry so good.'

He then wrote a general introduction to the series. After a number of re-draftings this came out as a very warm, humane document. In it appeared the following paragraphs.

The main strength of our military system had always laid in the fact that regimental roots were planted deep in the British countryside in the shape of the Territorial Army whose battalions are also subject to the cold winds of change. This ensured the closest possible link between civilian and military worlds, and built up a unique county and family esprit de corps which exists in no other Army in the world. A Cockney regiment, a West Country regiment and a Highland regiment differ from each other greatly, though they fought side by side in a series of battles. In spite of miserable conditions and savage discipline a man often felt he belonged with the regiment – he shared the background and the hopes of his fellows. This was a great comfort for a soldier. Many times, at old comrades' gatherings, some old soldier has come up to me and said, referring to one of the world wars, 'They were good times, sir, weren't they?'

They were not good times at all. They were horrible times but what these men remember and now miss was the comradeship and esprit de corps of the old regular regiment. These regiments, which bound men together and helped them through the pain and fear of war, deserve to be recalled.

Regimental histories are usually terribly dull, as the authors are forced to include the smallest operation and include as many names as possible. In this series we have something new. Freed from the tyranny of minute detail, the authors have sought to capture that subtle quary, the regimental spirit.

These sentences provide an interesting insight on Horrocks himself. He knows that war is an appalling, boring, experience but that some people do very well out of it. He sees too his potential readers as an army to be conquered, in this case by a mixture of realism and blandishment. He hops from one side of the fence to the other without hesitation, one minute mocking slightly cynically, the other swelling with uncritical pride. But, as he concludes in one comment: 'Let us not be sentimental. Tradition in the army can be viewed in quite the wrong perspective. Albuera Day meant a great deal to us; but when the real testing time comes, a good Commanding Officer is worth a ton of tradition with mould on it.'

In editing this series he soon showed the clarity of mind, and ability to concentrate, which had served him well in the past. Of one early manuscript he wrote: 'I have now read the last paragraph on page 6 several times and to be frank I dislike it more each time. It combines a sort of intellectual arrogance with a cheap form of mentality which would kill the series stone dead.' One sentence he compared to 'an undergraduate debate where everybody is trying *so* hard to be clever'.

Hamish Hamilton's editor for the series was Leo Cooper, who subsequently went on to become Britain's most discriminating military publisher. The relationship in the early days was formal: Horrocks addressing him as 'Dear Cooper' and Leo Cooper replying 'Dear Sir Brian'. Later this became a close friendship but never quite lost the touch of formality, although it was 'Dear Leo' and 'Yours, Brian'. Horrocks took his responsibilities as editor very seriously, sometimes offering advice where advice was not needed. Leo Cooper replied to every point with courteous efficiency, rather like a wicket-keeper dealing with fast balls, slow balls and an occasional wide. Horrocks constantly emphasised the need for 'sparkle', otherwise each would just become 'a somewhat dreary abridged regimental history'.

He had no need to worry. The series attracted a number of entertaining, well-informed writers. Two early writers were Tim Carew and Cyril Ray. His own most valuable contribution was to give a balanced appraisal of the regiment's history as outlined in the synopsis. He was flatly opposed to long descriptions of battles and sceptical about the real value of the achievements of certain regiments. He felt that Victoria Crosses had often been awarded for deeds which did not merit them: he recalled that although he had recommended certain people for VCs on some of his own campaigns none had ever been awarded and he felt that standards varied too widely. In one letter he finished with the remarks: 'I hope these notes are not too incoherent but I am surrounded by lists of Christmas cards which I have not sent, television scripts which I have not prepared, and my wife getting rather restless because I won't come out to a meet of the local hounds as it happens to be, for once, a beautiful day in Somerset.'

It is hardly surprising that he was finding life rather too full. While waiting for the house at Shepton Mallet to be made habitable the Horrockses were living near Frome. They moved to their new address; The Manor House, East Compton, Shepton Mallet on 25 July 1967. The fact that they were moving the following day did not prevent him dictating a long letter for Leo Cooper on the twenty-fourth. It contained an illuminating comment on the official history of the war. He said: 'As usual the authors of the *Official History* have obviously got the story wrong. I hate to say this, but it always irritates me when people allude to the genius of Field Marshal Alexander and then proceed to decry Monty. I know very well that Monty behaved in a most unusual manner. I know that he made many foolish statements at the end of the war but there is no question at all as to who was responsible for the entire strategy of the desert campaign. When I arrived out I was interviewed by Alexander in Cairo and he said to me, "You're going up to join Monty, he's got a plan for driving Rommel back. I hope he knows what he is up to." I then went up and saw Monty who'd only been there for five days and he gave me one of the most illuminating appreciations that I have ever heard. Furthermore, I have seen Alexander in Monty's caravan with a note book and Monty saying all the things that he wanted to do and Alexander making a note of them. Unfortunately, the more Monty misbehaved himself the more people liked Alexander; he was a most charming man but the brain behind the whole thing, believe me, was Monty. I am afraid the *Official History* will be rather irritating to read so I shall refrain from doing so.'

Nigel Nicolson, in his illuminating biography of Alexander (*Alex*, Weidenfeld & Nicolson, 1973) wrote:

His visits to Eighth Army were deliberately pitched in so low a key that even some of the Corps Commanders scarcely knew him – like Horrocks, to whom Alexander appeared 'remote from the battle ... as if he lived in a world of his own which few others were encouraged to enter'. De Guingand, who admired Alexander greatly, wrote of him unwittingly in terms which suggest a wholesaler's routine calls on the manager of Fortnum and Mason's: 'I often used to sit in the Army Commander's caravan. When Alexander paid his visits to Eighth Army before the battle of Alamein Monty would rattle out his requests, troops, commanders, equipment, whatever it might be. His Commander-in-Chief took short notes, and with the greatest rapidity these requests became accomplished facts.'

It seems surprising that even at this late stage Horrocks did not realise that the plan for driving Rommel back was neither Alexander's nor Montgomery's but Auchinleck's. The 'illuminating appreciation' was based entirely on the conversation Montgomery had had with Auchinleck at the time of Auchinleck's dismissal. Subsequently Montgomery had said that the conversation was all about retreating to the Nile, a statement repeated in his memoirs but which was subsequently withdrawn. It seems that in this letter Horrocks was leaping to the defence of Montgomery because he felt that if credit should be given to anyone it should be given to Montgomery, not Alexander. But, as we know, the plan for the battle of Alam Halfa was Auchinleck's, made in August before Montgomery arrived, and Auchinleck had also made an outline plan for the later, last battle of Alamein which began on 23 October. This particular volume of the *Official History* has been much criticised, and it is unnerving to think that what will be regarded as a totally authentic account of the Second World War in future years is by no means a version agreed by all the participants.

Many of Horrocks' comments on the texts of *Famous Regiments* show that even if he was short on editorial knowledge he was long on military wisdom: 'The author has managed to capture the atmosphere without too much "Huntin', Shootin' and Fishin'"', of which there is always a great risk when dealing with the cavalry. The trouble with our cavalry right up to the last World War has always been that in spite of the greatest courage and dash they have always lacked control.' And: 'The more I read of history the more surprised I am at the different aspects which are produced of the same battles.' He went on to say that the Royal Fusiliers always consider Albuera as their great battle. 'This, of course, was the Middlesex's greatest pride, but in regimental accounts neither regiment mentions the other's part in the battle.'

He was constantly checking attempts by authors to sing the praise of their subjects too loudly. He said: 'We only read of the "ups" and not of the "downs", and it is just as well to record these from time to time. Let me give you just one example from the last war. The 51st Highland Division in Normandy were very "sticky" indeed and nobody wanted them in their corps. The thick bocage country was very different from the desert and I think they were stale and perhaps they had had too much patting on the back in Eighth, anyhow it was a bad period for the division. Then a new divisional commander was introduced and he really set about them with the result that by the end of the war there was no better division in Europe and it takes a very good formation to make a recovery like that.'

In November 1968 there was a suggestion that Horrocks should take part in a BBC broadcast on the *Famous Regiments*. His response was brisk. 'I am afraid your letter filled me with alarm. By the time (end of March) I have finished my fifteenth programme for TWW I shall have had enough of broadcasting to last me for some time and an hour's programme involves a vast amount of work.

'You say that you will do all the hard grind but I have heard this so often before and it never works out like that. For a programme of this sort to be any good it must be a personal affair.'

However, he did not turn down the idea completely although he finished up by saying: 'I intend to enjoy my summer come what may!'

By this time he was experienced enough to be wary. He said: 'You say the BBC will pay. I am afraid my participation will depend largely on how much. I have had many arguments in the past with the BBC on fees. This sounds terribly commercial and horrid but since leaving the Army I have come to realise that money is not a dirty word.'

Leo Cooper sent back an understanding reply and Horrocks replied: 'Thank you for your nice letter. As usual, having despatched my last one to you I felt very ashamed of myself for being such a boorish old brute. The real trouble is that I am stale and thoroughly fed up with TV. . . .'

However, it was the TWW series which gave way. He decided he simply could not go beyond thirteen programmes and told them so. The BBC programme offered a change of scene, the fee was apparently reasonable, and he agreed. But he was working extremely hard for a man of seventy-three with a long history of war wounds and indifferent health. For that reason, and the fact that he was tired of re-creating military scenes, he declined an offer to write a book incorporating the material he had used in 'The Peace Keepers'. Later, in the autumn, he said, 'he might feel better about it', but not now.

But the *Famous Regiments* went on. He displayed a wide knowledge of military history and was quick to pick on any inaccuracies. This was sometimes made easier by his own experiences. 'C Coy of the 1st Hampshires *were not* the first troops to enter Belgium. This advance was carried out by my Corps and unless I have gone mad in the meantime the Household Cavalry (Armoured Cars) and the 11th Armoured Division were the leading troops into Belgium.'

The BBC broadcast, which he had baulked at giving, was a great success. He was overwhelmed with letters from admirers and replied personally to each of them.

Some of the authors who offered to write about regiments impressed him from the start; others perturbed him. Of one he wrote: 'I knew him well in the war. He was extremely brave but I am afraid extremely stupid. So before engaging him I should have a talk with him and see something he has written. I am always suspicious of people who say "I can write", as he does.'

But it was not all plain sailing. When Field Marshal Sir Gerald Templer was shown a draft of a history of the Royal Irish Fusiliers in the hope that he would write an introduction for it, he declined to do so, saying that the book was 'utter rubbish'. His annoyance was eventually traced to one paragraph. Very occasionally, regiments objected to the style in which a book was written even though they had personally approved the author.

By 1972 he felt he was getting stale and said so. But in that year he also mentioned to Leo Cooper that he was always getting letters from people who had been unsuccessful in obtaining a copy of his autobiography *A Full Life*. Would it, he asked, be possible to have it reprinted? Leo Cooper thereupon decided to buy the rights from Collins, the publishers of the first edition, and produce a later, more up-to-date version, with extra photographs. This was duly done and the book was published in 1974. Horrocks asked that there should be a photograph of Baron, the Boxer dog which had succeeded Maxie.

By this time the number of famous regiments in the series numbered fifty. He was also doing occasional broadcasts, and writing articles. His health varied. After an attack of jaundice his heart had given some cause for concern, but in 1974 he seemed as full of energy as ever. He was always saying, 'I am a very old man', and proceeding to act like a young one.

In 1977 the public was surprised to see yet another book by Sir Brian Horrocks. This time it was called *Corps Commander*. It had originally been planned to amplify and elucidate the information given in his own life story. Since writing the introduction to the *Famous Regiments*, and taking part in so many broadcasts and television presentations, he had developed a much clearer picture in his mind of the battles in which he himself had fought. He had intended to write it with the assistance of his old friend, Major-General Hubert Essame CBE, DSO, MC, who, after a distinguished career in the Army described himself in *Who's Who* as 'military lecturer, broadcaster, journalist and TV advisor'. He was a year younger than Horrocks and had served under him as a brigadier in 43rd Division. They had discussed the book together and it was a sad setback when Essame died soon after the book had been begun. However, in the preliminary talks Essame had suggested that they should bring in a third author, Eversley Belfield. Belfield was an inspired choice for he had been Senior Lecturer in the Military History Department of Southampton University for twenty-five years and supervised many courses run by that department for aspiring Staff College students. He had also written a number of books on military history. His outstanding asset, as far as Horrocks was concerned, was that he had served throughout the war with the Royal Artillery and was an Air Observation Pilot with the Canadian Army; this included the Polish Division and was operating on the left flank of 21st Army Group. 'His official title was "Air Observation Post Pilot with the Canadian Army" which meant in simple terms two things. Firstly that, flying above the battle in a very small aircraft all on his own, he reported the fall of shot. . . . Secondly, good Air Observation Pilots were in short supply and played such an important and dangerous part in the battle that they were privileged people and welcome to attend conferences at all levels. They therefore had an almost unique opportunity of viewing and understanding the battle as a whole.'

Horrocks, in his introduction, mentioned that during the battle he was so involved with his own corps that he knew nothing about the operation of the other corps taking part in the battle. Belfield, on the other hand, knew what was going on in the whole theatre. *Corps Commander* does not, unfortunately, deal with any campaigns earlier than August 1944. We are not therefore given further information about Alam Halfa, the third Alamein battle, or Mareth. However, it is clear that even at that distance in time, thirty years later, his admiration for Montgomery never wavers. Clearly he feels that Montgomery was a brilliant general: it does not occur to him that Montgomery might have been less brilliant in Africa and Europe if he had not had the thrust and loyalty of Horrocks to call on.

In hindsight he can see where major mistakes lay. The halt at Brussels seems to him to have been unnecessary and inexcusable. The reason given was that they were already too far ahead of their administrative resources: petrol, in particular, was dangerously short. Yet at that stage the only German division between them and the Rhine was a totally inexperienced formation of elderly Germans with stomach ailments. 'I cannot believe that Eisenhower's Intelligence did not realise that this was all the opposition there was in front of us. We could have brushed them aside without difficulty and might easily have bounced a crossing over the Rhine. It was infuriating because we still had 100 litres of petrol per vehicle, plus a further day's supply within reach.' They had already captured Brussels airport and petrol could have been airlifted to that. 'We also heard on the grapevine that at the end of August Patton's Third Army on my right flank had been halted for a similar reason.'

The delay was for purely political reasons. The 'broad front' policy was a top-level American-influenced decision. It seemed so mistaken in retrospect that the order for Horrocks to halt is often explained as being necessary in order to rest his troops. 'Some historians have suggested that the troops were exhausted,' he says. 'This is completely untrue. . . . I had rarely seen morale higher . . . the fighting troops were raring to go.'

But he blamed himself over Antwerp. With recollection of the way in which the Germans had destroyed or immobilised ports as they retreated along the North African coast, he had determined to save the Antwerp docks from destruction if he could. And he did, aided by the Belgian resistance, the 'Armée Blanche'. But he adds: 'It never entered my head that the Scheldt would be heavily mined so that Antwerp could not be used as a forward base for some time – or worse still that the Germans would succeed in ferrying across the estuary the remaining troops of the German Fifteenth Army, which had been holding the coast.' In hindsight, he considered that if he had ordered 11th Armoured Division to bypass Antwerp and advance fifteen miles north-west, the whole of that evacuated German force, which caused them great difficulty later, would have been destroyed or forced to surrender. 'Napoleon, no doubt, would have realised this, but I am afraid Horrocks didn't,' he commented.

He blames himself. He does not blame Montgomery, nor Dempsey, nor the Intelligence services, nor anyone else. Plenty of people should have known about the German capability of arranging a surprising and enormous evacuation. They had done so in Sicily. But when they had evacuated over 60,000 men across the Straits of Messina, Horrocks had been lying in hospital in danger of his life. After losing Antwerp they evacuated even more, 82,000 (on their own counting). While accepting the blame for a wrong decision in deciding to send 11th Armoured Division into Antwerp, he was unable to understand why he had been left in complete ignorance of what was happening outside his corps area. 'Of the Canadians and Poles,' he said, 'I had no information at all.' When he wrote *Corps Commander*, the 'Enigma' story had not been released, so he could only make a very vague reference to learning later that the experts had broken a German service code 'so that our corps commanders were always well informed of German intentions all over the world'. In fact he cannot blame the Enigma team entirely, for their information could only come from intercepted messages. Clearly they were not getting intercepted messages from the Terneuzen area when the evacuation was taking place.

Eventually he finds a rather more disturbing reason for the lack of information about the forces then to face 30 Corps. He believes that the villain of the piece was the Allied Airborne Army. This was still in the United Kingdom but straining to get into the battle. Owing to the speed of 30 Corps' advance, the AAA had already had sixteen operations cancelled. 'Back in Washington, General Marshall, the Chief of Staff of the US Army, was urging Eisenhower to use this immensely powerful force in one great operation to finish the war in 1944, so Patton's two flanking thrusts on the right of my 30 Corps and on the left were halted.' Horrocks felt that if the transport aircraft in Allied Airborne had been used to supply the armies on the ground the tragedy of Arnhem would never have occurred and the war would have been ended by the land armies in 1944. Instead he was ordered to halt and prepare for the Arnhem battle – a delay which proved fatal for it enabled the Germans to bring back their divisions to the point where they would do the most damage.

Further on in this book he gives a full and exciting account of the Arnhem battle. Essame, who would have been a co-author of the book, was at that time commander of 214th Brigade, the leading brigade of 43rd Division. The leading battalion was the 7th Somerset Light Infantry. Horrocks bitterly resented the accusation that 43rd Division had been 'slow and sticky', and went into detail in this chapter to prove they had not been.

The picture which emerges from this chapter is that Horrocks himself was always thinking rapidly, but constantly having to fight off a feeling that the whole operation was a terrible blunder. Montgomery had told him, 'However bad the situation, the commander must always radiate confidence.' 'I did my best,' said Horrocks, 'but this was becoming increasingly difficult day by day.' So far in this campaign everything had gone right, now at Arnhem, everything seemed to be going wrong.

As we saw earlier, when the Ardennes battle looked like becoming a disaster, various emergency moves were made; one of these was to put the 84th US Division under Horrocks' command. When he went forward in his jeep to look at the battlefield he was surprised to be halted by an American sentry who leapt from behind a tree and pointed his rifle at Horrocks' stomach. As he did so he shouted: 'Who the hell are you?' Horrocks got out of his jeep and said: 'I am a Britisher – and what's more your division has just been placed under my command.' The soldier looked at him with astonishment, not unmixed with scepticism. 'What's your rank then?' he asked. 'Three-star general,' said Horrocks. The man was suitably impressed. 'Holy Moses, we don't see many of them up here,' he said. After that all went very well indeed.

Horrocks went on to say that although the American Army impressed him in many ways he felt that the senior officers, with exceptions, lacked close contact with their troops. He felt that this was probably because the American Army had not had enough experience in the field. The British Army had learnt the vital importance of officers looking after their men in the First World War. There, the regimental officers had been good but the senior officers remote, selfish, uncaring, or so it seemed. When the regimental officers of the First World War, like Montgomery, became the senior officers of the Second World War they behaved in a way they wished their own senior officers had behaved in the earlier war. Montgomery's expertise in this field is well known: he wore distinctive but casual dress, an Australian hat or a beret with two badges, and he kept men as fully informed as was militarily possible. Horrocks mentions that he also used to visit hard-worked units and while sympathising with their difficulties would add in little pieces of good news. He was careful not to paint too bright a picture, in case that should seem improbable. Horrocks called this technique 'smelling the battlefield'.

The Ardennes battle, which was preceded by the Germans concentrating over two hundred thousand men and all their guns and stores into the Eifel, caught the Allies by surprise. Horrocks was never able to understand how this vast concentration could have been made without Allied Intelligence having the least idea that it was going on. But, of course, there was so much information at that time that its assessment was a major difficulty. And throughout history it has been proved that in warfare commanders like to believe that the enemy will do what they think he should do. Whenever, therefore, an enemy does the unexpected, such as the Germans coming twice through the Ardennes in the Second World War, or the outnumbered English relying entirely on longbows at Crécy and Agincourt, Intelligence forecasts go badly awry. Before the Ardennes battle the Allies discounted any possibility of Germany being able to mount a massive counter-attack at that stage in the war, but equally the Germans underrated the tenacity of the average American soldier; those, whatever their jobs in the Army, fought like the most experienced infantry. Eisenhower waited forty-eight hours at the start of the battle but then took the courageous step of putting Montgomery in charge of the northern sector. Although many people think that if the Germans had not been checked they might have reached Brussels and Antwerp, cutting the Allied armies in two and destroying each in turn, Horrocks does not agree. He thinks the British would have checked them before they reached Brussels and the Americans could then have caught the Germans in a pincer movement. This might have ended the war much sooner because the Germans would then have lost the bulk of their remaining best troops.

Although *Corps Commander* is in many ways only an expansion of what he wrote in his own autobiography, it presents Horrocks in a slightly different light. Usually he makes everything seem easy, as if commanding a hundred thousand men or more was a responsibility which was not over-burdensome. In *Corps Commander*, the reader senses the immense strain that it must have been, particularly as his general health was not good and his particular style of command was intensely active. He was not a general who could sit in a rear headquarters, studying reports and maps, and clinically analysing the situation before resolving on his next move. He had to be there, up with the leaders. Major-General Borradaile, who commanded the 7th Somerset Light Infantry, saw a lot of Horrocks, and Borradaile's regiment was always in the thick of the battle. There were times when there was so much going on that it was impossible to form a clear, overall picture, but Horrocks appears to have had a remarkable instinct for sensing the general drift of a situation and whether it was favourable or unfavourable.

Borradaile had known Horrocks for a long time. He had been in Horrocks' syndicate at the Staff College as early as 1939, and Dempsey had been Borradaile's platoon commander when the latter was a cadet at Sandhurst. After commanding the Somersets Borradaile was made GSO 1 (Senior Staff Officer) in 30 Corps HQ. He was therefore involved in the planning for the Rhine crossing. Horrocks worked his staff very hard, he recalls. Often Borradaile would stay up most of the night, occasionally all of it, preparing material for the next morning's conference. Borradaile used to drive Horrocks around the area. He noticed that Horrocks was never really fit: he used to take a succession of powders and pills to ward off fevers and pains from his old wounds. He had to be very careful of his diet, which was austere, but 'he was like a human dynamo; he never stopped, never relaxed'. He ate very little and only drank a little champagne. 30 Corps had captured the German Army's entire stock of champagne at Brussels. In the opinion of the experts, of which there were a surprising number available, the champagne was not of the 'keeping' variety, but needed immediate drinking.

Horrocks was excellent at explaining what was to be done, warmer and less clinical than Montgomery. Borradaile recalls that when he was a battalion commander he saw more of Horrocks, the corps commander, than he did of his own divisional commander. In briefings Horrocks never, ever used notes; he knew exactly what he wanted to say and never hesitated.

In this campaign Horrocks wanted to be the leader of the fastest moving corps; he did not want to be less than the star performer. This may have been a flaw in his character but it certainly motivated him. Some of those who observed him felt that this urge for the first prize stopped just short of being obsessional. Yet it must be remembered that he was conscious of his own limitations. Within those limitations he wished to be top of his group.

His 'style' never varied. All through his military career he had been accustomed to get up early, sleep on a groundsheet or in a trailer, and eat the same food as his men. He believed that if he was to lead men successfully, he must share their hardships. His active service wear was brown corduroy trousers, a battledress jacket, and a beret or peaked cap; he never wore a steel helmet even when he was under heavy shellfire. The privilege of high rank was, in his view, to be used to move wherever he wanted on the battlefield, and mingle with his fighting soldiers. That was his life, that was his material and spiritual home.

Chapter 15

Some Assessments

Sir Denis Hamilton felt that the combination of Horrocks as a corps commander and Montgomery as an army commander, both soldier-generals, made an unbeatable team. Both liked to be as far forward as possible and to talk to soldiers. The result was that soldiers, whatever they thought of their own officers, were convinced that Montgomery and Horrocks were really on their side. Both men realised that it was a civilian army they were commanding, and those civilians in uniform would not be content merely to be told what to do without asking why. Before questions could be asked, Montgomery and Horrocks were there with the answers. They knew that men wished to get home but were prepared to work hard to achieve it at the earliest possible time. Montgomery seems to have taken this philosophy to the limit with 50th (Northumbrian) Division, which fought arduous battles in North Africa and then landed on the most important part of the D-Day beaches. By that time the division was beginning to be weary but it went on, unflagging. Hamilton felt that the build-up to D-Day, followed by the landing and the difficult fight to get well inland created an unendurable strain for many of the senior officers, particularly if they were regulars who had been brought up to expect events to conform to a certain pattern. Horrocks seemed immune to the stress of setbacks: they merely spurred him to greater efforts.

Hamilton considered that Horrocks' poor opinion of his own intellectual abilities, a view shared by certain other people, was unjustified. He felt that the autobiography showed a striking ability to reflect constructively on past events, as well as the ability to concentrate over a long period. Horrocks wrote at remarkable speed. In Hamilton's view, Horrocks showed exceptional versatility and adaptability in being able to command widely differing units, e.g. infantry and armour, on battlefields which varied from the sandy desert of Alam Halfa to the flooded plains of Holland.

Harold Young, Horrocks' longest serving ADC, considered that a principal feature in Horrocks' success was his personal drive (what Borradaile called the 'human dynamo'). He would never tolerate the second-rate.

In his early days in France he used to get high temperatures and bouts of sweating. He had a very bad spell just before the Ardennes. Montgomery came along one day, saw how ill he was, brushed aside Horrocks' excuses and put him in an aeroplane to go back to England for a day or two to get over it. (In Horrocks' absence the corps was commanded by Major-General G.I. Thomas of 43rd Division). Horrocks drove himself as hard as he drove the troops. Young said that in spite of the chain of command below him – brigade, regiment, company and platoon commanders – Horrocks himself was the driving force. Possibly because he was so often seen being active but also because his enthusiasm was infectious, he managed to motivate everyone in 30 Corps to give of his best – all the time. His enthusiasm did not merely influence British soldiers. As we saw above, he quickly made friends with American private soldiers who were not very amicably disposed to generals or the British as a whole. The most impressive example of Horrocks creating cheerful enthusiasm was seen by Young when they used to be invited to lunch by the Russians when Horrocks was in the Hanover district. 'There was I,' said Young, 'sitting next to some fat Russian woman commissar, with scarcely a word being spoken, while further along the table was Horrocks happily chatting away, surrounded by apparently cheerful, affable Russians.'

Young, as we have mentioned, was in the desert before Horrocks arrived. His job at that time was with Light Armoured Brigade HQ where he was a staff officer (G3) and combined this with being ADC to the brigade commander. He spent much of his time in the southern half of the Alamein line where they were working on the plan for the next battle, marking up maps and so on. This plan, the one which was subsequently employed in the battle of Alam Halfa, was Auchinleck's. Neither Montgomery nor Horrocks were in the area when this plan was made. It went exactly as foreseen by Auchinleck, Young said.

Horrocks, according to Young, had a great ability to select the people he wanted for certain jobs, and in this he could be quite ruthless. He was not so much concerned with military details as with broad concepts. Thus his admiration for Montgomery was based on his recognition of the latter's overall ability. He felt that he himself owed everything to Montgomery, but was not blind to his patron's faults. He was not above pestering Montgomery for a certain person to be a brigade or regimental commander until he got the man he wanted. However, having got his man, he did not try to supervise him.

Young recalls that life as Horrocks' ADC never lacked excitement. The worst moments were when there was a general feeling of frustration at being unable to reach Arnhem. He felt that the disaster was largely due to lack of co-ordination, the responsibility for which lay with 2nd Army. The best times were in the desert, particularly at Mareth. All through the war they had a Tactical Headquarters in a tank. The Tac HQ consisted of Horrocks, Young or another ADC, a signaller and a staff officer. The guns were taken out of this Sherman tank but they had an escort of two other tanks. Their tank was always in the front line – with no guns. The fact that they were often travelling over minefields added to the possibilities of sudden disaster. When they went through gaps in minefields they were often observed by German gunners who had guns permanently trained on these corridors. Once, as he was reconnoitring in a jeep before Alam Halfa, Horrocks was going up through a lane in a minefield when the Germans began shelling it. His driver slowed down. Horrocks looked at him and said, 'What are you doing?' 'Well, sir,' said the driver, 'I was waiting for this burst of shelling to ease up.' 'Drive on,' said Horrocks. 'If I want to go somewhere no bloody German is going to stop me.'

Throughout his time with Horrocks Young found him always completely straightforward. Although he was ambitious – up to a point – he was never devious, and never tried to advance his own career. If any of his actions exposed others to risks he made sure that he shared those risks himself.

Chapter 16

Hindsight

In old age his memory has faded, though parts of it remain clear. At the age of eighty-eight he is still able to walk without sticks, in spite of being partly paralysed on his left side. His determination never to give in is reinforced by his wife who, in the fifty-sixth year of their marriage, is looking after him entirely by herself. Her sight is failing, and she cannot read, so she finds some relaxation in household chores and walks in the Sussex countryside. He drives her in their Mini Metro and waits while she takes a daily walk on the downs. They have acquired a boxer puppy, which they called Jez (short for Jezebel); it shares some of the characteristics of its biblical namesake and causes them a lot of trouble but they love it dearly.

Old friends keep a watchful eye on them. Sir Denis Hamilton, who has a farm nearby, ensures that they always have adequate supplies of fruit and vegetables, Neville Vincent, in company with John Shelford, relieves them of any financial and administrative problems. It is not easy to help the Horrockses, for they are firmly independent, so everything is done unobtrusively.

When some of the many thousands who have met him in the past write to him at Christmas or for his birthday, he is saddened if he cannot remember much about them. Whenever he speaks of events in his past life no trace of bitterness or envy ever creeps in. He laughs at humorous events in the distant past, particularly when they spring from the sardonic humour of British soldiers. He still thinks the world of Montgomery who, he said, 'was not really half as tough as people think. Monty had a job to do and he did it as he thought best. But in his later life he was often sad and lonely. Like many old soldiers he had nostalgic dreams, not of winning battles or moments of triumph but of being in his garden with his beloved wife, long since dead.' Horrocks too dreams, but his dreams are less pleasant; and when thunder wakes him at night he will sometimes leap out of bed, thinking it was the crack of guns in a long past battle.

The Horrockses' greatest sorrow was the death of their daughter Gillian who was drowned in the Thames in 1979. She had bathed at that place many times and at first it seemed she had either been sucked under by a mysterious eddy in the current, or perhaps had

had cramp and been unable to get help. Subsequently it was established that the coldness of the water on a day in May when the air temperature was warm had caused her heart to stop. She was in her fiftieth year. She had had three children, a daughter from a first marriage and two sons from her second marriage to John Herbert, son of the writer Sir Alan (A.P.) Herbert. There were no other close relatives. Horrocks' sister, who had spent many years looking after his father, was dead too.

He is always totally unassuming, and is much loved in the village. His only lament is that in old age he should have to walk so slowly and so carefully when in his modern pentathlon days he had been so mobile. He has some pain but never mentions it. In spite of the various injuries to his stomach he has somehow retained a good digestion: he is as happy eating in a country pub as in a luxury hotel. His hearing is excellent; his speech unimpaired.

Sometimes they both speak regretfully of never being able to sail again (he gave it up in 1972). Otherwise, he is contented enough. He has a justified pride in his rank, title and honours. They were earned in danger and hardship. He does not realise how great his contribution to Allied victory was, seeing Montgomery as the architect of success and himself as a mere assistant. Horrocks used to say of himself that he was a first-rate subaltern officer and that the highest rank a subaltern officer could achieve was corps commander. A subaltern is a lieutenant or second lieutenant whose duties are in the forefront of a battle. He usually commands approximately thirty men. In the early days he tends to rely heavily on the knowledge of his platoon sergeant, who is older and more experienced. The subaltern spends most of his time with his platoon (called a 'troop' in some regiments), leads them, and often dies in battle while doing so. This was the Army job Horrocks liked best and perhaps explains why he was never happier, whatever his rank, than when with fighting soldiers in forefront of battle. 'God,' he said, 'never meant me to be an army commander.' He never liked problems of politics or logistics on which you had to brood; he did not think he could achieve intellectual detachment. He felt he had limited aims in accordance with limited ability; and had reached the highest point at which that ability could be used successfully.

It is, of course, the reasonable view of a modest man. Yet looking over his career and comparing it with others, one cannot but wonder whether he was underrating himself. 'In the country of the blind the one-eyed man is King.' Montgomery recognised Horrocks' talents and realised that here he had a lively, loyal, uncomplaining instrument. Montgomery brought Horrocks out to the desert and immediately gave him an important command although he knew Horrocks had no desert experience. Neither, of course, had Montgomery. Horrocks had at least commanded an armoured division for a few months so was familiar with its problems; Montgomery had no experience in command of armour and very limited success in command of infantry. It seems that if Montgomery did much to help Horrocks, Horrocks did even more to help Montgomery. And in underrating himself – as he does to this day – Horrocks overlooks the fact that he made a success of other appointments than being an Army officer. One cannot imagine Wavell or Montgomery or Leese or Dempsey as Black Rod, nor Alexander, Auchinleck, Slim or Ironside as popular broadcasters.

It has been a long, interesting life, full of variety, a life of service to his country. During the First World War he had been wounded and captured when fighting the enemy; subsequently he had given that enemy as much trouble as he could in trying to escape. Soon after release he had volunteered for dangerous duty in Russia. During the years of peace he had represented his country in the Olympic Games. At the Staff College he had been an inspiring teacher who had communicated enthusiasm and a passion for efficiency to many students who would benefit by his teaching and pass on the lessons. Subsequently he had shown himself to be a dashing, fearless, successful commander of troops in battle. He had always been a genial colleague. After the war he had done much to rehabilitate the defeated enemy and then, after retirement, accepted the important post of Black Rod whose duties he had performed with efficiency and distinction. He had achieved national fame as a television programme presenter and in the process given much pleasure and interest to millions. Even while doing this he had been an active director of a large construction company and made a valuable contribution. Finally he had made a success of writing, in newspaper articles, in books, in editing other people's books.

All these activities had been useful, wholesome, of benefit to the people of his country. But his greatest achievements have been on the battlefield. Chester Wilmot said of him, when he took over 30 Corps: 'Within a few days his fresh and fiery spirit had transformed the corps. A tall, lithe figure, with white hair, angular features, penetrating eyes and eloquent hands, he moved among his troops more like a prophet than a general.'

In pondering Horrocks' effect on morale and fighting quality, one is reminded of Wellington's comment on Napoleon: 'I used to say of him that his presence on the field made the difference of forty thousand men.'

Lieutenant General Sir Brian Horrocks, KCB, KBE, DSO, MC, died on January 4th, 1985. His funeral, a few days later, was a simple ceremony with no hymns, no flowers and a plain coffin. This was his own request.

On February 26th, 1985 a thanksgiving service for his life was held in Westminster Abbey. He had said firmly that if such a service were to be held it was not to be a memorial service, but an occasion of thanksgiving for the life he had been privileged and happy to live.

In the congregation were representatives of every unit he had commanded. The Abbey was full, not merely with colonels and brigadiers, whom you would have expected to see, but also with soldiers who had held much lesser ranks or no rank at all. They were all paying their last respects to someone whom they knew had been a friend. Battle is a good test of friendship.

Horrocks would have been astonished if he had been there to see how many people wished to attend a thanksgiving service for his life. He was a modest man.

Appendix I

Lt-General Sir B.G. Horrocks issued a Personal Memorandum on 23rd August 1942 shortly after taking over the command of 13 Corps:

Para 3 (a)
(ii) I feel that a certain aspect of our propaganda is bad. The troops have been told so much that we are certain to win the war that they accept this as a fact, but do not realise their individual responsibility in the matter. It should be pointed out to them that unless each individual soldier fights to the last ounce, the war may go on for years and years. NO situation is ever hopeless provided a man has guts.

General Horrocks also made an unfavourable comment about another characteristic of the Eighth Army.

(b) I have noticed on several occasions that when an order is issued from a higher formation, staff officers in subordinate formations ring up staff officers at the formation above them and protest about certain aspects of the order – in other words 'bellyache'. This is no good in battle. The Comd. of a subordinate formation always has the right to protest, but this must be done *to the Comd. above in person or on the telephone*, not to the staff. I want this clearly understood throughout all formations in the 13 Corps.

Appendix 2

Letter from General James Gavin, Commander 82nd US Airborne Division

Dear Mr Warner:

I was very pleased to receive your letter telling me that you are doing a biography of Sir Brian Horrocks, because he was truly a unique general officer and his qualities of leadership were greater than any I have ever seen.

In lecturing at the American Service schools I stated frequently that General Horrocks was the finest general officer I met during the war, and the finest corps commander.

I had not met him before Market-Garden. My work prior to that operation was with 'Boy' Browning and his staff. As I recall, when link-up occurred, at D+3,* early in the morning, we were immediately involved, that is the 82nd, with the Guards Armoured Division. I met General Horrocks for the first time that afternoon. He seemed to be very easy-going and very relaxed. I remember him saying to me, 'Jim, don't ever try to fight a Corps off one road.' To add to his complications in fighting off the one road, at that moment the Germans had a complete plan of the operation and they were counter-attacking quite successfully to cut the road.

I was impressed by his kindness, lack of any pomposity, and his willingness to talk about any aspect of the operation with complete candor. He was neither promising nor wishful, just simply trying to do the best job that he possibly could with the resources that he had. When I asked him if he had boats, he turned to one of his staff and they soon figured out that they had some. An American Corps in that situation would have had an engineer battalion which, in turn, would have a boat company. Unfortunately, the boat company was down the road, miles away, and although the staff assured me they would be up by daylight, they did not arrive until the following afternoon.

* Three days after the beginning of Market Garden.

I did not see General Horrocks again for about a day. He was terribly busy with all the problems that he had, and he was getting little news from Arnhem. After that the Arnhem force was withdrawn, 2,500, and the battle settled down to tidying up the battlefield and getting ready for what was next. In about a day General Horrocks came up to see me. He had his aide bring along a picnic lunch and we spent the day going from front line unit to front line unit. At noon we stopped to lean against a haystack and we enjoyed our lunch and talked about many things. He expressed some concern about the future of the British Empire after the war came to an end. The inevitability of colonialism being out was in the offing and he wondered what the British were going to do. We talked some about our units and his relationship with the combat forces was one that I admired very much. He was the one who said to me, 'You must go to where you get the smell of the battle in your nostrils', and I agreed with him entirely. And so, we went to see every battalion commander in the division as well as several company commanders. He was impressed with the 82nd Airborne Division and later said to me, 'You know, they are professional killers'. But he remembered them and when the heavy fighting was over, he talked to each battalion as a group as they came out of the line. They were assembled in a Dutch meeting hall or cinema, and he explained to them what they had been doing, or at least trying to do, and what they could expect to do next. He talked to them about their weapons, rations, etc., and then he asked them what they wanted. Somewhat to my embarrassment the Americans said they wanted more to eat. The trouble was they didn't like the kind of food. They were accustomed to the American C. Ration. He doubled the ration. We then spent time in the rear areas and all of his troops were busy cleaning and repairing their weapons, tanks and other vehicles. Some, who had caught up on those chores, were playing football. But, he was available to be seen. He was very strict and demanding of them and worked hard to achieve a standard of readiness for the next battle. He made that quite clear, so he combined to a unique degree obvious empathy and consideration for the troops, while he was very firm and tough in making clear to them what he expected of them in battle. He was an exceptional leader; but for his wounds he certainly could have commanded an army and probably could have gone higher.

As you write, he was a quick thinker and he did have an open mind. He was quite unaffected and could converse with the privates on the same level of mutual understanding as with the senior generals. The troops trusted him and had great confidence in him.

Your recollection is quite correct. I did lecture at Sandhurst. That was quite a few years ago now. As I recall, General Horrocks came down and introduced me.

With best regards,
James M. Gavin

PS. As the days grew shorter, and colder, in the fall of '44, and the Dutch dampness of Holland seemed to penetrate everywhere, his staff inquired about a rum ration – I declined. Finally on our last evening with 30 Corps he sent me a message, "You will issue a rum ration this evening" – a nice Horrocks touch. We enjoyed it.

Appendix 3

13 CORPS
(Lieut-General B.G. Horrocks)
(BGS: Brigadier George Erskine)

7th Armoured Division (Major-General A.F. Harding):

4th Light Armoured Brigade (Brigadier M.G. Roddick): 4/8th Hussars, The Greys and 1st King's Royal Rifle Corps (motor battalion).

22nd Armoured Brigade (Brigadier G.P.B. Roberts): 1st and 5th Royal Tank Regiment, 4th Cty of London Yeomanry and 1st Rifle Brigade (motor battalion).

131st Lorried Infantry Brigade. (See under 44th Infantry Division.)

Divisional Troops:

Household Cavalry Regt, 11th Hussars and 2nd Derbyshire Yeomanry (armoured cars).

Royal Artillery (Commander, Brigadier Roy Mews): 3rd Royal Horse Artillery, 4th and 97th (Kent Yeomanry) Field Regts, 65th Anti-Tank Regt, 15 Light Anti-Aircraft Regt.

Royal Engineers: 4th and 21st Field Squadrons, 143rd Field Park Sqn.

Others: 7th Armoured Div Signals, 2nd and 14th Light Field Ambulances.

Under command: 1st and 2nd Free French Brigade Groups and 1st Free French Flying Column.

44th Reconnaissance Regt (from 44th Division).

44th Infantry Division (Major-General I.T.P. Hughes):

131st Infantry Brigade (Brigadier W.D. Stamer): 1/5th, 1/6th and 1/7th The Queens' (became incorporated in 7th Armd Div on 1/11/1942).

132nd Infantry Brigade (Brigadier L.G. Whistler): 2nd Buffs, 4th and 5th Royal West Kent Regt.

133rd Infantry Brigade. (see under 10th Armd. Div.)

Divisional Troops:

RA (CRA, Brigadier H.R. Hall): 57th, 58th, 65th and 53rd Field Regts, 57th Anti-Tank Regt, 30th Light AA Regt.

RE: 11th, 209th and 210th Field Coys, 211th Field Park Company and 577th Army Field Park Coy.

Others: 44th Div Signals, 6th Cheshire Regt (machine-gun battalion), 131st and 132nd Field Ambulance.

50th Infantry Division (Major-General J.S. Nichols):

69th Infantry Brigade (Brigadier E.C. Cooke-Collis): 5th East Yorkshire Regt, 6th and 7th Green Howards.

151st Infantry Brigade (Brigadier J.E.S. Percy): 6th, 8th and 9th Durham Light Infantry.

1st Greek Infantry Brigade Group (Colonel Katsotas): 1st, 2nd and 3rd Greek Battalions, 1st Greek Field Artillery Regt, 1st Greek Field Engineer Coy, 1st Greek Machine Gun Coy, 1st Greek Field Ambulance.

Divisional Troops:

RA (CRA, Brigadier Claude Eastman): 74th, 111th, 124th and 154th Field Regts, 102nd (Northumberland Hussars) Anti-Tank Regt, 34th Light AA Regt.

RE: 23rd and 505th Field Coys, 235th Field Park Coy.

Others: 50th Div Signals, 2nd Cheshire Regt (machine-guns), 149th and 186th Field Ambulances.

13 Corps Troops 118th and 124th RTR (dummy tanks):

4th Survey Regt, RA (part), 578th Army Field Coy and 576th Corps Field Park Coy, RE, 13 Corps Signals.

10 CORPS

(Lieut-General Herbert Lumsden; Lieut-General B.G. Horrocks from December 1942)

(BGS: Brigadier Ralph Cooney)

1st Armoured Division (Major-General Raymond Briggs):

2nd Armoured Brigade (Brigadier A.F. Fisher): The Queen's Bays, 9th Lancers, 10th Hussars and Yorkshire Dragoons (motor battalion).

7th Motor Brigade (Brigadier T.J.B. Bosvile): 2nd and 7th Battalions of the Rifle Brigade and 2nd King's Royal Rifle Corps (60th Rifles).

Divisional Troops:

12th Lancers (armoured cars).

RA (CRA, Brigadier B.J. Fowler): 2nd and 4th RHA, 11th RHA (Honourable Artillery Company), 78th Field Regt (less troops with other divisions), 76th Anti-Tank Regt and 42 Light AA Regt.

RE: 1st and 7th Field Sqns, 1st Field Park Sqn.

Attached: 9th Field Sqn and 572nd Field Park Coy.

Others: 1st Armd Div Signals, two companies Royal Northumberland Fusiliers, 1st and 5th Light Field Ambulances.

184

Attached: 'Hammerforce' (artillery and armd cars).

10th Armoured Division (Major-General A.H. Gatehouse):

8th Armoured Brigade (Brigadier E.C.N. Custance): 3rd RTR, Nottinghamshire Yeomanry (Sherwood Rangers), Staffordshire Yeomanry, 1st Buffs (motor battalion).

24th Armoured Brigade (Brigadier A.G. Kenchington): 41st, 45th and 47th RTR and 11th KRRC (motor battalion).

133rd Lorried Infantry Brigade (Brigadier A.W. Lee), added from 44th Division: 2nd, 4th and 5th Royal Sussex Regt and one company R. Northumberland Fusiliers.

Divisional Troops:

The Royal Dragoons (armoured cars).

RA (CRA, Brigadier W.A. Ebbels): 1st, 5th and 104th (Essex Yeomanry) RHA, 98th Field Regt (Surrey and Sussex Yeomanry), 84th Anti-Tank Regt, 53rd Light AA Regt.

RE: 2nd and 3rd (Cheshire) Field Sqns, 141st Field Park Sqn.

Attached: 6th Field Sqn, 571st and 753rd Army Field Coys.

Others: 10th Armd Div Signals, 3rd, 8th and 168th Light Field Ambulances.

8th Armoured Division (Major-General Charles Gairdner). This division was reduced to a headquarters staff and some non-operational troops only.

10 Corps Troops: 570th Corps Field Park Coy, RE, 10 Corps Signals, 12th and 151st Light Field Ambulances.

30 CORPS (Africa)
(Lieut-General Sir Oliver Leese, Bt.)
(BGS: Brigadier G.P. Walsh)

51st (Highland) Infantry Division (Major-General D.N. Wimberley):

152nd Infantry Brigade (Brigadier G. Murray): 2nd and 5th Seaforth Highlanders, 5th Cameron Highlanders.

153rd Infantry Brigade (Brigadier D.A.H. Graham): 5th Black Watch, 1st and 5/7th Gordon Highlanders.

154th Infantry Brigade (Brigadier H.W. Houldsworth): 1st and 7th Black Watch, 7th Argyll and Sutherland Highlanders.

Divisional Troops:

RA (CRA, Brigadier G.M. Elliot): 126th, 127th and 128th Field Regts, 61st Anti-Tank Regt, 40th Light AA Regt.

RE: 274th, 275th and 276th Field Coys, 239th Field Park Coy.

Others: 51st Div Signals, 1/7th Middlesex Regt (machine-guns), 51st Div Reconnaissance Regt, 174th, 175th and 176th Field Ambulances.

2nd New Zealand Division (Major-General B.C. Freyberg, VC):

9th Armoured Brigade (*United Kingdom*) (Brigadier John Currie): 3rd Hussars, Royal Wiltshire Yeomanry, Warwickshire Yeomanry and 14th Foresters (motor infantry).

5th NZ Infantry Brigade (Brigadier Howard Kippenberger): 21st, 22nd and 23rd NZ Battalions, 28th Maori Bn.

6th NZ Infantry Brigade (Brigadier William Gentry): 24th, 25th and 26th NZ Bns.

Divisional Troops:

2nd NZ Divisional Cavalry Regt (light tanks).

NZ Artillery (CRA, Brigadier C.E. Weir): 4th, 5th and 6th NZ Field Regts, 7 NZ Anti-Tank Regt, 14th NZ Light AA Regt.

NZ Engineers: 6th, 7th and 8th NZ Field Coys, 5th NZ Field Park Coy.

Others: 2nd NZ Div Signals, 27th NZ Bn (machine-guns), 5th and 6th NZ Field Ambulances and 166th Light Field Ambulance (for 9th Armd Bde).

9th Australian Division (Major-General L.J. Morshead):

20th Australian Infantry Brigade (Brigadier W.J.V. Windeyer): 2/13th, 2/15th and 2/17th Australian Infantry Bns.

24th Australian Infantry Brigade (Brigadier Arthur Godfrey): 2/28th, 2/32nd and 2/43rd Australian Infantry Bns.

26th Australian Infantry Brigade (Brigadier D.A. Whitehead): 2/23rd, 2/24th and 2/48th Infantry Bns.

Divisional Troops:

RAA (CRA, Brigadier A.H. Ramsay): 2/7th, 2/8th and 2/12th Aust Field Regts, 3rd Aust Anti-Tank Regt, 4th Aust Light AA Regt.

Engineers: 2/3rd, 2/7th, 2/13th Aust Field Coys, 2/4th Aust Field Park Coy, 2/3rd Aust Pioneer Bn.

Others: 9th Australian Div Signals, 2/2nd Aust Bn (machine-guns), 2/3rd, 2/8th and 2/11th Aust Field Ambulances.

4th Indian Division (Major-General F.I.S. Tuker):

5th Indian Infantry Brigade (Brigadier D. Russell): 1/4th Essex Regt, 4/6th Rajputana Rifles, 3/10th Baluch.

7th Indian Infantry Brigade (Brigadier A.W.W. Holworthy): 1st Royal Sussex Regt, 4/16th Punjabi Regt; 1/2nd Gurkha Rifles.

161st Indian Infantry Brigade (Brigadier F.E.C. Hughes): 1st Argyll and Sutherland Highlanders, 1/1st Punjabi Regt, 4/7th Rajputs.

Divisional Troops:

RA (CRA, Brigadier H.K. Dimoline): 1st, 11th and 32nd Field Regts, 149th Anti-Tank Regt, 57th Light AA Regt.

RE: 2nd, 4th and 12th Field Coys, 11th Field Park Coy.

Others: 4th Indian Div Signals, 6th Rajputana Rifles (machine-guns), 17th and 26th Indian Field Ambulances and 75th Light

Field Ambulance.

1st South African Division (Major-General D.H. Pienaar):

1st SA Infantry Brigade (Brigadier C.L. de W. du Toit): 1st Royal Natal Carabiniers, 1st Duke of Edinburgh's Own Rifles, 1st Transvaal Scottish.

2nd SA Infantry Brigade (Brigadier W.H.E. Poole): 1/2nd Field Force Bn, 1st Natal Mounted Rifles, Cape Town Highlanders.

3rd SA Infantry Brigade (Brigadier R.J. Palmer): 1st Imperial Light Horse, 1st Durham Light Infantry, 1st Rand Light Infantry.

Divisional Troops:

SA Artillery (CRA, Brigadier F. Theron): 1st, 4th and 7th Field Regts, 1st SA Anti-Tank Regt, 1st SA Light AA Regt.

SA Engineers: 1st, 2nd, 3rd and 5th SA Field Coys, 19th SA Field Park Coy.

Others: 1st SA Div Signals, Regiment President Steyn and one Coy Die Middelandse (machine-guns), 12th, 15th and 18th SA Ambulances.

(Divisional Reserve Group, including 2nd Regiment Botha, was dissolved a week after Alamein began.)

30 Corps Troops and Troops in Corps Reserve:

23rd Armoured Brigade Group (Brigadier G.W. Richards): 8th, 40th, 46th and 50th RTR, 121st Field Regt RA, 168 Light AA Battery, RA, 295th Army Field Coy, RE, 7th Light Field Ambulance.

Armoured Cars: 4/8th South African Armoured Car Regt.

RA: 7th, 64th and 69th Medium Regts.

RE: 66th Mortar Company

30 Corps Signals.

30 CORPS (Europe)
(Lieut-General B.G. Horrocks)

Corps Troops:

RAC: 11th Hussars (Armoured Car).

RA: 73rd A/Tk., 27th LAA and 4th Survey Regts.

RE: 30th Corps Troops Engineers.

R. Signals: 30th Corps Signals.

Guards Armoured Division (Major-General A.H.S. Adair):

5th Guards Armoured Brigade: 2nd (Armoured) Grenadier Guards, 1st (Armoured) Coldstream Guards, 2nd (Armoured) Irish Guards, 1st (Motor) Grenadier Guards.

32nd Guards Brigade: 5th Coldstream Guards, 2nd Scots Guards, 3rd Irish Guards, 1st Welsh Guards.

Divisional Troops:

2nd Armoured Recce. Welsh Guards

RA: 55th and 153rd Field, 21st A/Tk and 94th LAA Regts.

RE: Guards Armoured Division Engineers.

R. Signals: Guards Armoured Divisional Signals.

11th Armoured Division (Major-General G.P.B. Roberts):

29th Armoured Brigade: 23rd Hussars, 2nd Fife and Forfar Yeomanry, 3rd Royal Tank Regt, 8th Bn. The Rifle Brigade (Motor).

159th Infantry Brigade: 1st Cheshire Regt (ex-115th Bde), 4th King's Shropshire Light Infantry, 1st Herefordshire Regt.

Divisional Troops:

RAC: 15th/19th King's Royal Hussars.

RA: 13th Regt RHA, 151st Field, 75th A/Tk, and 58th LAA Regts.

RE: 11th Armoured Divisional Engineers.

R. Signals: 11th Armoured Divisional Signals.

15th (Scottish) Division (Major-General C.M. Barber):

44th (Lowland) Brigade: 8th Royal Scots, 6th Royal Scots Fusiliers, 7th King's Own Scottish Borderers.

46th (Highland) Brigade: 9th Cameronians, 2nd Glasgow Highlanders, 7th Seaforth Highlanders.

227th (Highland) Brigade: 10th Highland Light Infantry, 2nd Gordon Highlanders, 2nd Argyll and Sutherland Highlanders.

Divisional Troops:

RAC: 15th Recce Regt.

RA: 131st, 181st and 190th Field, 97th and 102nd (ex-50th Division) A/Tk and 119th LAA Regts.

RE: 15th Divisional Engineers.

R. Signals: 15th Divisional Signals.

Machine Gun: 1st Middlesex Regt.

43rd (Wessex) Division (Major-General G.I. Thomas):

129th Brigade: 4th Somerset Light Infantry, 4th and 5th Wiltshire Regt.

130th Brigade: 7th Hampshire Regt, 4th and 5th Dorsetshire Regt.

214th Brigade: 7th Somerset Light Infantry, 1st Worcestershire Regt, 5th Duke of Cornwall's Light Infantry.

Divisional Troops:

RAC: 43rd Recce Regt.

RA: 94th, 112th, 121st and 179th Field, 59th A/Tk and 110th LAA Regts.

RE: 43rd Divisional Engineers.

R. Signals: 43rd Divisional Signals.

Machine Gun: 8th Middlesex Regt.

50th (Northumbrian) Division (Major-General D.A.H. Graham to 16.10.44, Major-General L.O. Lyne to 21.11.44, Major-General D.A.H. Graham from 27.11.44):

69th Brigade: 5th East Yorkshire Regt, 6th and 7th Green Howards.

151st Brigade: 6th, 8th and 9th Durham Light Infantry.

231st Brigade: 2nd Devonshire Regt, 1st Hampshire Regt, 1st Dorsetshire Regt.

Divisional Troops:

RAC: 61st Recce Regt.

RA: 74th, 90th and 124th Field, 102ns A/Tk and 25th LAA Regts.

RE: 50th Divisional Engineers.

R. Signals: 50th Divisional Signals.

Machine Gun: 2nd Cheshire Regt.

51st (Highland) Division (Major-General T.G. Rennie, killed 24.3.45, Major-General G.H.A. Macmillan from 25.3.45):

152nd Brigade: 2nd and 5th Seaforth Highlanders, 5th Queen's Own Cameron Highlanders.

153rd Brigade: 5th Black Watch, 1st and 5th/7th Gordon Highlanders.

154th Brigade: 1st and 7th Black Watch, 7th Argyll and Sutherland Highlanders.

Divisional Troops:

Royal Armoured Corps: 2nd Derbyshire Yeomanry.

RA: 126th, 127th and 128th Field, 61st A/Tk and 40th Light Anti-Aircraft Regts.

RE: 51st Divisional Engineers.

R. Signals: 51st Divisional Signals.

Machine Gun: 1/7th Middlesex Regt.

52nd (Lowland) Division (Major-General E. Hakewill-Smith):

155th Brigade: 7th/9th Royal Scots, 4th King's Own Scottish Borderers, 6th Highland Light Infantry.

156th Brigade: 4th/5th Royal Scots Fusiliers, 6th Cameronians, 1st Glasgow Highlanders.

157th Brigade: 5th King's Own Scottish Borderers, 7th Cameronians, 5th Highland Light Infantry.

Divisional Troops:

RAC: 52nd Recce Regt.

RA: 79th, 80th and 186th Field, 1st Mountain, 54th A/Tk, and 108th LAA Regts.

RE: 52nd Divisional Engineers.

R. Signals: 52nd Divisional Signals.

Machine Gun: 7th Manchester Regt.

53rd (Welsh) Division (Major-General R.K. Ross):

71st Brigade: 1st Oxfordshire and Buckinghamshire Light Infantry, 1st Highland Light Infantry, 4th Royal Welch Fusiliers.

158th Brigade: 1st East Lancashire Regt, 7th Royal Welch Fusiliers, 1/5th Welch Regt.

160th Brigade: 6th Royal Welch Fusiliers, 2nd Monmouthshire Regt, 4th Welch Regt.

Divisional Troops:

RAC: 53rd Recce Regt.

RA: 81st, 83rd and 133rd Field, 71st A/Tk and 116th and 25th (ex-50th Division) LAA Regts.

RE: 53rd Divisional Engineers.

R. Signals: 53rd Divisional Signals.

Machine Gun: 1st Manchester Regt.

[*TEMPORARILY UNDER COMMAND*]

2nd Canadian Division (Major-General C. Foulkes to 9.11.44, Major-General A.B. Matthews from 10.11.44):

4th Canadian Brigade: The Royal Regiment of Canada, The Royal Hamilton Light Infantry, The Essex Scottish Regt.

5th Canadian Brigade: The Black Watch (Royal Highland Regt) of Canada, Le Régiment de Maisonneuve, The Calgary Highlanders.

6th Canadian Brigade: Les Fusiliers Mont-Royal, The Queen's Own Cameron Highlanders of Canada, The South Saskatchewan Regt.

Divisional Troops:

CAC: 8th Recce Regt (14th Canadian Hussars).

RCA: 4th, 5th and 6th Field, 2nd A/Tk and 3rd LAA Regts.

RCE: 2nd Canadian Divisional Engineers.

RC Signals: 2nd Canadian Divisional Signals.

Machine Gun: The Toronto Scottish Regt.

3rd Canadian Division (Major-General D.C. Spry to 22.3.45, Major-General R.H. Keefler from 23.3.45):

7th Canadian Brigade: The Royal Winnipeg Rifles, the Regina Rifle Regt, 1st Bn The Canadian Scottish Regt.

8th Canadian Brigade: The Queen's Own Rifles of Canada, Le Régiment de la Chaudière, The North Shore (New Brunswick) Regt.

9th Canadian Brigade: The Highland Light Infantry of Canada, The Stormont, Dundas and Glengarry Highlanders, The North Nova Scotia Highlanders.

Divisional Troops:

CAC: 7th Recce Regt (17th Duke of York's Royal Canadian Hussars).

RCA: 12th, 13th and 14th Field, 3rd A/Tk and 4th LAA Regts.

RCE: 3rd Canadian Divisional Engineers.

RC Signals: 2rd Canadian Divisional Signals.

Machine Gun: The Cameron Highlanders of Ottawa.

Select Bibliography

There have, of course, been many hundreds of books written on the Second World War. Many of these mention General Horrocks. The following list is a very small selection of the available titles.

Barnett, Correlli *The Desert Generals* (Allen & Unwin 1983)

De Guingand, Major-General Sir Francis *Operation Victory* Hodder & Stoughton 1947

Hervey, H.E. *Cage Birds* Penguin 1940

Hinsley, F.H. *British Intelligence in the 2nd World War*, Vols I & II HMSO 1981

Horrocks, Lt-Gen Sir B. *A Full Life* Leo Cooper 1974

Horrocks, Lt-Gen Sir B. with Maj-Gen H.E. Essame and Eversley Belfield *Corps Commander* Sidgwick & Jackson 1977

Hunt, Sir David *A Don at War* Kimber 1966

Lucas-Phillips, C.E. *Alamein* Heinemann 1962

Kennedy, Maj-Gen Sir J. *The Business of War* Hutchinson 1957

Montgomery, Field Marshal Lord *Memoirs* Collins 1958

Nicolson, Nigel *Alex* Weidenfeld & Nicolson 1973

North, John (ed.) *The Alexander Memoirs* Cassell 1962

Warner, Philip *Alamein* Kimber 1979

—— *Phantom* Kimber 1982

Wilmot, Chester *The Struggle for Europe* Collins 1952

Young, Brigadier Peter *World War II 1939-45* Arthur Barker 1966

Official Histories

The War in France and Flanders 1939-40 L.F. Ellis HMSO

The Defence of the United Kingdom B. Collier HMSO

The Mediterranean & the Middle East, Vols III, IV and V: I.S.O. Playfair & C.J.C. Moloney HMSO

Victory in the West L.F. Ellis HMSO

Index